Rage·Hate·Assault and Other Forms of Violence

Aggression and Violence
Edited by Denis J. Madden, Ph.D. and John R. Lion, M.D.

Volume 1:

Rage ● Hate ● Assault and Other Forms of Violence
Denis J. Madden and John R. Lion M.D.

Rage·Hate·Assault and Other Forms of Violence

Edited by
Denis J. Madden, Ph.D.
and
John R. Lion, M.D.

both of the
Institute of Psychiatry and Human Behavior
University of Maryland School of Medicine
Baltimore, Maryland

S P Books Division of
SPECTRUM PUBLICATIONS, INC.
New York

Distributed by Halsted Press
A Division of John Wiley & Sons

New York   Toronto   London   Sydney

SPECTRUM PUBLICATIONS, INC.
86-19 Sancho Street, Holliswood, N.Y. 11423

Distributed solely by the Halsted Press division of John Wiley & Sons, Inc., New York

Library of Congress Cataloging in Publication Data

Main entry under title:

Rage/hate/assault and other forms of violence.

   (Aggression and violence series ; v. 1)
   CONTENTS: Sarles, R. M. Child abuse.--Scratton, J. Violence in the family.--Donner, L. Violence in the media.--Steadman, H. J. Predicting dangerousness.--Penna, M. W. National and international violence. [etc.]
   1. Violence--Addresses, essays, lectures. I. Madden, Denis J. II. Lion, John R.
HM291.R315   301.6'33   76-131
ISBN 0-470-15022-X

Second Printing

Contributors

D. CHRIS ANDERSON, Ph.D.
Department of Psychology
University of Notre Dame
Notre Dame, Indiana

DIETRICH BLUMER, M.D.
Harvard Medical School
McLean Hospital
Belmont, Massachusetts

FRANCIS L. CARNEY, Ph.D.
State of Maryland, Patuxent Institution
Jessup, Maryland
Institute of Psychiatry and Human
    Behavior
University of Maryland School of
    Medicine
Baltimore, Maryland

LAWRENCE DONNER, Ph.D.
Institute of Psychiatry and Human
    Behavior
University of Maryland School of
    Medicine
Baltimore, Maryland

GEORGE GALLAHORN, M.D.
Director, Open Clinic
Department of Psychiatry
Institute of Psychiatry and Human
    Behavior
University of Maryland School of
    Medicine
Baltimore, Maryland

JOHN R. LION, M.D.
Director, Clinical Research Program for
    Violent Behavior
Department of Psychiatry
Institute of Psychiatry and Human
    Behavior
University of Maryland School of
    Medicine
Baltimore, Maryland

VICTOR LUPO, M.A.
Department of Psychology
University of Notre Dame
Notre Dame, Indiana

DENIS J. MADDEN, Ph.D.
Associate Director, Clinical Research
    Program for Violent Behavior
Institute of Psychiatry and Human
    Behavior
University of Maryland School of
    Medicine
Baltimore, Maryland

GARY MAIER, M.D.
Director of Social Therapy
Mental Health Centre
Penetanguishene
Ontario, Canada

HENRY MUSK, M.Ed.
Maryland Correctional Institution for
    Women
Jessup, Maryland

MANOEL PENNA, M.D.
Director, Inpatient Services, Inner City
    Community Mental Health
    Program
Department of Psychiatry
Institute of Psychiatry and Human
    Behavior
University of Maryland School of
    Medicine
Baltimore, Maryland

RICHARD SARLES, M.D.
Division of Child and Adolescent
    Psychiatry
Institute of Psychiatry and Human
    Behavior
Univeristy of Maryland School of
    Medicine
Baltimore, Maryland

JOAN M. SCRATTON, ACSW
Director, Family Clinic
Associate Professor
Institute of Psychiatry and Human
    Behavior
University of Maryland School of
    Medicine
Baltimore, Maryland

BOYLSTON D. SMITH, M.D.
Supreme Bench, City of Baltimore
Department of Psychiatry
Institute of Psychiatry and Human
    Behavior
University of Maryland School of
    Medicine
Baltimore, Maryland

HENRY. J. STEADMAN, Ph.D.
Director, Mental Health Research Unit
New York State Department of Mental
    Hygiene
Albany, New York

Preface

Violence and aggression have become popular concepts in our day. Whether there is indeed more violence today than in times past can be disputed but more is being written on this subject than ever before. Not only has this topic become more visible in the popular vein but it is an area of concern in journals, books and annual meetings of professional groups. We thus felt that an overview of the literature and present thinking on violence and aggression is called for now more than ever.

Since this subject has been approached by several disciplines, we have sought out contributors from different fields for this volume. What we feel further enriches the chapters is the fact that many of the authors are not only acquainted with the subject from an academic point of view, but many work as clinicians themselves with patients demonstrating problems in impulse control. It is thus felt that such a book will be valuable to clinicians, academicians and students interested in learning more about this subject.

In the past much has been written on violence from a psychological point of view, especially in the area of animal studies or nonhuman aggressive behavior. The organic or biological contributors to violence have also been written on, and for this reason we thought it important that chapters discussing these areas be included.

Today there is increasing interest in violence as it is demonstrated in the family and parent-child relationships. The role of violence in the media is also of great concern, as is also the issue of international violence. The chapters included in this book will provide the reader with a historical perspective as well as current thought in these areas.

Whenever there is a concern with an issue such as violence, attempts are made to learn how predictable this behavior is. Government agencies often seek out test batteries that will help to identify the violent offender. After the offender has been caught, the question arises as to what can be hoped for with regard to rehabilitation. Too often we forget that violence and aggression are symptomatic entities, and that they must be viewed within the context of human behavior where more often than not there are multivariate factors to be considered. We hope that this book will help bring all of this into perspective for the reader.

One must be humble when he approaches this subject, for there are still many unknowns. It has become more apparent to us that there are no quick or easy solutions to the problems of violence. Violent patients must be viewed with compassion and understanding as individuals with their own needs and qualities. Research, with its statistical analysis, has a tendency to blur the individual we are dealing with and place him within a proscribed category. As any clinician knows, this is not helpful in the therepeutic encounter.

There are many persons who should be thanked for their support and encouragement in producing this book. Although each is not mentioned by name, we hope they realize we are indebted to them. Ms. Patricia Lovell, our secretary, who proofed and provided valuable advice, must be mentioned as well as our colleagues at the Institute of Psychiatry and Human Behavior, University of Maryland School of Medicine.

Denis J. Madden
John R. Lion

Contents

Rage·Hate·Assault and Other Forms of Violence

Child Abuse

RICHARD M. SARLES

Child abuse is by no means a problem of modern society. However, review of the literature discloses virtually no mention of child abuse prior to Caffey's original description in 1946 of a syndrome of subdural hematoma and abnormal x-ray changes in the long bones (1). Since then a plethora of articles have appeared to focus attention on the magnitude of the problem. A selected bibliography of child abuse published by the National Institutes of Mental Health for the years 1968 through 1972 listed over 290 references (2).

Current statistics would also lead one to believe that child abuse is increasing. It is difficult to conclude whether this has been the result of more children actually being abused or better reporting of cases or both. In New York City, between the years of 1966 to 1970, the number of reported cases increased 549 percent (3). Gil in a research project in 1967 on child abuse control contacted control registries of all fifty states and found 5,993 cases of child abuse (4). Kempe (5) estimated 50,000 cases of child abuse occurred in 1970 alone, and some estimates run as high as 500,000 to 2.5 million cases per year. Fontana believes that child abuse probably is the greatest cause of death in children (6). Most authorities agree that the reported cases represent only the tip of the iceberg and the true incidence of child abuse in the United States has never been and probably never will be fully known. In any event, it is apparent that child abuse and neglect have reached epidemic

1

proportions, and represent major etiology factors in the morbidity and mortality of children (7).

In spite of the extensive literature amassed over the past twenty years and the statistical increase in the number of reported cases of child abuse, Radbill suggests that children today are exposed to less violence, mistreatment and neglect than at any other time in history (8).

DEFINITION AND DIAGNOSIS

Kempe and Helfer described the "battered child" as any child who received nonaccidental physical injury (or injuries) as a result of acts (or omissions) on the part of the parent or guardians (15). Other authors feel that the term "battered child" needs to be expanded: they prefer the term "maltreatment syndrome" to include emotional and nutritional deprivation, neglect and abuse, both physical and sexual (3). This acknowledges that the abuse need not be willful and that child abuse represents spectra of behavior, i.e., punishment-abuse, accident-abuse or neglect-abuse (16).

The clinical signs of child abuse range from the simple undernourished infant to the grossly battered, abused or neglected child. Fontana (3) has outlined several signs which may lend suspicion towards the diagnosis of child abuse: 1) parents' history of the event that is at variance with the clinical findings; 2) reluctance of parents to divulge information; 3) child brought to the physician with complaints other than the abuse; 4) parents' inappropriate reaction to the severity of the injury, either apathetic or overresponsive; 5) inconsistent social histories; 6) parents' aggressive or abusive behavior when questioned about problems concerning the child; 7) date of injury prior to examination; 8) multiple visits to various medical facilities and; 9) family discord, financial stress, alcoholism, psychosis, etc. Physical signs may be poor nutrition, bruises, lacerations and hematomas in various stages of healing, inability to move certain extremities due to old and new dislocation and/or fractures, unusual injuries such as cigarette burns or electric cord whip marks and neurologic signs of intracranial damage. It should be noted that little mention has been given to burns in child abuse cases. Smith found that one-fifth of their cases had serious burns or scalds. Burns of the perineum or buttocks from placing the child on a stove or hot metal surface was a particularly striking finding (17). Radiologic signs may be fractures in various stages of healing, previously healed periosteal calcifications, epiphyseal separations and subperiosteal hemorrhages among others.

Almost three decades following his original report, Caffey has described a variation of the "battered child syndrome." He states that the whiplash shaking of infants is a common primary type of trauma in the so-called battered infant syndrome and may be a frequent cause for later mental retardation and permanent brain injury (18). Subdural hematoma is the most common, most injurious, least detected and most common cause of death in these infants. It remains undiagnosed in most cases because of the lack of history of the trauma.

The clinical findings in the whiplash shaking syndrome (WLS) presents rather extraordinary diagnostic contradictions, which include massive intracranial and intraocular hemorrhages in the absence of signs of external trauma to the head or fractures of the skull, associated with traction of the periosteum of the long bones and the absence of fractures or traumatic changes in the overlying skin of the extremities. Habitual, moderate, casual manual whiplash appears to be practiced to some degree nearly everywhere by many types of parents or parent surrogates for a wide variety of reasons. the most common reasons are usually punitive and disciplinary. Caffey also hypothesizes that this syndrome may be a major cause or factor in the sudden unexplained infantile death SID—"crib death").

It should be emphasized that child abuse should be considered in every case of Sudden Infant Death. The inability to determine the etiology of a sudden death, however, should never be used to support the diagnosis of child abuse. The diagnosis of child abuse should not be one of exclusion.

Caffey warns that current evidence of WLS in SID is largely circumstantial and incomplete. He suggests educating the public to the potential dangers of casual whiplash shaking of infants and alerting the medical profession to consider this syndrome in all infants with unexplained convulsions, bulging fontanels, paralysis or other central-nervous-system symptoms.

HISTORICAL PERSPECTIVES

In order to achieve some perspective and understanding of the current interest and concern about child abuse, a historical approach to the treatment and mistreatment of children is needed. Infanticide is certainly the most lethal form of mistreatment of children and represents an extreme on one pole of the spectrum of child abuse. It was, however, practiced by almost all cultures, both civilized and uncivilized, throughout recorded history. It has been reported to be a regular feature of several cultures, including the American Indian, Polynesian, Egyptian and Australian Aborigine.

Female infanticide was permitted in China as late as the early nineteenth century. Solomon states that "infanticide has been responsible for more child death than any other single cause in history, other than possibly bubonic plague" (9).

Although many cultures have had laws against infanticide, beginning with the Code of Hummurabi approximately four thousand years ago, they were seldom enforced. Lack of enforcement was generally rationalized by the culture itself to lessen individual responsibility and to transfer it to the culture as a whole. Thus, the act was condoned for the general good of the group: 1) for appeasement of the gods to ward off disasters and doom; 2) as acts of faith for positive reward and proof of worthiness; and 3) for population control (8). Nevertheless, these ancient practices set the tone for the value of children in any society.

Physical mistreatment of children has also existed throughout history. "Spare the rod and spoil the child" is an ancient Roman dictum passed down to modern times. It was assumed that parents and guardians had the absolute right and the obligation to treat their children in any manner they saw fit in order to maintain discipline and to teach certain educational material and values. Physical punishment was also seen as necessary to please certain gods and to expel evil spirits.

Whipping children has already been the prerogative of teachers, as well as parents. Five thousand years ago, in the School of Sumer, there was "a man in charge of the whip" to punish on the slightest pretext. The ancient philosophers believed in beating their students; and stories and pictures of American and English schools in the eighteenth and nineteenth centuries depict the teachers with the birch switches.

In the United States today only three states—New Jersey, Maryland and Massachusetts—have laws expressly forbidding corporal punishment in the schools; seventeen states have laws expressly allowing physical punishment of children. In one school system which allows physical punishment, over 24,000 instances of corporal punishment were recorded in the school years 1970–1972, some of them so severe as to need medical attention and, in several cases, hospitalization (10).

Many children with learning disabilities are especially vulnerable targets for classroom cruelty. Some parents favor corporal punishment for their child, who they feel is lazy or obstinate because of chronic underachievement (11).

Children have also been exploited throughout history. Slavery was a common fate of many children until recent times, and Charles Dickens immortalized the fate of children in the early phase of the Industrial Revolution. The euphemism, "beating the dickens" out of the child persists today as proof of the extreme physical hardship and corporal punishment children received during his day.

It was not until 1871, when the Society for the Prevention of Cruelty of Children was founded in New York City, that children had any organization express concern for their welfare. This organization, in fact, grew from an appeal to the Society for the Cruelty to Animals on behalf of an abused child, Mary Ellen, who was removed from her home on the grounds that she was a member of the animal kingdom and could be included under the laws against animal cruelty (6).

In 1899, thirty-one such societies joined to form the National Society for the Prevention of Cruelty to Children, and the English Parliament passed "The Children's Charter" as a act for the prevention of cruelty to children. As a result of a White House conference on Child Health and Protection in the United States, the "Children's Charter" of the United States was adopted in 1930.

Following Caffey's original paper, Silverman in 1953 reported similar findings and described trauma as the unrecognized cause of the skeletal lesions (12). In 1955, Wolley noted that skeletal trauma were willfully inflicted in many cases (13).

In 1961, the American Academy of Pediatrics conducted a symposium headed by Kempe who had carried out the first large-scale survey for abused children in the early 1960's. He coined the phrase "the battered child syndrome" to indicate the seriousness of the problem of children who were injured through circumstances that pointed to willful rather than accidental causes (14). His efforts catalyzed nationwide interest and concern, and by mid-1967 all fifty states, Washington, D.C., and the Virgin Islands had enacted laws concerning the reporting of child abuse.

The professional literature and lay publications are replete with many hundreds of articles on the subject and countless symposia have been held. The focus of most of this work have been to 1) delineate the incidence and demographic distribution of the syndrome; 2) understand the dynamics involved; 3) increase professional and public awareness of the problem; 4) decrease the resistance of professionals to consider the diagnosis and report such cases; 5) protect the child from further injury or death; and 6) investigate various treatment modalities to help the parents, the child and the family.

Despite the extensive literature and the impressive progress that has been made thus far, it is discouraging to see how little is really known about the incidence and what little agreement there is about the demography, etiology, prevention, treatment and outcome.

ETIOLOGY

In order for an adult to maltreat and abuse a child, three factors have to be present, according to Helfer: 1) the potential for abuse; 2) a crisis or series of crises; and 3) a special child (15).

The potential for abuse appears to be rooted in several areas. As mentioned earlier, children have been subjected to corporal punishment and even death as an inherent right of parents and teachers throughout history. This took place under the guise of discipline, training and education. Corporal punishment remains the major method of discipline in child rearing in the United States today. Child abuse represents one end of the normal scale of discipline in our culture. That point which transgresses the culturally acceptable reasonable punishment and becomes abuse is often open to interpretation depending on the age of the child, socioeconomic setting, community and ethnic background. It is not surprising that a public opinion survey revealed that nearly 60 percent of adult Americans thought that "almost anybody could at some time or other injure a child in his care" (19).

Steele suggests that this potential exists in everyone (20). He comments that there is an instinctual drive or urge toward aggression as part of our biologic heritage. The growing child must come to grips with these aggressive impulses and learn to channel these drives into socially acceptable behavior. The superego, which is a combination of the social conscience and identification models of the child, generally acts as a mediator between the aggressive impulses and what is socially acceptable for that child in his particular family and culture. The social conscience develops by accepting the values and mores of the family and culture and by receiving the positive reward of love and approval or by the fear of punishment if the child does not accept these values. Thus, if violence is a method of problem-solving in a family, the child will incorporate these values as a positive means of gaining approval. The child also may respond to the violence he experiences by identifying with the perpetrator of the violence in an effort to gain some mastery over a situation he cannot control. Also, in an effort to deal with the anger generated from the physical aggression directed against him, the child often tries to become like the punishing person so he can then direct his own anger and aggression onto others as a strong attacker himself.

Steele summarizes this psychological mechanism by stating that, "the potency of this mechanism of identification with the aggressor in such children is markedly enhanced by the fact that the parent is the aggressor, the same parent who is the model for much of the rest of the superego's formation" (20). Thus, the potential for violence seems directly linked to early childhood experiences.

It is striking to note that most authorities have reported an almost universal occurrence in the lives of parents of abused children: the abusing parents were themselves, as children, abused or neglected physically or emotionally, (21, 22, 23, 24). The parents repeat the same child-rearing practices they themselves experienced as children. This supports the notion that parents often parent as they were parented. Oliver and Taylor's report of five generations of abused children in one family pedigree lends further credence to the evidence that violence begets violence (25).

The potential for abuse seems to be enhanced by a distortion in the parent-child relationship. The parents often perceive the child as capable and responsible to fulfil certain unmet needs for them as parents. In this role reversal the parents often view their child as a hostile, unloving, persecuting adult who is a competitor. Because the child cannot fulfill these unmet needs, the unconscious anger and pain of their own childhood is released on the child who acts as a "hostility sponge" (24). Galdston agrees with this concept and describes this behavior as a "transference psychosis" (26). He and others note (27) that these parents are incapable of understanding the normal developmental stages of their children. There is a tendency for the abusing parent to have high expectations for their young children and demand premature maturation and performance (28, 29). In Elmer's study most mothers asserted that a baby should know right from wrong by the age of 12 months and one-third of the mothers specified 6 months (30). There was a marked inability to emphathize with their child or sympathize with the feelings of others (23, 24). The abusing mother tended toward extreme reaction, judging their babies to be either all good or all bad (30).

The personality patterns of the abusing parents are difficult to catagorize by psychiatric diagnosis. Kempe (15) believes there is a defect in character structure. Steele and Pollock (21) describe the parent as depressed, immature and impulsive, and Holter and Friedman (22) found the abusive parent to have immature, dependent, impulsively acting-out personality patterns. Depression was present in about half of the mothers in Elmer's study, and several showed uncontrollable actions such as sexual promiscuity, aggression against other women and secret compulsive spending (30). They were lonely and isolated and were unable to use help from others when they felt "uptight." Smith found that 78 percent of the mothers in their study had abnormal personalities, with 48 percent being neurotic, the usual symptoms being depression, anxiety or a mixture of both (31). A high percentage of the fathers in this study were diagnosed as psychopaths. In other studies the spouses of the abusing parent were described as passive and nonsupportive.

Psychosis or severe personality disorders are present in only a small percentage of the child-abusing parents. Only the most violent parents inflicting the most bizarre injuries or deaths appear to be schizophrenic or psychotic and seem to form a distinct and separate group apart from other child-abusing parents (21, 24, 31).

Intellectual functioning is reported to be subnormal in from 10 (22) to 25 percent (31) of the cases and may be directly related to the common finding that the abusing parents generally have limited education (4, 26).

Electroencephalographic studies of child-abusing parents have been investigated to determine the possibility of organic dysfunction to account for the abusing behavior (32). Twenty-three percent of the electroencephalographs were found to show abnormalities ranging from marked asymmetry, dominant activity of low frequency, notable theta activity with some alpha activity to complex activity of the type associated with epilepsy. The authors concluded, however, that child-abusing parents are not a homogeneous group, and their behavior shows no clear-cut relationship to demonstrable abnormalities by electroencephalographic studies.

Steele states that the parents in their study did not give evidence of excessive aggressive behavior in other areas of their lives, and in fact were not much different from a random cross section of the general population (21).

It seems clear that there is no unanimity in the literature in classifying the personality patterns of the abusing parents. It is clear, however, that one basic fact does emerge from most studies: there appears to be a defect in the character structure of these parents which, during added stress, allows aggressive impulses to be expressed too readily and too severely.

CRISES AND STRESS

Although there are observations in the literature that child abuse is found in all socioeconomic classes and "has nothing to do with race, color, creed, sex, income, education or anything else" (33), there is a disproportionate representation of the working and lower class in those studies which report the socioeconomic data (4, 22, 30, 31). This may be due to the differential reporting of all crimes according to socioeconomic status and the fact that the majority of the studies are conducted in medical facilities used by the lower classes. There is evidence, however, that lower socioeconomic groups tend to use "normal violence" as a means of problem-solving to a greater degree than upper classes (34, 35). "The poor tend to discharge aggressive impulses more directly as they seem less inhibited in expressing feelings through action" (4). In contrast, middle-class parents tend to utilize verbal interactions with their children and use psychological approaches in disciplining them. The types of behavior punished also vary with social class. Mothers of the upper class punished primarily for aggressive acts; middle-class mothers for activity, dangerous and otherwise; and lower-class mothers for conduct, such as excessive demands, disobedience and crying (30).

This disproportionate representation may also be due to the lack of resources, both internal and external, available to the lower classes. When faced with stress the middle-class mother can afford to "get away from it all" by a vacation apart from their children or can utilize outside help for relief, such as baby-sitters, a personal physician, psychological intervention or medication. The middle-class physician often tends to be more tolerant and empathetic to his middle-class patients' behavior. The middle-class mother has, in the past, also had greater access to birth control and abortion services.

The birth of a sibling less than one year before or nine months after the abuse of a child was found to be an important consideration (30). The abused child is often a product of an unwanted pregnancy either because of being conceived out of wedlock or because of inconvenience to the parents and family (15, 22, 24, 31). This finding appears to be directly related to the fact that the abused child is often very young and either the youngest or the only child in the family (27, 31, 37). Gil found that abuse occurred most often in families with four or more children, suggesting that the burden of another, perhaps unwanted, child placed additional stress on the parents (19). Elmer (30) stated that those families that had successfully begun to use contraception were better able to recover from stress and to stop venting their frustrations on their children. Several authors (30, 31, 37) indicate that the parents are often young with little experience in child rearing, many struggling with adolescent developmental problems and faced with economic hardships. Gil (19) and others (22, 26, 31, 38) found a high proportion of unemployment and mobility, thereby depriving the parents of family roots and support.

Opinions vary concerning the influence of alcoholism and drug abuse and their contribution to child abuse. Wertham (39), Gil (19) and Young (38) agree that alcoholism is a causal or contributing factor of extreme importance. Gartner noted that "about 70 percent of the child battering deaths in New York City involve children of drug addicted parents" (40). Smith (31) and Steele and Pollock (21) found no association with alcoholism or drug abuse.

Significant health problems such as mental retardation, seizures, heart disease and emotional difficulties were present in over 50 percent of the parents in Elmer's study (30). Holter and Friedman found close to 60 percent of the families in their study to have definite and marked psychopathology or mental retardation present (22). There does seem to be general agreement in the literature about social factors contributing to added stress in the parents of child-abusing families. In general, all the authors mentioned above describe a high incidence of marital strife, separation and divorce. Unwanted pregnancies, youthful marriage and children born out of wedlock, born in close succession or into large families, seem to bring added stress. The disproportionate representation of the lower socioeconomic classes contributes to the high incidence of unemployment, poor education and high mobility in the reported studies. It should be emphasized, however, that child abuse occurs in all socioeconomic groups and that not all families in the lower classes abuse their children (26, 28, 38, 41). These stresses should be recognized as the precipitating factors and not the cause of the abuse.

SPECIAL CHILD

It is unusual for multiple children in one family to be abused. In almost every normal family, however, parents can describe one of their children who is "different." This difference may be some indefinable feeling on the part of the parents or may be a child with a "birth" defect hyperactivity, slow development, mental retardation or even the overly bright child. There is a high incidence of premature babies who are abused, and also infants with colic, teething difficulties or problems with toilet training. Children described as "irritable," "demanding," "always crying" or "never sleeping" are more likely to be abused.

A MULTIDIMENSIONAL MODEL

It would seem that the etiology of child abuse cannot be limited to a psychopathology model, a socioeconomic model or a cultural model.

No one single theory can explain why a parent allows his or her aggressive drives to transgress the boundary of normal, culturally acceptable child-rearing practices. The potential for abuse seems to exist in everyone. Added stress and crisis may weaken the defect in the character structure of the parent to the point of uncontrolled physical aggression toward the special child.

OUTCOME

Little is known of the long-term sequela of abuse upon children. The mortality in child-abuse cases varies from zero percent (42) to five percent (28) to 15 percent (30, 31) in individual case studies; and from 27 percent in a study by the American Humane Society to an estimate of 50 percent by Fontana (6). The morbidity from child abuse is strikingly high. Neurological impairment, including spasticity, paraplegia, blindness and other sequela requiring long-term rehabilitation, developed in 15 percent of Smith's cases (17). These figures support those of Martin (43) and Helfer (28). A high incidence of mental retardation is reported by Elmer (44), Morse et al. (42) and Martin (43). Smith noted that 38 percent of the cases without head injury or neurological impairment still showed a significant lower overall ability than controls (17). Caution must be exercised in evaluating these figures, since the retardation or neurologic impairment may have preceded the abuse through previous trauma, genetic endowment, prematurity or environmental deprivation.

Language retardation is described by Martin (43) and Smith (17). However, little information is available concerning the personality development and structure of the abused child. Martin (43) described the child as one who lacks basic trust, tends to be a loner and may perpetuate abusive behavior as adult. There is ample evidence that children who are abused tend to show later evidence of juvenile delinquency (20). In studies of murderers, a common history of abuse as a child is present. Elmer (30) states that the abused children in her study had marked difficulty with impulse control and control of anger. They tended to either have outbursts of rage or had serious inhibitions of negative feelings. Morse et al. (42) found 70 percent of their study population in a three-year follow-up to exhibit behavior outside the normal range in social and motor development. With therapeutic intervention over a prolonged period of time the child may appear superficially quite nice and healthy, according to Martin (43), but on closer inspection the child is shallow, suspicious and has poor peer relationships.

At the present time, we do not know what the ultimate effect child abuse has on the growing child. One could suspect severe damaging results, since the abuse typically occurs during the early formative years of personality development. The finding of a history of child abuse in juvenile delinquency, murders and child-abusing parents casts an ominous light. Yet many abused children do not murder or abuse their own children. We have only begun to learn some of the parameters of a child abuse but meanwhile must search for solutions to the problem.

TREATMENT

The thought of a parent physically battering his or her own child generally evokes a strong feeling in the observer. The anger at the parents for beating a child and for awakening the fear of one's own potential for abuse often causes those professionals involved in child abuse cases to respond by demanding punishment for the parents or by denying the existence of the abuse. Through the efforts of Kempe and the American Academy of Pediatrics, all fifty states, the District of Columbia and the Virgin Islands enacted laws concerning the reporting of child abuse by mid-1967. Laws have subsequently been enacted to require physicians to report abuse in many states, and other laws have been passed to protect the physician from criminal prosecution when reporting these cases. Until recently, legislators have not supported public agencies to implement the care for these children and families once they have been identified. Legislation is now undergoing changes in some states to include funding to support Protective Services and to mandate what services must be provided for these children and their families.

Treatment of child abuse in the past occasionally centered around criminal prosecution and incarceration of the abusing parent. It must be noted, however, that few cases ever go to court. Experience has shown that the potential for rehabilitation in a correctional facility was not as great as when the parent remained in the home and received therapeutic intervention in that setting. Only in a small percentage of families in which the parent or parents are overtly psychotic should separation of parents and child definitely be considered.

Wasserman (24) feels the act of rushing a child to a hospital carries a message, "Please stop me from going out of control." The parent is asking for firm control and wants it. As a group, however, such parents are difficult to work with because of their demanding, hostile, inconsistent behavior and their need to ward off human interactions and relationships (45). Generally, conventional individual and group therapy has proven to be unsuccessful (46, 47).

Several authors suggest a team approach and indicate it must be nonpunitive and nonjudgmental (22, 48-51). The team often consists of pediatrician, social worker, nurse, psychiatrist or psychologist and a community aide. Much of the primary service is often provided by the community aide, a member with the least formalized training, but who is available twenty-four hours a day, is accepted and trusted in the community and serves as a model of the behaviors that constitute good mothering (48). Other authors suggest the public health nurse, alone or together with the medical social worker as the most helpful in visiting the home (22, 52).

Several other innovative approaches have been attempted, generally modeled after Kempe and Helfer's work (15). Parent's aides (foster grandparents) are assigned to help with the care of the abused child while in the hospital and with aftercare in some cases. The focus is on the parents and not the children, and close supervision and conference time are provided to support these aides.

Comprehensive emergency services, including a 24-hour hot line, 24-hour intake, emergency caretakers, emergency foster homes, emergency shelter for families, emergency shelter care for adolescents and outreach programs, are further examples of innovative programs. Homemaker services are yet another step to provide the parent with some relief from the stresses of home and to provide another sympathetic support.

Parent Anonymous, a nonprofessional, self-help group, is "one of the brighter lights that has appeared on the horizon of therapeutic interventions . . . and could have as significant an impact on child abuse as AA has had on alcholism" according to Kempe and Helfer (15).

Treatment requires a long-term commitment to these families in which the parents often test the helpers to ward off interpersonal relationships or to recapitulate their experiences of rejection. Actually, Wasserman suggests that the helping person or agency must become the "hostility sponge" instead of the child (24). The professional working with these parents also serves as an "external superego" by making the parents aware of society's expectations of acceptable parental behavior, by assisting and directing them in assuming their parental responsibility and by restricting their abusive behavior (22). Additional goals are to help the parents effectively use other adults and resources in times of crisis and to help these parents find satisfaction of their dependency needs without turning to the infant or child.

A major goal of treatment is to create a positive shift of personal and family dynamics to aid these parents in maintaining their parental responsibilities and ensuring a safe and nurturant environment for the growth and development of their children. Inherent in this goal is the need for education for parenting, community education about abuse and neglect, a change in attitudes about working mothers, and the development of day-care centers, nurseries and community crisis-intervention centers.

The necessity for adequate communication between various hospitals and agencies is accentuated in child abuse cases because it is characteristic of the parents to seek medical attention at several emergency rooms, clinics and private physicians' offices. Visits to multiple facilities may be interpreted as a means to avoid detection or may mean that the parents' cry for help is not being heard (53). Unfortunately, many cases go undiagnosed until the abuse and neglect are blatant. A computer-based system (54) to provide a cumulative record of all injuries and medical visits, as well as a tracking system, may facilitate an earlier diagnosis when utilized by the medical profession. In addition, child abuse resource coordinating centers are needed to correct the common problem of poor coordination between various community agencies.

Despite extensive studies and reviews over the past fifteen years, the field of child abuse is still wide open to discovery. There are still more questions than answers; and growth and change are slow. Major shifts will need to occur in our society to bring about these changes. Our society thinks of itself as child oriented, yet bills supporting day-care centers are repeatedly vetoed and school bond bills are voted down as being too expensive.

In the meantime, appropriate prevention and treatment models must be sought while researchers continue their attempt to develop criteria for identifying parents who represent a potential high risk of child abuse prior to the onset of the abuse.

REFERENCES

1. Caffey J: Multiple fractures in the long bones of children suffering from chronic subdural hematoma. *Am. J. Roentgenol* 56:163-173, 1946.
2. *Selected References on the Abused Child and Battered Child.* DHEW Publication No. (HSM) 73-9034, 1973.
3. Fontana VJ: The Diagnosis of the maltreatment syndrome in children. *Pediatrics* 51:780-782, 1973.
4. Gil DG: *Violence against Children: Physical Abuse in the United States.* Cambridge, Mass., Harvard University Press, 1970.
5. Kempe HC: Paediatric implications of the battered baby syndrome. *Arch. Dis. Childhood* 46:28-37, 1971.

6. Fontana VJ: *The Maltreated Child. Springfield, Ill., Charles C Thomas, 1971.*

7. Blumberg ML: *Psychopathology of abusing parents. Amer J Psychotherapy* 28:21-29, 1974.

8. Radbill SX: A history of child abuse and infanticide in the battered child, in Helfer RE & Kempe H (eds.): Chicago, University of Chicago Press, 1968.

9. Solomon T: History and demography of child abuse. *Pediatrics* 51:773-776.

10. Maurer A: Corporal punishment. *Amer Psychologist* 29:614-626, 1974.

11. Kline C: Child abuse in class. *World medical Reports* August, 1973.

12. Silverman FM: The Roetgen manifestations of unrecognized skeletal trauma in infants. *Am J Roentgenol Radium Therapy Nucl Med* 69:413-427, 1953.

13. Wooley PV, Jr., Evans, WA, Jr.: Significance of skeletal lesions in infants resembling those of traumatic origin. *J Am Med Assoc* 158:539-543, 1955.

14. Kempe HC, Silverman FM, Steele BF, et al: The battered child syndrome. *J Am Med Assoc* 181:17-24, 1962.

15. Kempe HC, Helfer RE: *Helping the Battered Child and His Family.* Philadelphia, JB Lippincott, 1972.

16. Newberger EH, Haas G, Mulford R: Child abuse in Massachusetts. *Mass Physician* 32:31, 1973.

17. Smith SM, Hanson R: 134 battered children: A medical and psychological study. *Brit Med J* 3:666-670, 1974.

18. Caffey J: The whiplash shaken infant syndrome: Manual shaking by the extremities with whiplash induced intracranial & intraocular bleedings, linked with residual permanent brain damage and mental retardation. *Pediatrics* 54:396-403, 1974.

19. Gil DG: Violence against children. *J of Marriage and the Family* 33:644-648, 1971.

20. Steele BT: Violence in our society: The Pharos of Alpha Omega Alpha. 33:42-48, 1970.

21. Steele BT, Pollack CB: A psychiatric study of parents who abuse infants and small children, in Helfer RE, Kempe CH (eds.): *The Battered Child,* Chicago, University of Chic Press, 1968.

22. Holter JC, Friedman SB: Principles of Management in Child Abuse Cases. *Am J Orthopsychiat* 38:127-136, 1968.

23. Melnick B, Hurley HB Jr: Distinctive personality attributes of child abusing mothers. *J Consult Clin Psychol* 33:746-749, 1969.

24. Wasserman S: The abused parent of the abused children. 14:175-179, 1967.

25. Oliver JE, Taylor A: Five generations of ill-treated children in one family pedigree. *Brit J Psychiat* 119:473-480, 1971.

26. Galdston R: Observation on children who have been physically abused and their parents. *Am J Psychiat* 122:440-443, 1965.

27. Holter J, Friedman SB: Child abuse: Early case findings in the emergency department. *Pediatrics* 42:128-138, 1968.

28. Helfer RE, Pollock CB: The battered child syndrome. *Advances in Pediatrics* 15:9-27, 1967.

29. Gregg GS, Elmer E: Infant injuries: Accident or abuse. *Pediatrics* 44:434-439, 1969.

30. Elmer E, Gregg GS, Wright B, Reinhart JB: *Studies of Child Abuse and Infant Accidents.* DHEW Publication No. (HSM) 72-9042, 58-59, 1971.

31. Smith SM, Hanson R, Noble S: Parents of battered babies: A controlled study. *Brit Med J* 4:388-391, 1973.

32. Smith SM, Honigsberger L, Smith CA: EEG and personality factors in baby batterers. *Brit Med J* 3:20-22, 1973.

33. Kempe HC: The battered child and the hospital. *Hosp. Practice* 4:44, Oct. 1969.

34. Blumberg M: When parents hit out. *Twentieth Century* 39-41, Winter, 1964-65.

35. *Steinmetz SK, Straus MA: Intra-family Violence in Violence in the Family.* 3-25. New York, Dodd, Mead.
36. Zalba SR: The abused child: A survey of the problem. *Social Work* 11:3-16, 1966.
37. Lauer B, TenBroeck E, Grossman M: Battered child syndrome: Review of 130 patients with controls. *Pediatrics* 54:67-76, 1974.
38. Young LR: Wednesday's children: A study of child neglect and abuse. New York, McGraw Hill, 1964.
39. Wertham F: Battered children and baffled adults. *Bull, NY, Acad Med* 48:887-898, 1972.
40. Gartner LM: Neonatal addiction seen as increasing problem. *Pediatric News* Dec., 1974.
41. Zalba SR: The abused child: A typology classification and treatment. *Social Work* 12:70-79, 1967.
42. Morse CW Sahler OJZ, Friedman SB: Three year follow-up study of abused and neglected children. *Am J Dis Child* 120:439-445, 1970.
43. Martin H: The Child and His Development. Kempe HC, Helfer RE, (eds.): *Helping the Battered Child and His Family,* 93-114, Philadelphia, JB Lippincott, 1972.
44. Elmer E, Gregg: Developmental characteristics of abused children. *Pediatrics* 40:596-602, 1967.45. Reiner BS, Kaufman I: *Character Disorder in Parents of Delinquents.* Chicago, American Public Welfare Association, 1958.
46. Helfer RE, Kempe CH, (eds.): *Battered Child.* Chicago, Univ. of Chicago Press, 1968.
47. Paulson MJ, Blake DR: The abused, battered and maltreated child: A review. *J Trauma* 9:1-136, 1967.
48. Chabon RS, Barnes GB, Hertzberg LJ: The problem of child abuse: A community hospital approach. *Md State Med J 22:* 50-55, 1973.
49. Newberger EH, Hagenbuch JJ, Eblling NB, Colligan EP, Sheenan JS, McVeigh SH: Reducing the literal and human cost of child abuse: Impact of a new hospital management system. *Pediatrics* 51:840-848, 1973.
50. Galdston R: Violence begins at home. *Am J Child Psychiatry* 10:336-350, 1971.
51. Delnero H, Hopkins J, Drews K: The medical center child abuse consultation team, in Kempe HC, Helfer RE, (eds): *Helping the Battered Child and His Family.* 161-176. Philadelphia, JB Lippincott, 1972.
52. Savino AB, Sanders RW: Working with abusing parents, group therapy and home visits. *Am J Nursing* 73:482-484, 1973.
53. Holter J: Personal Communication. December 26, 1974.
54. Diggle G, Jackson G: Child injury intensive monitoring system. *Brit Med J* 3:334-336, 1973.

Violence in the Family

JOAN SCRATTON

Those who maintain the conventional, idealized view of the family as a haven of gentleness, nurturance and love, may need to repudiate the concept of the family as "cradle of violence" within which physical violence is an everyday occurrence (1). A middle-class abhorrence of violence, coupled with the functional purpose of perpetuating the myth of the idealized, timeless, universal nuclear family (2), seems to have resulted in some kind of tacit agreement among students of human behavior to ignore the reality and extent of intrafamilial violence. If violence in the family is acknowledged at all, it is typically considered within the context of abnormality, yet there is growing evidence to support the view that violence is indeed fundamental to family life.

The Steinmetz and Straus (3) definition of violence in the family as "the intentional use of physical force between family members" is adopted as a working definition for the purposes of this review of the literature on violence in the family. If, however, the definition of acts of violence is extended to include overtly *threatened* as well as overtly accomplished acts of force (4), the evidence for its incidence in family life seems overwhelming.

17

HISTORICAL PERSPECTIVES

Viewed historically, the concept of the family as cradle of violence gains perspective and plausibility. While violence in the family probably dates back to the predawn of history, within the Judeo-Christian context we find the first account of intrafamilial violence recorded in the Old Testament story of Cain killing his brother, Abel, in a fit of sibling rivalry. The wrath of the Lord notwithstanding, Cain went on to take a wife and to ensure the continuance of humankind. We find a pattern of societally sanctioned intrafamilial violence early established with the swift and bloody dispatch with which Jacob's sons avenged the violation of their sister. A generation later, Absalom made explicit the incest taboo by arranging the death of his brother, Ammon.

Such selective societal sanction of intrafamilial violence has its counterpart in the gradations of violence sanctioned within many modern cultures, given a complex set of contingencies (5). Examples of values and attitudes which will condone and even approve violence in certain circumstances include the tolerant judicial and public attitude toward the wronged husband who avenges his wife's seducer and the father who beats an errant daughter. Claude Brown (6) graphically portrays the value system with respect to the violence which operated in the black ghetto of his youth in the early 1940's. Succinctly stated, you "don't mess with a man's money, his woman, or his manhood." He goes on to spell it out with unequivocal clarity:

> If somebody messed with your brother, you could just punch him in his mouth, and that was all right. But if anybody was to mess with your sister, you had to really f . . . him up—break his legs or stab him in the eye with an ice pick, something vicious.

Violence in the family reached a literary peak with the compelling and timeless tragedies of Greek mythology, including the Oedipus fable which Freud was later to translate into the universal family drama underlying all intrafamilial tensions and rivalries. If we omit the Dickensian chronicles of child abuse and neglect in Victorian England which probably reflected quite accurately the child-rearing practices of the day, a veil seems to have been drawn over violence within the family, at least in the pages of fiction, ever since the great dark tragedies of Shakespeare compelled attention to family violence in all its force and starkness.

Violence within the family has received relatively scant attention from sociologists, anthropologists, psychologists and other students of family behavior. Yet child abuse, both in the home and in industry, has a long and shameful history of exploitation, brutality and neglect of children that is surely difficult to ignore. Only as we abandon the modern American concept of the idealized functional nuclear family and take a closer look at the actual changing nature of the intimate human relationships between adults and children at different points in human relationships between adults and children at different points in history, can we get a more accurate perspective on the subject of violence in the family. History refutes the concept of the timeless and universal nuclear model of the family. In medieval society, the idea of childhood simply did not exist, inasmuch as there was no awareness of the "particular nature" of childhood that distinguishes the child from the adult (7). The grave face of miniature adults which stare forth from medieval family portraits mutely testify to this fact. The concept of extension of formal education into young adulthood and, in some cases, beyond.

In the introduction to a provocative, but poorly documented, recent publication, Skolnick and Skolnick (8) invite us critically to reexamine conventional assumptions about the family. They question the sacredness of motherhood in particular and the assumption that the least powerful (i.e., the children) in the family are the most indulged. This assumption ignores the fact that the tyrannical Victorian fathers and the Dickensian child-abusers live on in modern-day America and that violence is indeed an everyday occurrence in twentieth-century American life.

Taking an historical perspective on violence within the family is difficult, if not impossible, without reference to the long and chronicled history of socially condoned child abuse to which children have been subjected in Western society, not only by parents but by teachers and others entrusted with the rearing of children, and quite apart from the well-documented history of exploitation of both woman and child labor which characterized the Industrial Revolution. As child abuse is the subject of a separate chapter in this review on aggression, it is not my intention to do more than draw attention to this phenomenon and to relate it to the child-rearing practices which have wittingly or unwittingly produced a situation where intrafamilial violence is an everyday occurrence in our society.

Those who naïvely perceive the twentieth-century as the Age of Violence need only a cursory glance at the annals of Western civilization to appreciate the major role that legally and societally sanctioned violence has played in the regulation of society throughout the ages. Both capital and corporal punishments, publicly carried out, have been historically endorsed and administered by church, court and prison systems. Until quite recently, cruel and unusual sanctions imposed by both church and state for minor offenses committed by women and children went largely unchallenged.

The incidence of violence between spouses (short of murder) is much less well documented, both in fiction and in history, but the evidence in police annals is overwhelming. Perhaps a literal interpretation of the sacredness of a man's home and family has led to an implicit sanctioning of violent behavior between spouses and between parents and children which does not suffer outside interference except in dire and unusual circumstances. Be that as it may, as recently as 1885, a certain Mr. Adams during a session of the legislature of Pennsylvannia sought unsuccessfully to pass legislation which would make wife-beating a crime punishable by the infliction of a number of lashes, not exceeding thirty-five, on the offender's bare back. Adams quoted 1883 Maryland legislation which punished wife-beaters by whipping them, "it being well understood that corporal punishment is to be inflicted solely in cases of wife-beating" (9). One doubts, however, that wife-beating has completely disappeared from the Maryland scene, although it seldom comes to official notice. Lex talionis may have a certain crude appeal, but in this case, the message is clearly conveyed that use of violence is the proper and only effective recourse in family matters of gravity. Against such a backdrop of institutional violence, it is scarcely surprising that parents have been given a clear legal mandate to use violence or the threat of violence as a means of socializing their children.

THEORETICAL PERSPECTIVES

While it is clearly beyond the scope of this chapter to include a review of theories of violence, the phenomenon of family violence requires a theoretical framework for its analysis. The reader is referred to Megargee's scholarly report on the psychology of violence (10), which was one of the five major critical reviews of theories of violence prepared for the President's Commission, 1969. The author seeks to integrate and evaluate comparative theories and data derived from a variety of disciplines. He examines ethological theories to support the hypothesis of instigation and inhibition of aggression as being innate—(Ardrey 1966 (11); Lorenz, 1966 (12); Morris, 1967 (13)—as well as others that arise from environmental factors, showing the pendulum swinging away from the concept of an innate aggressive instinct to more emphasis on environmentalism and sociocultural factors—(Dollard et al., 1939 (14); Bateson, 1941 (15).

Social learning and environmental theories have particular relevance to a consideration of the etiology, incidence and prevention of violence within the family. Most theories of environmentally acquired inhibitions against the expression of aggressive behavior rely on the principles of learning theory, either implicitly or explicitly. This also holds true of the psychoanalytic approach to human behavior. Most learning theorists agree that behavior that successfully meets an individual's needs will be repeated and become habitual, while unsuccessful behavior tends to drop out of the individual's response repertoire through the process known as "extinction." What is often overlooked is that social learning has had, regrettably, its greatest effect in teaching the child that aggression *can* satisfy a number of needs (16).

In 1970 an extensive search of the literature on violence and the family, involving a bibliography of over four hundred items, was undertaken for the National Council on Family Relations. A welcome outcome of this library research and a significant contribution to the literature is a 1974 publication, edited by Steinmetz and Straus (17), which brings together selected theoretical articles, reports on original research, and summaries of research. The authors approach the topic of violence and the family from a conflict theory perspective, suggesting that "a focus on conflict and violence may, in fact, be a more revealing approach to understanding the family than a focus on family consensus and solidarity" (18). Their selections from the literature to some extent reflect this bias while persuasive evidence is offered to support the view that violence is indeed a fundamental, if undesirable, part of all family life.

In an introductory article, William J. Goode (19) provides a thoughtful overview of the literature and attempts a theoretical synthesis based on the assumption that human society requires a minimum degree of social order and control if it is to survive. He advances a social control or resource theory of family violence which argues that violence is a resource which can be used to achieve desired ends: that violence tends to be used when other resources are lacking or found to be insufficient, as is all too often the case with families living at the poverty level in slum neighborhoods.

Sociologists, such as Cohen (20), Becker (21), and Erikson (22), who have begun to focus attention on deviance as a societal process rather than a social disease would seem to support the adoption of a conflict model for the study of intrafamily relationships. Kai Erikson (23) claims that deviant forms of behavior actually support rather than undermine the social order, by providing the framework within which people develop an orderly sense of their own cultural identity. The social theorist Georg Simmel (24) views antagonism as a central feature of intimate social relationships, hypothesizing that the closer and more intimate an association, the greater the likelihood of aggression and violence. From this theoretical perspective, some measure of violence within the family would seem inevitable rather than pathological, though the line between pathology and normality still awaits definition.

O'Brien's (25) study of violence in divorce-prone families suggests that violence in the family, as with violence in the larger society, most often represents a response to certain status imbalances in the social structure, no doubt to be increasingly exacerbated by the current thrust toward liberalization of woman from her traditionally subordinate status in Western society.

INCIDENCE AND DEMOGRAPHY

There is little doubt that the idealized view of the family has served as a deterrent to objective analysis of the extent and incidence of intrafamilial violence, yet the skeptic about the incidence of violence among intimates should ask a policeman. According to the Federal Bureau of Investigation, as cited by Sullivan (26), "one of every five policemen killed in the line of duty dies trying to break up a family fight." "That murder tends to be a family affair has been documented in a number of studies and reports, including the Uniform Crime Reports: the significant fact emerges that most murders are committed by relatives of the victim or persons acquainted with the victim" (27).

A significant factor in the distribution of homicide by sex is that "although women exhibit a much lower homicide rate than men, when they do kill they are more likely to kill their husbands than any other category of persons" (28). Goode hypothesizes that battles of words lead to physical violence in the absence of rules for ending verbal confrontations and that "women are socialized to use far less physical violence than men, but typically do not feel that the words they use justify violence against them. Men are trained differently and recognize far more clearly that certain degrees of verbal violence will have a high probability of eliciting a physical counterattack, not only a verbal counterattack" (29). He notes that differences in verbal skills are substantial between classes. The middle-class child is taught how to mediate and talk himself out of difficulties, thereby avoiding physical confrontations. Also, middle-class couples are more likely to discuss their differences openly and seek solutions. The greater inhibition in matters of violence and a higher evaluation of nonviolence in intimate relations among the middle and upper social class strata are reflected in the statistics on crimes of violence. Clearly, such an explanation does not suffice to explain the greater incidence of violence among lower-class families reared in a culture of poverty. For this disadvantaged segment of urban society, violence is born out of hopelessness, frustration and despair, and is seen by some to be essential to survival. Regardless of class differences, however, there are many studies and reports to attest to the fact that violence is indeed a family affair and that violence among intimates accounts for the largest category of homicides and serious assaults—(Goode, 1969 (30); Wolfang, 1958 (31); Mulvihill and Tumin, 1939 (32); Ward et al. 1969 (33); Parnas, 1967 (34); Ennis, 1967 (35); Federal Bureau of Investigation reports (36).

Within this context, Lizzie Borden's horrendous act, immortalized in doggerel, may prove less exceptional than we like to believe. Turning from the statistical evidence of the high incidence of serious crimes of violence among family members, the most universal type of physical violence present in American families is the corporal punishment of children by parents. Certainly this is violence of a different order, but violence nonetheless. Steele and Pollock (37) conclude a study of the battered child syndrome with the observation:

> There seems to be an unbroken spectrum of parental action toward children ranging from breaking of bones and the fracturing of skulls through severe bruising, through severe spanking and on to mild "reminder" pats on the bottom. To be aware of this, one has only to look at the families of one's friends and neighbors, to look and listen to the parent-child interactions at the playground and the supermarket, or even to recall how one raised one's own children or how one was raised oneself. The amount of yelling, scolding, slapping, punching, hitting, and yanking acted out by parents on very small children is almost shocking. Hence, we have felt that in dealing with the abused child we are not observing an isolated, unique phenomenon, but only the extreme form of what we would call a pattern or style of child-rearing quite prevalent in our culture.

A survey by the National Commission on the Causes and Prevention of Violence (38) revealed that about a third of the population had been spanked frequently as children (and almost all at some time) and one out of five husbands could approve of slapping a wife's face. No significant social class differences in either approval of slapping or in reports of spankings in childhood were reported in this study.

The evidence is conflicting when it comes to examination of the widely held myth that intrafamilial violence is primarily a lower- or working-class phenomenon. Whereas most studies report more use of physical punishment by working-class parents (39, 40), some find no difference. A recent comprehensive review of studies of social class differences in the use of physical punishment (41) concluded that although the weight of the evidence supports the view of less use of physical punishment among the middle class, the differences are small. Sizable differences do occur, however, with the analysis of such factors as race, the sex of the child and the parent, occupation of the father, etc., suggesting the variation *within* social classes is at least as important as differences *between* classes. It has been suggested that such class differences as do exist are not so much due to the existence of a lower-class "culture of violence" as cultural factors impinging on lower-class families, such as a lack of resources within the social system sufficient to maintain a family member's position and status within the family (42).

A British study (43) tends to support the resource theory of violence in the family, which may yet tragically be put to the test in the face of spiraling inflation and rising rates of unemployment in this country. Statistics from Birmingham, England, showed a sharp increase in wife-beating during a six-month period when unemployment also rose sharply. It was also found that the lower the job satisfaction, the higher the incidence of harsh treatment of children, even when the social class factor was controlled.

Steinmetz and Straus (44) reported that they were unable to locate a single study giving figures for a representative sample of the percentage of couples who engage in physical fights. Similarly, O'Brien (45) reports that in the Index for all editions of the *Journal of Marriage and the Family,* from its inception in 1939 through 1969, not a single entry can be found which contains the word "violence" in the title, although discussions of "conflict" in the family were quite common. The proliferating literature in the family therapy field is singularly innocent of reference to violence in the family in general and to husband-wife fights in particular. This reviewer found no reports of clinical studies of violence-prone families or of suggested modes of intervention in the family therapy literature. Social work journals generally reflect a similar reluctance to confront the issue of intrafamilial violence except for isolated references to child abuse.

Whatever the reasons for this lack of data on husband-wife fights, the incidence of physical fights between spouses is clearly an area for much-needed research. A study by Levinger (46) of physical abuse among applicants for divorce shows that of the 600 wives in the study, 37 percent complained of "physical abuse." Complaints differed significantly across socioeconomic lines with respect to physical abuse, lower-class wives being considerably more likely to complain of physical abuse than their middle-class counterparts. "In general, the evidence indicates that spouses in the middle-class marriages were more concerned with psychological and emotional interaction, while the lower-class partners saw as most salient in their lives financial problems and the unsubtle physical actions of their partner . . ." (47).

ORIGINS OF INTRAFAMILIAL VIOLENCE

Rather than attempt a comprehensive overview of the theoretical explanations of the origins of violence in the family, attention will be narrowed to those interrelated areas of empirical observation which represent major foci of research in this field: the family as agent of socialization; child-rearing practices conducive to violence; societal sanction and training for violence within the family; and conflict theory applied to the family system.

The Family as Agent of Socialization

Historically the family has been viewed as the central institution of human society with a major responsibility for the socializaiton of its members (48). The structural-functional school of sociology (49) give preeminence to the nuclear family as the functional institution *par excellence* in terms of its contributions to social order, stability and continuity. There seems little dissent that the primary goal of most parents is to socialize their children in accordance with those things which they approve and those they disapprove. So long as parental values are in harmony with those of the larger culture the nuclear family generally fulfills its prescribed functional role. Yet it is to socially sanctioned and broadly accepted child-rearing practices that many researchers attribute the origins of violence within the family. The question arises as to whether the isolated nuclear family of modern industralized society has within itself sufficient resources to perform the functional roles traditionally ascribed to it.

What is abundantly clear is that parents are given nearly absolute power over children, with minimal social regulation of parent-child relationships; so that "one can be as irrational as one pleases with one's children so long as severe damage does not attract the attention of the police" (50). According to Erik Erikson (51), "It is in the daily life, and especially in the life of children that the human propensity for violence is founded; we now suspect that much of that excess of violence which distinguishes man from animals is created in him by those child-training methods which set one part of him against another."

Child-Rearing Practices

Although the belief in the efficacy of punishment as an inhibitor of aggressive behavior is reflected in our modern code of law, the fact remains that punishment alone is relatively ineffective in eliminating aggressive habits. Indeed there is considerable evidence in child development literature that physical punishment, particularly when the punishment is severe, not only is ineffective in suppressing undesired behavior, but is actually productive of increased aggressivity in children—(Glueck and Glueck, 1950 (52); Sears et al., 1957 (53); Bandura and Walters, 1959 (54); Miller and Swanson, 1960 (55); McCord et al., 1961 (56); Becker, et al., 1962 (57); Veron, et al., 1963 (58); Lefkowitz, et al., 1963 (59); Delaney, 1965 (60); Jenkins, 1968 (61); Aronfreed, 1968 (62)).

Regardless of parental motivation, physical punishment represents physical attack. The implications are obvious when we consider that children learn behavior patterns not only on the basis of reward and punishment but also on the basis of imitation and identification. Yet there is little doubt that parents will continue to resort to physical punishment of aggressive behavior, particularly if directed toward themselves, because of short-term restitution of power and status, as well as the lack of alternative solutions available to them.

Societal Sanction and Training for Violence in the Family

We have everyday evidence through the media of the extent to which we have become acculturized to accept violence as a societally sanctioned norm in Western society. The glorification of masculinity epitomized in the code of machismo with its corollary deprecation of so-called female characteristics is seen by some as a powerful force toward violent sexuality (63). This is closely allied to Jackson Toby's "compulsive masculinity" syndrome (64).

Goode (65) notes that not all socialization experiences mold the child against violence. Indeed, what emerges from close examination of many parent-child relationships is a systematic pattern of training for violence. While parents, teachers, police and other authority figures preach nonviolence to children, at the same time they exhibit their own belief in the efficacy of force and the threat of force when used on intimates and subordinates. The child learns early that violence can play a useful role in protecting his property and his rights, or in imposing his will on another. Within the socialization process the child learns the various gradations of sanctioned violence specific to certain circumstances. As part of the socialization toward degrees of violence, Goode (66) notes that we acquire a range of rationalizations to justify our lapses into physical aggressivity.

McCandless (67) has described rewards for aggressiveness in the world of the lower-class child brought up in the culture of poverty. Environmental deprivation can produce instigation to aggression not only through frustration (68), but also by teaching the child that aggression is the best if not the only way to satisfy basic needs and ensure his survival (69-70).*

Conflict Theory Applied to the Family System

A conflict approach to the study of family process throws new light on the etiology of violence both from intrapsychic and sociological perspectives. Conflict theory emphasizes violence as a means of bringing about social change and thereby ensuring the viability of social systems such as the family. From this perspective, the tensions and violence which occur among family members would be viewed as a normal part of individual and societal growth and development. While the Eriksonian concept of deviance as actually supporting the social order is lent credence by a close study of violence among family members, it is difficult to remain sanguine in the face of mounting evidence as to its pervasiveness and the extent to which that most sacrosanct of institutions, the family, is credited with actually training its members to violence. In a classic paper, Adelaide Johnson (71) has described the conflict between consciously stated standards of parents and their unresolved underlying feelings about behavior, such as violence and aggression, that may prompt the child to act out the behavior as part of his relationship with his parent. An extreme manifestation of the powerful concept of superego lacunae is provided by Sargent's 1962 study of children who kill (72). Other studies (73, 74) lend support to the Johnson thesis, while Campbell (75) hypothesizes the conflict between verbally transmitted rules and actual behavior of parents as an explanation for so-called good-home delinquents.

Viewed from a broader sociological perspective, O'Brien (76) relates violence in the family to violence in the larger society as representing a response to certain status imbalances in the social structure. Goode (77) suggests the contribution of the victim to the dynamics of violence among intimates as a fertile area for further study, but the phenomenon of victim-precipitation has been fairly extensively

---

*For an example of training for violence in a middle-class family see Jules, Henry. "Making Pete Tough," in Suzanne K. Steinmetz, and Murray A. Straus, (eds.), *Violence in the Family* (New York: Dodd, Mead and Company, 1974), pp. 238–240.

covered in the literature—Tarde, 1912 (78); Hentig, 1948 (79); Wolfang, 1967 (80); Schafer, 1968 (81); Palmer, 1974 (82)).

SUMMARY AND RECOMMENDATIONS

This far from comprehensive overview of the literature on violence in the family is suggestive only of the extent and complexity of a problem which has deep societal implications. The intent was to give an indication of the present state of knowledge in this field, but the literature on violence in the family requires a rigorous and critical review beyond the scope of this chapter. The Steinmetz and Straus (83) well-edited and documented 1974 publication of significant readings in the field represents a major step in this direction and should prove a useful resource to researchers on family violence, particularly as they have made available two extensive bibliographies to aid other researchers (84).

There are various models of intervention and prevention of family violence described in the literature ranging from a successful program in police family crisis intervention in New York City (85), to the emergence of fight-training workshops in which warring couples are taught to handle their conflicts constructively with an emphasis on fighting for positive change and growth (86). While this educative, behavior-modification approach may hold promise for some couples and their children, further research is certainly indicated before it can be prescribed universally. The same reservation applies to attempts to train parents to control an aggressive child (87). Most of such attempts to reduce individual violence are based on little or no research evidence and fail to take into account the larger social system within which violence occurs. Any concerted effort to reduce the incidence of violence both within the family and industrialized society as a whole will need to address itself to such global and interrelated problems as ignorance, poverty, overpopulation, racial and sex discrimination, social inequality, mass migration and anomie (88).

The dynamics of violence are sufficiently complex to preclude any definitive conclusion with respect to which of many theoretical positions approximates the seminal truth. It is therefore not surprising that an attempt to narrow the investigation to the area of intrafamilial violence has resulted in a diversified and sometimes conflicting range of theoretical explanations for the etiology of violence within the family. What emerges from empirical findings is that intrafamilial violence cannot be encompassed within any one dimensional perspective. Genetic, biopsychological and social factors interact with intrafamilial variables to produce the phenomenon under review. While the doctrine of Original Sin may be sufficient explanation for the layman, the search for more sophisticated explanations must go on, based on an understanding of the complex interface between environment and family system.

At this point in our knowledge it is clear that no one single explanation will suffice, and available data can do no more than suggest modes of prevention and intervention in the violence-producing social system known as the family. Further research is needed to differentiate between types of violent acts and those who commit them and the circumstances conducive to their occurrence. In the present alarmist atmosphere of urgency with respect to violence in our society the need for ongoing critical basic research and sharing of information among behavioral and social scientists should not be overlooked in favor of simplistic solutions and expediency.

REFERENCES

1. Steinmetz SK, Straus MA: The family as a cradle of violence. *Society 10*: Sept, Oct 1973: 50-56.
2. Ferreira A: Family myth and homeostasis. *Arch Gen Psychiatry 9*:457–463, 1963.
3. Steinmetz SK, Straus MA (eds): *Violence in the Family*. New York, Dodd, Mead & Company, 1974. Footnote 1, p 4.
4. Megargee EI: A critical review of theories of violence, in Crimes of Violence. Edited by Mulvihill D, Tumin MM National Commission on the Causes and Prevention of Violence. Washington, D.C., U.S. Government Printing Office, Staff Study Series 13, December, 1969, Appendix *22*:1036–1115.
5. Goode W: Violence among intimates. Ibid. Appendix *19*: pp 941–997.
6. Brown C: *Manchild in the Promised Land*. New York, Signet Books, 1965.
7. Aries P: *Centuries of Childhood: A Social History of Family Life*. New York, Alfred A. Knopf, 1962.
8. Skolnick AS, Skolnick JH: Family in Transition: Rethinking Marriage, Sexuality, Child Rearing and Family Organization. Boston, Little, Brown and Company, Inc, 1971.
9. Steinmetz SK, Straus MA (eds) op. cit., 43.
10. Megargee EI: op. cit.
11. Ardrey R: *The Territorial Imperative*. New York, Atheneum, 1966.
12. Lorenz J: *On Aggression*. New York, Bantam Books, 1966.
13. Morris B: The Naked Ape. New York, McGraw-Hill, 1967.
14. Dollard J, Doob LW, Miller NE, et al: *Frustration and Aggression*. New Haven, Yale University Press, 1939.
15. Bateson G: The frustration-aggression hypothesis and culture. *Psychol Rev 8*:350–355, 1941.
16. McNeil EB: Psychology and aggression. *J Confl Resol 3*:195–293, 1959.
17. Steinmetz SK, and Straus MA (eds): op cit.
18. Ibid, p 6.

19. Goode WJ: Ibid. pp 26-43.

20. Cohen AK: *Deviance and Control.* New Jersey, Prentice-Hall Inc, 1966.

21. Becker HS: *Outsiders: Studies in the Sociology of Deviance.* New York, The Free Press, 1963.

22. Erikson KT: Notes on the sociology of deviance. *Soc. Probl* 9:307-314, 1962.

23. Ibid.

24. Simmel G: Conflict and the Web of Group Affiliations. (Translated by Wolff KH, and Bendix R) Illinois: The Free Press, 1955.

25. O'Brien JE: Violence in divorce-prone families. *J Mar Fam* 33:692-698. 1971.

26. Sullivan R: Violence, like charity, begins at home. *New York Times,* November 4, 1968.

27. Ward DA, Jackson M, Ward RE: Crimes of violence by women, in *Crimes of Violence.* Edited by Mulvihill D, Tumin MM. National Commission on the Causes and Prevention of Violence. Washington, D.C., U.S. Government Printing Office, Staff Study Series 13: 1969, Appendix 17: 843–909.

28. Goode W: Violence among intimates. Ibid, p 954.

29. Ibid, p 960.

30. Ibid, pp 941–997.

31. Wolfang ME: *Patterns in Criminal Homicide.* Philadelphia: University of Pennsylvania Press, 1958.

32. Mulvihill DJ, Tumin MM: Suicide and violent auto fatality data and computational method, in *Crimes of Violence.* Edited by Mulvihill D, Tumin MM. National Commission on the Causes and Prevention of Violence. Washington, D.C., U.S. Government Printing Office, Staff Study Series 13: 1969, Appendix 10: 187–194.

33. Ward DA, et al: op. cit., pp 843–909.

34. Parnas RI: The police response to the domestic disturbance. *Wis Law Rev* 914:914–960, 1967.

35. Ennis PH: Crime, victims and the police. *Transaction* 36–44, 1967.

36. Federal Bureau of Investigation Law Enforcement Bulletin 27: (January), 1963.

37. Steele BF, Pollock CB: A psychiatric study of parents who abuse infants and small children, in *The Battered Child.* Edited by Helfer RE, and Kempe CH. Chicago, University of Chicago Press, 1968.

38. Stark R, McEvoy J: Middle class violence. *Psychol Today* 4: 52–65, 1970.

39. Bronfenbrenner U: Socialization and social class through time and space, in *Readings in Social Psychology.* Edited by Maccoby EE, Newcombe TM, Hartley EL. New York, Holt, Rinehart, and Winston, 1958.

40. Kohn ML: *Class and Conformity: A Study in Values.* Homewood, Illinois, Dorsey Press, 1969.

41. Erlanger HS: Social class differences in parents' use of physical punishment, in *Violence in the Family.* Edited by Steinmetz SK, Straus MA, op. cit., pp 150–158.

42. Steinmetz SK, Straus MA: *Violence in the Family,* op. cit., p 9.

43. Ibid, p 9.

44. Ibid, p 85.

45. O'Brien JE: Ibid, pp 65–66.

46. Levinger G: Source of marital satisfaction among applicants for divorce. *Am J Orthopsych* 36: 804–806, 1966.

47. Ibid, p 88.

48. Campbell JS: The family and violence. Law and Order Reconsidered. Edited by Campbell JS, Sahid JR, Stang DP. Washington, D.C., U.S. Government Printing Office, 1969.

49. Parsons T: The normal American family, in *Man and Civilization: The Family's*

Search for Survival. Edited by Farber, Mustachi, Wilson. New York, McGraw-Hill, 1965.

50. Henry J: *Culture Against Man.* New York, Random House, 1963.
51. Erikson E: *Gandhi's Truth.* New York, W.W. Norton and Company, Inc, 1969.
52. Glueck S, Glueck E: *Unravelling Juvenile Delinquency.* New York, Commonwealth Fund, 1950.
53. Sears RR, Maccoby EE, Levin H: *Patterns of Child Rearing.* White Plains, NY, Row, Peterson and Company, 1957.
54. Bandura A, Walters RH: Dependency conflicts in aggressive delinquents. J Soc Issues 14:525–565, 1958.
55. Miller DR, Swanson GE: *Inner Conflict and Defense.* New York, Holt, Rinehart, and Winston, 1960.
56. McCord W, McCord, J, Howard A: Familial correlates of aggression in non-delinquent male children. *J Abnorm Soc Psychol* 62:79–83, 1961.
57. Becker WC, Peterson DR, Luria Z, et al: Relations of factors derived from parent interviews ratio to behavior problems of five year olds. *Child Dev* 33:509–535, 1962.
58. Veron LD, Walder LO, Toigo R, et al: Social class, parental punishment for aggression and child aggression. *Child Dev* 34:849–867, 1963.
59. Lefkowitz MM, Walder LO, Eron L: Punishment, identification, and aggression. Merrill-Palmer *Q Dev Behav* 9:159–174, 1963.
60. Delaney EJ: Dissertation Abstracts, 28:938, 1965.
61. Jenkins R: The varieties of children's behavioral problems and family dynamics. *Am J Psychiatry* 124:1440–1445, 1968.
62. Aronfreed J: Conduct and Conscience: The Socialization of Internalized Control over Behavior. New York, Academic Press, 1968.
63. Steinmetz SK, Straus MA (eds): op. cit. p 20.
64. Toby J: Violence and the masculine ideal. Ibid. pp 58–65.
65. Goode W: Violence among intimates, in *Crimes of Violence.* Edited by Mulhivill DJ, Tumin MM. National Commission on the Causes and Prevention of Violence. Washington, D.C., U.S. Government Printing Office, 1969.
66. Ibid, p 951.
67. McCandless BB: *Children: Behavior and Development.* (Second edition) New York, Holt, Rinehart and Winston, Inc, 1967.
68. Dollard J et al: op. cit.
69. Brown C: Manchild in the Promised Land. Op. cit. pp 263–272.
70. Grier WH, Cobbs PM: *Black Rage.* New York, Bantam Books, 1969.
71. Johnson A: Sanctions for superego lacunae of adolescence, in *Searchlights on Delinquency.* Edited by Eissler KR. New York, International Press, 1949.
72. Sargent D: Children who kill—a family conspiracy? *Soc Work* 7:35–42, 1962.
73. Van Amerongen ST: Permission, promotion and provocation of antisocial behavior. *J Am Academy Child Psychiatry* 2:99–117, 1963.
74. Gellenkamp KR, Rychlak JS. Parental attitudes of sanction in middle-class adolescent male delinquency. *J of Soc Psychol* 75:255–260, 1968.
75. Campbell JS: op. cit. p 258.
76. O'Brien JE: op. cit., p 74.
77. Goode WJ: Force and violence in the family. Ibid., pp 36–37.
78. Tarde G: *Penal Philosophy.* Boston, Little, Brown and Company, 1912.
79. Hentig H: *The Criminal and His Victim,* New Haven, Yale University Press, 1948.
80. Wolfang ME, Ferracuti, F: *The Subculture of Violence.* New York, Barnes and Noble, 1967.

81. Schafer S: *The Victim and his Criminal*. New York, Random House, 1968.
82. Palmer S: Family members as murder victims, in *Violence in the Family*.
83. Steinmetz SK, Straus MA (eds) *Violence in the Family*, op. cit.
84. Op. cit. footnote[10], p 22.
85. Bard M, Zacher J: The prevention of family violence: dilemmas of community intervention. *J Marriage Fam. 33*:677–688, 1971.
86. Bach G, Bernhard Y: *Aggression Lab: The Fair Fight Training Manual*. Dubuque, Iowa, Kendal-Hunt Publishing Company, 1973.
87. Patterson GR, Cobb JA, Ray RS. Training parents to control an aggressive child, in *Violence in the Family*. Ibid.
88. Merton RK: *Social Theory and Social Structure*. Glencoe, Illinois, The Free Press, 1957.

Violence in the Media

LAWRENCE DONNER

The depiction of violence has existed since prehistoric times, as evidenced by the remarkable, well-preserved works of early man discovered in caves in southern France (1). Speculation as to the rationale for these cave paintings of scenes involving man's confrontation with and killing of prey ranges from an attempt to record and document successful hunts to a technique of preparing the young novice for what he would confront on his virgin hunt.

These pictures remind us on the one hand that man was from the beginning violent and killed like other animals for food but also, on the other hand, that he was above the other animals in his ability to think creatively and leave his mark for future generations to admire and study.

GREEK AND ROMAN TIMES

Ancient man continued this interest in the portrayal of physical confrontations. With his developing engineering and technological skills he built mammouth self-aggrandizing edifices on which large-scale conquests were depicted in relief for all the population to admire and find vicarious pride in. Later, man's fascination with physical confrontation found expression in a far more dangerous arena where human life was at stake. The Roman Colosseum filled to capacity with citizens watching gladiators wielding all types of destructive gadgets and weaponry as they vigorously tried to annihilate their opponents. No doubt the bloodletting was followed by lusty shouts of the viewing audience and cries for greater violence (remarkably paralleling in many ways today's professional football battles). For a diversion, lest the regular audience be satiated or, even worse, all the gladiators destroy each other, the Romans turned periodically to the violent "sport" of throwing Christians to hungry and starved lions to be mercilessly mauled for the delictation of the cheering throngs of both the elite and the general citizentry.

In time, drama was increasingly substituted for actual violence; it was thought that this allowed the spectator the opportunity to vicariously vent his own strong emotions through identification with the actors on the stage. Until recently this concept of the value of being exposed to contrived depictions of violence as being a constructive event and harmless opportunity for catharsis has largely gone unchallenged. We shall see in the following discussion that this erroneous assumption has rather far-reaching and increasingly dangerous implications.

VIOLENCE OUR BIRTHRIGHT?

The first conclusion drawn by the National Commission on the Causes and Prevention of Violence was that "America has always been a relatively violent nation. Considering the tumultuous historical forces that have shaped the United States, it would be astonishing were it otherwise" (2).

Generally speaking, America was settled by two categories of individuals: those trying to escape religious persecution and those seeking their fortune, eager for adventure and challenge. This country was first and foremost a nation of immigrants of diverse cultural and social backgrounds. The American frontier itself further stimulated individualism, demanded self-reliance, encouraged assertion and aggression while obliterating distinctions of class. Although the frontier experience undoubtedly strengthened the American character, it did so at the expense of the Indians, whose numbers were brutally and violently cut in half from 850,000 to 400,000. A wasteful brutalization and exploitation not only of people but of our natural resources also took place.

With the availability of affordable newspapers the frontier exploits of a few were devoured by many, (especially the urban Easterners). Murderers like Billy the Kid and thieves like Jesse James were transformed overnight into folk heroes, and their antisocial exploits were described in great detail in papers and books. If one could not personally help win the West, at least one could read about it.

Our democratic tradition also grew out of international and national violence beginning with the French and Indian War and the War of Independence. Violence was apparent in the labor movement, and it was at the core of such frontier practices as vigilantism and lynching. Violence not only affected the lives of union workers and disadvantaged minorities but also those holding the most powerful positions of our land. Presidential assassination claimed the lives of four of our Presidents. And more recently in the last decade the protest against the Vietnam war saw a sizable proportion of middle-class students, largely without the right to vote, resorting at times, to violence, to challenge the national conscience.

THE CONTEMPORARY SCENE

We might review the contemporary scene by looking at some of the media that stimulate individuals in our country today and examine the amount and form that violence plays in each.

Motion Pictures

The movie industry is a new medium, relatively speaking, dating back to the turn of the century. Financially it has come a long way: movie theaters gross over one billion dollars a year.

We would venture to say that violence has had some part in the industry's remarkable success; it is worth noting that one of the first feature-length movies. The Great Train Robbery (1903), contained incidents of armed robbery, physical assault and murder (3). The marketing of crime and violence has continued to ensure success for the industry, and it is not surprising that one recent film, Mark of the Devil, was advertised as follows: "Most horrifying film ever made, guaranteed to upset your stomach. The first film rated V for violence. Due to horrifying scenes, no one will be admitted without a stomach distress bag." The movie makers' preoccupation with violence is shown in such films as Straw Dogs, Clockwork Orange, Beyond the Valley of the Dolls and The Godfather. Recently a series of films glorifying kung fu and other martial arts showed audiences, in explicit gory detail, how to maim, torture and brutally kill human beings. Inner-city youngsters are entertained for hours by double features showing man's inhumanity to man.

The glories of violence as depicted on the screen affect even middle-class suburbanites in a film such as *Death Wish,* which shows a contemporary middle-class man who is driven to take the law in his own hands following a revolting and graphic brutal beating of his wife and rape of his daughter. As a one-man vigilante, he walks the streets and rides subways shooting felons who cross his path so effectively that the crime rate drops in Manhattan and the police are ordered not to arrest him when they find out his identity. Viewers of the film cheer wildly as the star cuts down one criminal after another. Ironically this film came to Baltimore just at the time the city police department was giving rewards to individuals for turning in their handguns, since handguns are by far the most frequent weapon found in homicides.

Today scenes of violence seem clearly to be the rule and not the exception. It is a strange twist that the film industry has chosen to police and scrutinize films for their sexual content while casting a blind eye or deaf ear to violent content and language. The message is clear: "Make war not love."

FILMS AND ANTISOCIAL BEHAVIOR—SOME CHANCE OCCURRENCES?

Born Innocent, a made-for-TV movie, was shown in September 1974. It included a scene in which a girl is raped by her reformatory classmates with the end of a broomstick. The very next day four children raped a nine-year-old California girl and her eight-year-old playmate in an identical manner. The parents of the nine-year-old victim are suing NBC, the sponsors and the local affiliate for eleven million dollars.

Duplicating the scene of a show some young boys had seen the night before, they doused a drifter with alcohol and put a match to him, burning him alive.

In Baltimore, within the week of the showing of *Hawaii Five-O* featuring a sniper dressed in Army fatigues who systematically shoots people crossing his line of fire, a disgruntled employee of Pittsburgh Plate Glass Company dressed in Army fatigues systematically cut down five of his fellow workers.

Another movie made for television, *The Doomsday Flight,* whose plot involves the possibility of a plane being blown up in midair unless ransom is paid, was shown in 1971. Immediately thereafter, telephone threats to airline offices increased twofold. In May 1971 the film was rebroadcast. Within several days following the broadcast, Qantas paid approximately $500,000 in ransom to protect 116 passengers aboard one of their flights to an individual following the movie's script.

Early Questions Concerning the Effects of Motion Pictures

> Motion pictures are not understood by the present generation of adults. They are new; they make an enormous appeal to children; and they present ideas and situations which parents may not like. Consequently when parents think of the welfare of their children who are exposed to these compelling situations, they wonder about the effect of the pictures upon the ideals and behavior of the children. Do the pictures really influence children in any direction? Are their conduct, ideals, attitudes affected by the movies? Are the scenes which are objectionable to adults understood by children, or at least by very young children? Do children eventually become sophisticated and grow superior to pictures? Are the emotions of children harmfully excited? In short, just what effect do motion pictures have upon children of different ages?

So wrote W.W. Charters, chairman of the Committee on Educational Research of the Payne Fund. This group of university psychologists, sociologists and educators was brought together by the Motion Picture Research Council to conduct investigations over a four-year period, from 1929 to 1932. Two of the committee's researchers, Herbert Blumer and Philip Hauser, summarized their findings as follows, over forty years ago (4).

> It is evident that motion pictures may exert influences in diametrically opposite directions. The movies may help to dispose or lead persons to delinquency and crime or they may fortify conventional behavior. Motion pictures may create attitudes favorable to crime and the criminal or unfavorable to them . . . The child in the high-rate delinquency area tends to be sensitized and the child in the low-rate delinquency area immunized to delinquent and criminal attitudes and forms of behavior depicted on the screen. On the other hand the forms of thought and behavior presented by the movies are such as to provide material and incentive to those sensitized to delinquent and criminal suggestions.

> Motion pictures play an especially important part in the lives of children reared in socially disorganized areas. The influence of motion pictures seems to be proportionate to the weakness of the family, school, church and neighborhood. Where the institutions which traditionally have transmitted social attitudes and forms of conduct have broken down, as is usually the case in high-rate delinquency areas, motion pictures assume a greater importance as a source of ideas and schemes of life.

> Motion pictures are a relatively new factor in modern life. While primarily a form of recreation, they play an appreciably important role in developing conceptions of life and transmitting patterns of conduct. They may direct the behavior of persons along socially acceptable lines or they may lead, as has been indicated, to misconduct. They may be, therefore, an agency of social value or of harm. As the former they raise no issue, as the latter they raise problems of social control.

Have these implications been heeded in the last four decades? Have the number of violent movies been decreased?

MAGAZINES AND BOOKS

Besides movies, the contemporary American is stimulated by a variety of mass media, including magazines, books, radio and television. The impact of these media is likely to be different because some are dependent on more active participation on the part of the audience and some are less so. Some of the media require greater use of imagination on the part of the subject, while others present concrete, explicit data.

Let us first explore the medium which is thought by most to be the least immediate and having the most meager sensational impact: magazines and books.

The violence done by man to his brothers is at the foundation of almost all religions, and so it is not surprising that in the Bible one finds the story of Cain and Able, the sons of Adam and Eve. The creation of mankind in Genesis is immediately followed by the account of filial violence and murder. In their Sunday School classes children are instructed: "Thou shalt not kill" and "Treat thy Neighbor as thyself." But what impact can the Bible have on children when they are addicted to comic books? At one point in time a hundred million comic books were published every month; this figure has never been approached by any other form of publication. And what was the format of the vast majority of these comic books? Not Donald Duck and Mickey Mouse, as most adults might think, but crime comics dealing primarily with violence and criminal activity. Killings through conventional and unconventional means were and still are depicted. Shooting policemen is a favorite theme in some of these comics.

Many regard comic books as trivia and not worth investigating, although, as a Saturday Evening Post article in December of 1964 pointed out, the huge profits in the business amounted to about $100 million a year. Parents and government authorities may continue to say that "crime does not pay," but even a superficial perusal of comic books will show that it does.

And what of adults? The best-selling hard-cover novel of the past was The Godfather, whose theme was clearly that "violence pays." The reader was beguiled into identifying with the "bad guys" and relishing the ingenuity and brutality with which those who crossed the organization were dispatched.

TV—IN-HOME EDUCATION OF THE MASSES

In 1949 there were approximately one million TV sets in American homes. In 1951 that figure had increased tenfold, and within ten years the figure had reached over fifty million. In 1975 more homes were likely to have television than indoor plumbing. By the time a child born today would reach eighteen he or she would likely have spent more time watching television than being involved in any other single activity with the exception of sleep.

American television, which is probably the most effective and far-reaching sales medium in the world, is primarily directed to adults who buy the products of companies that pay to put programs on the air. Television programing as a whole is really not directed to children; the adolescent child is not the audience that the TV executives, producers and writers are thinking about when they put programs on the air. This is not to say that there are not a few TV programs intended for children on Saturday mornings and late afternoon hours, but what most of what young children watch on TV is actually meant for adult viewers—one can only hope they are more capable in distinguishing between fact and fancy in advertising and between fact and fantasy in the programs they see.

By the time a child is able to walk efficiently he is also likely to have learned to turn on the TV set. By the age of three he is probably a regular watcher of TV. He has learned much from TV long before he enters a classroom. During elementary school he continues to learn from TV watching it after school, in the evenings, on weekends and all through the summer.

It is interesting to note that many parents are concerned about where a child goes to school, who his teacher is, what he is taught. If one or more of these concerns do not successfully meet their satisfaction, the parent is off to the school principal, teacher or school board to try to rectify the situation. State law further mandates that educators must meet strict criteria before they are allowed to get their teaching degrees and given access to the classrooms. The same is usually true about curriculum and books used within the classroom.

But what of television, which can intrude ideas and attitudes into the home simply through the physical ability of a two-year-old to turn on the set. What are the effects of this exposure?

TELEVISION'S STEREOTYPES AND ATTITUDES

Television not only can teach antisocial activities but can also provide a biased, distorted view of the world which may foster prejudice and misunderstanding. As Himmelweit, Oppenheim and Vince point out: "A whole range of values, however, never find expression in Westerns—those to do with family, work, education, and manners. The characters do not need them in their way of life; they are rarely encumbered by parents, wives or children, and seldom eat or go into their homes. . . ." (5). Gerbner reports that "foreigners and those not identifiable as Americans, as a group were (in 1969) increasingly more likely to become involved in violence and to pay a higher price for it than were Americans (6). Racial bias and stereotypes were clear in the fifties, when blacks were hardly ever seen on TV, with the exception of such programs as *Amos and Andy,* where the portrayal was that of lovable and lazy buffons. People outside of the United States who saw American TV programs might have well wondered if there were any black people living in the United States.

In the last half dozen years some changes have occurred, with an increasing number of blacks having prominent nonstereotyped roles, which nonetheless have placed them in the position of being "regulators" (7)—staunch supporters of the status quo (as in *The Rookies, Ironside).* Blacks are portrayed as law enforcers today, which conveys the implicit message to the black viewers that they should support the present social structure.

Bias is also clearly portrayed in the types of occupational roles presented. Managers, officials, professionals, service workers and servants compromised 51 percent of the television characters but only represent approximately 11 percent of the U.S. population (8). The occupations which were overrepresented were also stereotypically depicted. "Lawyers were very clever, and usually legally unorthodox. Members of artistic professions were almost always temperamental and eccentric. Police officials were generally hardened, and often brutal. Private investigators were always resourceful and clearly more capable than the police. Nurses were cold and impersonal. Salesmen were glib. Journalists were callous. Taxi, bus and truck drivers were burly and aggressive" (9).

A very recent study of TV watchers by Gerbner and Gross (1975) indicated a distorted perception of reality among the heavy viewers. This survey found that heavy viewers believe at least 5 percent of all male workers in the United States are police officers, whereas light viewers estimate 1 percent, which is much closer to the actual percentage.

Those viewers who watch over nine hours daily also believe that they have a one-in-ten chance of being the victim of a violent assault. The lighter viewers estimated that they had at least a one-in-a-one-hundred chance, which is still higher than what actual crime statistics indicate.

Fear of potential violence and insensitivity to the value of others' lives may be increasingly apparent in the indifference of bystanders to intervene to help victims of violent crimes, e.g., the brutal, drawn-out stabbing murder of Kitty Genovese while over a dozen of her neighbors passively watched.

Stereotyped roles for women are dominant particularly in TV advertising, as Marge Mannes points out: ". . . television commercials . . . reinforce, like an insistent drill, the assumption that a woman's only valid function is that of wife, mother, and servant of men: the inevitable sequel to her earlier function as sex object and swinger" (10). After studying over twelve hundred commercials, the National Organization for Women reported: "Almost all of them showed women inside the home. In 42.6% they were involved in household tasks; in 37.5% they were domestic adjuncts to men, and in 16.7% they were sex objects. That doesn't leave very many, and a lot of commercials don't even have people in them. Only 3% showed women as autonomous people leading independent lives of their own" (11).

Since the advent of public television some violence has always been shown, but in recent decades it has insidiously and consistently proliferated. From 1951 to 1953 the National Association of Educational Broadcasters reported that there was a 15 percent increase in violent incidents on TV. A study by Greenberg, in 1969, of four major cities indicated that in 1954, 17 percent of prime time was devoted to violence, and by 1961 this figure had risen to 60 percent (12). The National Association for Better Radio and Television reported that by 1964 almost two hundred hours per week were devoted to crime scenes involving over five hundred murders. Furthermore, the bulk of this violence (two thirds) occurred before 9 P.M. The NABRT estimated in 1968 that "the average child between ages 5 and 15 watches the violent destruction of more than 13,400 persons on TV" (13).

Gerbner reports that in 1969 "about eight in ten plays still contained violence, and the frequency of violent episodes was still about five per play and nearly eight per hour," but maybe what is more important is that the most violent shows were cartoons strictly designed for children. "The average cartoon hour in 1967 contained more than three times as many violent episodes as the average adult dramatic hour. The trend toward shorter plays sandwiched between frequent commercials on fast-moving cartoon programs further increased the saturation. By 1969, with a violent episode at least every two minutes in all Saturday-morning cartoon programing (including the least violent and including commercial time), and with adult drama becoming less saturated with violence, the average cartoon hour had nearly six times the violence rate of the average adult television drama hour, and nearly twelve times the violence rate of the average movie hour" (14). Evidence continues to pile up that the nightly progression of violence in the guise of entertainment is hardening the viewer and reducing his sensitivity to the value of human life by making murder an ordinary and acceptable part of everyday living.

The question might be asked has TV violence been on a decline since 1969? According to Gerbner's more recent finding, "new programs in 1971 spearheaded the trend toward more lethal violence by depicting record high proportions of screen killers. Contrary to a history of network officials' promises to curb violence, the industry has done little to bring about any change in the situation.

In January 1974 the networks promised that in September they would create an early evening "family viewing" hour. What was not stated was that this meant a nightly two-hour period in which there would be no discrimination in programming.

WHAT ABOUT GOVERNMENT INQUIRIES INTO VIOLENCE?

Probably the earliest formal government inquiry occurred in 1959, when Senator Estes Kefauver, at that time chairman of the Senate Subcommittee on Juvenile Delinquency, questioned the use of violent content in television programing. Following claims by the networks that research on the effects on children of watching television was inconclusive, the president and chairman of the board of the National Association of Broadcasters promised that NAB would undertake research in this area.

Seven years later this same subcommittee, this time under the chairmanship of Senator Thomas Dodd, held hearings and took testimony on the same issue. The testimony revealed that violent programming remained both "rampant" and "opportunistic." At the same time, it became apparent that the previously promised NAB research had not been carried out. The hearing mentioned many network series as being particularly violent, and one committee aide noted years later that these particular programs had been syndicated and shown on independent stations through the country: "it's as if they used our 1961 hearings as a shopping list!" (15). In addition, many of these particularly violent programs were shown at earlier hours than before and consequently were now reaching younger audiences. Again in 1961 an industry spokesman stated that research would be undertaken. By 1966 the promised research was still nonexistent.

In the 1968 hearings conducted by the National Commission on the Causes and Prevention of Violence, the networks argued that they should not be the ones to do research. Additionally, network executives were suggesting that research could not in fact be done because of methodological limitations.

RESEARCH FINDINGS: THE SURGEON GENERAL'S REPORT ON TELEVISION AND SOCIAL BEHAVIOR

On March 5, 1969, Senator John O. Pastore, chairman of the Senate Subcommittee on Communications, wrote to Robert Finch, then Secretary of Health, Education and Welfare:

> I am exceedingly troubled by the lack of any definitive information which would help resolve the question of whether there is a casual connection between televised crime and violence and antisocial behavior by individuals, especially children . . . I am respectfully requesting that you direct the Surgeon General to appoint a committee comprised of distinguished men and women from whatever professions and disciplines deemed appropriate to devise techniques and to conduct a study under his supervision using those techniques which will establish scientifically insofar as possible what harmful effects, if any, these programs have on children (16).

Exactly one week later, Surgeon General William M. Steward stated that he would appoint an advisory panel of experts. Forty scientists were recommended as candidates for the panel by a variety of academic and professional associations and the major broadcasting networks; seven on the list were rejected by the National Association of Broadcasters and the major networks as being unacceptable to them. By eliminating distinguished scientists and researchers, they were able to secure five of the twelve panel positions for their own network consultants and executives. The panel began its work on June 16, 1969, and a million dollars was made available to support research. The National Institute of Mental Health was directed to assume responsibility for the functions of the panel and to provide technical staff for the study. The research consisted of twenty-three independent projects which addressed a variety of related questions through a multidimensional approach to the assessment of television's impact and provided an interrelated set of results.

The report pointed out that television is the most widely used form of mass communication in the United States and perhaps the whole world. According to census statistics, 96 percent of American homes have one or more television sets with the average set being turned on more than one-quarter of each day every day of the year. Most adults and most children watch *at least* two hours daily.

Both the quality and quantity of television changes as the viewer grows older. Regular viewing begins at about three years of age and remains relatively high until puberty (around eleven). At this time it begins to decline, reaching a low point during the teenage years. With marriage and parenthood there is an increase in television viewing, which reaches a plateau through middle age, and then when the children leave home it increases once more (17).

A major component of all mass media, including television, in the United States is violence. What, if any, is the relationship between violence in television content and its effect on the viewers' attitudes and actual behavior?

The advisory panel's report suggested a clear causal relationship between viewing television violence and aggressive behavior for some youngsters. However, this relationship was expressed in such a deliberately tentative and hedging manner as to actually lead to mitigating the negative aspects of the findings. The report was clearly a compromise between the networks' defenders and the other panel members. A number of the researchers involved with the project were of the opinion that their work had been inaccurately represented in the direction of minimizing a clear relationship between the viewing of violence on TV and aggressive behavior on the part of youngsters. In a letter to Senator Pastore, Dr. Monroe Lefkowitz, principal research scientist of the New York State Department of Mental Hygiene wrote:

> The Surgeon General's Scientific Advisory Committee on Television and Social Behavior in my opinion ignores, dilutes, and distorts the research findings in their report, "Television and Growing Up: The Impact of Television Violence." As a contributor of one of the technical reports whose study dealt with television violence and aggressive behavior . . . I feel that the Committee's conclusions about the casual nature of television violence in producing aggressive behavior are hedged by erroneous statements, are overqualified, and are potentially damaging to children and society . . . (18).

In a report called "Social policy research and the realities of the system: violence done to TV research," it is indicated that fully half of the twenty committee researchers who responded to a questionnaire about the representation of their results felt that their research had not been adequately reported by the committee (19).

These twenty investigators were asked: "Whatever the findings of your own research suggest, which of the following relationships of violence viewing to aggressiveness do you feel now is the most plausible?"

(a) Viewing television violence increases aggressiveness.

(b) Viewing television violence decreases aggressiveness.

(c) Viewing television violence has no effect on aggressiveness.

(d) The relationship between violence viewing and aggressiveness depends on a third variable or set of variables.

(e) Other, please specify.

Seventy percent of these twenty respondents selected (a); none selected (b) or (c). The remaining qualified their responses by selecting alternate (d) or (e).

TWO-THEORIES OF MEDIA VIOLENCE AND ITS EFFECT

The Cathartic Theory

Aristotle stated in his *Art of Poetry* that drama is "a representation .. . in the form of actions directly presented, not narrated: with incidents arousing pity and fear in such a way as to accomplish a purgation of such emotions" (20). He speculated that the members of the audience witnessing a dramatic portrayal of grief, fear and pity would themselves be purged of those feelings. The Cathartic Theory, as it is applied to aggression, predicts that viewing violence reduces aggression in the observer because he purges himself of anger through vicarious identification. The major contemporary proponents of this theory are Seymour Feshback and Robert Singer, who suggest that aggressive fantasy serves to reduce aggression. The mass media stimulate fantasy, which "substitutes for overt behaviors which are partly rewarding in themselves and which may reduce arousal, as coping or adapting mechanisms useful when delays in gratification occur, and as aids to arousal possibly culminating in overt behavior." Television violence may also reduce aggression in another way: "It may frighten the viewer of violence and its possible consequences; it may create overaggressive impulses and the eventuality that they may be acted out. The viewer consequently avoids aggressive behavior in order to reduce his fear of what he may do or what may be done to him" (21).

The Imitative Learning Theory

This approach suggests that individuals learn by example. Exposure to a model who acts in a certain way leads one to acquire the particular behavioral sequence observed. However, whether this acquired behavior is performed or not depends on whether it will be rewarded or punished and whether the original model is of high status or low status.

This theory's major proponents are Albert Bandura and Richard Walters, who feel that a child does not just learn new behavior from watching others but just as important he also learns whether it is or is not appropriate to act in a certain manner, and when to act or when not to act in this manner. When the model's behavior leads to positive outcomes (reward) and when the model is of high status (high-status individuals are those who are presumed to know what is permissible or acceptable behavior), it will be imitated.

Some Research Findings Regarding These Two Theories

A very carefully constructed multiple correlation study sponsored by the Surgeon General's Scientific Advisory Committee on Television and Social Behavior was undertaken in 1971 by McLeod, Atkin, and Chaffee to examine the relationship between the viewing of television violence and a number of measures of aggressive behavior in two relatively large samples of students in junior and senior high schools, one in Maryland and one in Wisconsin. The authors concluded "that adolescents viewing high levels of violent content on television tend to have high levels of aggressive behavior, regardless of television viewing time, socioeconomic status, or school performance" (22).

McIntyre and Teevan (23) note from their research that "those adolescents whose favorite programs are more violent more frequently approve of a teenage boy punching or knifing another teenage boy. If the favorite program is described as depicting violence as a means to an end, or violence rewarded, teen violence is approved more often than if the program were not so described. Whether or not the program "shows the way people ought to act" does not influence frequency of approval.

Liebert, in his overview on "Television and Social Learning: Some Relationship Between Viewing Violence and Behaving Aggressively," concludes his evaluation and summary of research results with the following: "At least under some circumstances, exposure to television aggression can lead children to accept what they have seen as a partial guide for their own actions. As a result, the present entertainment offerings of television medium may be contributing, in some measure, to the aggressive behavior of many normal children. Such an effect has now been shown in a wide variety of situations" (24).

Summarizing research results, Liebert goes on to say that "evidence supporting the assertion that television violence can reduce aggression is scant and is directly at odds with correlational data based on widely varied samples as tapped by many different researchers." He concludes:

1. It has been shown convincingly that children are exposed to a substantial amount of violent content on television, and that they can remember and learn from such exposure.

2. Correlational studies have disclosed a regular association between aggressive television viewing and a variety of measures of aggression, employing impressively broad samples in terms of range of economic background and geographic and family characteristics.

3. Experimental studies preponderantly support the hypothesis that there is a direct, causal link between exposure to television violence and observer's subsequent aggressive behavior.

Following the publication of the technical reports, Senator Pastore held further hearings. At those hearings the following testimony was heard:

Twelve scientists of widely different views unanimously agreed that scientific evidence indicated that viewing of television by young people causes them to behave more aggressively. (Ithiel de Sola Pool, a member of the Surgeon General's Advisory Committee) (25)

Commercial television makes its own contribution to the set of factors that underlie aggressiveness in our society. It does so in entertainment through ceaseless repetition of the message that conflict may be resolved by aggression, that violence is a way of solving problems. (Alberta Siegel, another committee member (26)

We agree with you that the time for action has come. And of course, are willing to cooperate in any way together with the rest of the industry. (Julian Goodman, president of NBC) (27)

Now that we are reasonably certain that television can increase aggressive tendencies in some children we will have to manage our program planning accordingly. (Elton H. Rule, ABC) (28)

Certainly my interpretation is that there is a causative relationship between televised violence and subsequent antisocial behavior, and that the evidence is strong enough that it requires some action on the part of responsible authorities, the TV industry, the government, the citizens. (Surgeon General Steinfeld) (29)

WHAT CAN BE DONE?

The Private Citizen and the Profit Motive

A member of the Surgeon General's advisory panel and a former editor of the journal *Child Development*, Alberta Siegel, has made the following suggestion:

> The purpose of commercial television is to sell products. If consumers boycott products that are advertised on programs glorifying aggression and teaching techniques of mayhem and massacre, perhaps the producers of these products will turn their energies to finding other techniques of attracting customers. Many investors today are guided in their investing by social concerns. Churches, universities, foundations, union pension plans, and others are seeking to invest funds in ways that benefit society. If these groups know who the violence vendors are, they may withdraw investment funds from their firms and instead invest their funds in those manufacturers who sponsor wholesome entertainment for the next generation (30).

The Advertisers and the Profit Motive

Advertisers might withdraw all advertising from violent programs and purchase advertising time on constructive, creative, wholesome programing, as, for example, the president of Miracle White has done. Sponsors who direct their resources to improve programing might themselves be rewarded by private individuals purchasing their products and through public letters of commendation from citizen groups.

The Government

Since 1960 the Consumers Union has urged the more forceful and efficient functioning of the FCC:

> Make hearings mandatory in all license renewals. . . . To obtain its highly prized license to operate—the right to use the public domain: an air channel on TV or radio station vies with other contestants by, among other things, promising programs of quality. Every three years, according to law, a broadcasting license must be renewed. Although the FCC has the power to hold a renewal hearing to determine how well the licensee has carried out his promises, it has been most lax on this score. In 1958, for example, out of 1500 or so radio and TV renewals granted, only two renewal hearings, were held . . . hold all such renewal hearings, as well as new license hearings, in the locale of the broadcasting station so that the community to be served may be heard.
>
> Since community tastes and interests may differ, local set owners are, obviously, the ones best situated not only to know what they want over the

air, but what the actual program content has been. It makes little sense, therefore, to hold license hearings in Washington, D.C., where attendance is limited, practically speaking, to the industry's lobbyists, attorneys, and public relations personnel. Publicize the renewal hearings over the stations involved for a given number of days at fixed hours, and invite public participation in the proceedings.

A public hearing of which the public is unaware is hardly public.

Require each broadcaster to maintain for public investigation the commitments he made with regard to programing and advertising when he was granted his license.

The promise made by the broadcaster as a condition to his receipt of a license are not, practically speaking, a matter of public record unless access to such commitments is made easily available to the particular consumers whose sets receive the particular licensee's broadcasts (31).

An independent agency to monitor these practices would be critical for success, as Alberta Siegel pointed out:

... We need an independent monitoring agency to provide regular reports on the level of violence in television entertainment. This agency could issue periodic "smog bulletins," alerting the public to the level of violence pollution currently being emitted by their TV receivers. I suggest that this agency might be privately financed, by one of the foundations, and that reports should be issued at least monthly. These reports should be broadcast over television and should appear in newspapers and magazines. . . . They should indicate how much violence is occurring, which networks and stations are broadcasting it, the times it is being broadcast and how many child viewers are estimated to be watching and those times. They should also indicate who the sponsors are for the violent shows (32).

In an attempt to strengthen FCC authority, Congressman John M. Murphy introduced Bill HR 15408 on June 8, 1972.

... In introducing a bill for regulation of the networks, I am fully aware that, in the last analysis, it is those who have been licensed by the Federal Communications Commission to operate the nation's television stations who must bear the ultimate responsibility for the violence and triviality that today dominates American television . . .

Past experience has shown that it will be a long time—perhaps never—before the TV broadcasters eliminate violence from TV. That is, unless there is a vigorous move by government to force them to stop. But members of the Senate Communications Committee themselves professed frustration when it came to recommending a solution to TV violence because of First Amendment considerations. . . . Previous attempts at eliminating TV violence by relying on the "good faith" of the TV industry by several House and Senate Committees, the Federal Communications Commission, and the President's Commission on Violence have been marked by failure. Failure because these groups all deplored violence on television; with varying degrees of sophistication they pointed to TV violence as a negative influence on human behavior; and, they were lulled into inaction with promises from the TV industry that there would be a diminishment of violence if the industry were allowed to "clean up its own house." And, as of May, 1972, the net result of all this has been a lamentable cipher. Over and above the question of whether TV violence is harmful, the networks have, for the past 18 years, assiduously violated their own codes of ethics and standards of broadcasting. In the face of an 18-year history of failure of self-control, I feel it is safe to conclude that we cannot depend on the TV industry to clean its own house of TV violence. They obviously will not. . . .

I have decided to introduce legislation to give the FCC the authority to regulate the networks in the area of prime time programing. The recent antitrust suits by the Justice Department would divest the networks of their production of these shows altogether. I am against such drastic action.

As I pointed out, given our system, the networks, and only the networks, have the capability to produce quality television on a sustained basis. We need them. My bill would not take this function away from them—it would only make them produce programs more in the public interest (33).

REFERENCES

1. Bronowski J: *The Ascent of Man.* Boston/Toronto. Little, Brown and Co., 1973.
2. US National Commission on the causes and prevention of Violence, US Government Printing Office, 1969.
3. *The Film Index.* Vol. 1. *The Film as Art,* 562b, New York, The Museum of Modern Art Film Library and the HW Co., 1941.
4. Blumer H, Hauser PM: *Movies, delinquency, and Crime.* New York, Macmillan, 1933.
5. Himmelweit H, Oppenheim AN, and Vince P.: *Television and the Child: An Empirical Study of the Effects of Television on the Young.* London, Oxford University Press, 1958.
6. Gerbner G.: Violence in television drama: Trends and symbolic functions. In GA Comstock and EA Rubinstein (eds) *Television and Social Behavior* Vol 1: Media Content and Control. Washington, US Government Printing Office, 1972.
7. Clark CC: Communication, conflict and the portrayal of ethnic minorities: A minority perspective. Unpublished manuscript, Stanford University, 1972.
8. Smythe DW: Reality as presented by television. *Public Opinion Quarterly,* 18:143–156, 1954.
9. Defleur, M: Occupational roles as portrayed on television. *Public Opinion Quarterly,* 28:71, 1964.
10. Mannes M: Television: The splitting image. *Saturday Review,* 66–67, November 14, 1970.
11. Hennessee JA, Nicholson J: NOW says: TV commercials insult women. *The New York Times Magazine,* p 12, May 28, 1972.
12. Greenberg BS: The content and context of violence in the mass media. In RK Baker, SJ Ball (eds) *Violence and the Media.* Washington, US Government Printing Office, p 9, 1969.

13. National Association for Better Radio and Television. Crime on television: *A survey report*. Los Angeles: National Association for Better Radio and Television, 1964.
14. Gerbner G: Violence in television drama: Trends and symbolic functions. In GA Comstock, EA Rubinstein (eds) *Television and Social Behavior*, Vol 1: Media content and control. Washington, US Government Printing Office, p 36, 1972.
15. Gerbner G: The violence profile: Some indicators of the trends in and the symbolic structure of network television drama 1967-1971. Unpublished manuscript, The Annenberg School of Communications, University of Pennsylvania, p 3, 1972.
16. Barnouw, E: A history of broadcasting in the United States. Vol. III - from 1953: The image empire. New York, Oxford University Press, p 203, 1972.
17. Cisin IH, Coffin TE, Janis IL, Klapper JT, Mendelsohn H, Omwoke E, Pinderhughes CA, Pool I deSola, Siegel AE, Wallace AFC, Watson AS, Wiebe GD: *Television and Growing Up: The Impact of Televised Violence*. Washington, US Government Printing Office, 1972.
18. ibid.
19. Paisley MB: Social policy research and the realities of the system: violence done to TV research. Institute of Communication Research: Stanford University, 1972.
20. Berkowitz L: The effects of observing violence. *Scientific American* Vol 210, No. 2, p 35, 1964.
21. Feshbach S, Singer R: *Television and Aggression*. San Francisco, Jossey-Bass, 1971.
22. McLeod JM, Atkin CK, Chaffee SH: Adolescents, parents and television use. *Television and Social Behavior*, Vol 3, 1971.
23. McIntyre JJ, Teevan JJ: Television and deviant behavior. *Television and Social Behavior*, Vol 3, 1971.
24. Liebert, M: Television and Social Learning. Some relationships between viewing violence and behaving aggressively (overview). *Television and Social Behavior*. Vol 2, Television and Social Learning. Washington, US Government Printing Office, pp 1–34, 1972.
25. US Congress, Senate Hearings before the Subcommittee on Communications of the Commerce Committee, March 1972, p 47.
26. ibid (p 63).
27. ibid (p 182).
28. ibid (p 217).
29. ibid (p 28).
30. ibid (p 64).
31. Here, we would suggest, is a program for the FCC Consumer Reports, February 1960. (Copyright Consumers Union).
32. op. cit. (pp. 63–66).
33. Murphy JM: Statement of Representative John M. Murphy on the introduction of a bill to regulate the television networks. June 8, 1972.

Predicting Dangerousness

HENRY J. STEADMAN

Why a chapter on predicting dangerousness in a book on aggression?* Primarily because most people are not really concerned about prediciting aggression. Scientists may be, but the public and policy makers are not, *unless* it is aggression directed by one person against another or occasionally against self. In other words, until aggression becomes the type that is a threat to the well-being of self or others, it is of minimal concern to society as a whole.

One may examine the varied dimensions of aggression and violence indefinitely without touching on their most significant policy issues. The issues arise from the links of aggression and violence with the concept of dangerousness. As long as the aggression and violence is controlled or appropriately channeled, these concepts do not enter the social control realms of the criminal justice and mental health systems. As long as these activities relate to war or sport or remain at sufficiently low levels in the family or community, who cares? It is the fear of the shadowy stranger attacking in the night that elicits public fear and reaction. When the aggression or violence poses a threat, it is considered a danger. Then legislation for societal protection is demanded. It is my thesis here that it is in the concept of

*The substantive and editorial inputs of Joseph J. Cocozza on earlier drafts of this chapter are greatfully acknowledged.

dangerousness that the ideas of aggression and violence take on their most important implications. Therefore in any overview of these topics, dangerousness is an essential component.

Given that dangerousness is to be explained, why concentrate on "predicting dangerousness"? The answer to this question is inherent in the concept itself. Dangerousness is necessarily a prediction. As we will discuss in greater detail below, to say someone (or someplace) is dangerous, is to make an evaluation of what might happen in the future. Dangerousness is not anything innate in the person, place or event. Rather, it is an estimation by someone as to the expectation that something they see as dangerous may happen with a fairly high probability in the future. Thus, to analyze the concept of dangerousness and its relationships to aggression and violence, one must deal with its estimation—its prediction.

To proceed with this analysis, we will first consider how the concepts of aggression, violence and dangerousness are conceptually linked. Following this exercise, we will survey the areas where dangerousness is regularly employed, and then evaluate the empirical evidence for the various professionals who are permitted or mandated to make predictions of dangerousness that have serious implications for much of society through the criminal justice and mental health systems.

AGGRESSION, VIOLENCE AND DANGEROUSNESS

To analyze what is actually meant by dangerousness it is important to systematically consider the relationships between the terms "aggression," "violence" and "dangerousness." The two things most shared by these terms are vague conceptualization and imprecise measurement. What they do not share, unfortunately, is a consistent, integrative body of work either in clinical practice or in research. With few exceptions, notably Rubin (1), the genetic, biochemical, experimental and clinical research on aggression and violence have rarely been linked with developing work on dangerousness. Yet these three terms are intimately interrelated.

To obtain a preliminary handle on any concept, it is often helpful to examine the fields' standard reference works. Utilizing four such references from medicine, psychiatry, psychology and sociology (Stedman's Medical Dictionary, Psychiatric Dictionary, Encyclopedia of Psychology and The International Encyclopedia of the Social Sciences), it is striking to note that all offer some discussion of aggression but none has an entry for violence or dangerousness. This surely reflects a greater generalization for Ervin and Lion's (2) observation specific to psychiatry that as a field it "... generally shunned the subject of violence."

Having noted this omission, one finds little of use in these sources pertaining to aggression. As the *Encyclopedia of Psychology* reports, "Controversy reigns in the study of human aggression." A primary controversy involves various arguments about whether aggression is a drive, instinct or behavior, and if it is behavior, how it is learned or stimulated. Most basically, the conceptualizations of aggression grossly dichotomize into ideas defining aggression as instinct or drive and ideas defining aggression as behavior. The modal group of definitions would certainly be those defining it as behavior, and for the purposes of my presentation I will use "aggression" to mean assertive behavior.

Concerning violence, Gilula and Daniels (3) seem to reflect a consensus view defining violence as "destructive aggression." This conceptualization implies the use of physical force to injure persons or property, and this is the core of most definitions of violence. Two major variant views on definitions of violence are found in the report of the President's Task Force on the Causes and Prevention of Violence. The first is the Commission's own extremely broad definition, which includes overt *threats* of force even toward the reputation of persons, as well as actual application of force toward persons or property. A second major variant definition is found in one of the Commission's staff reports by Ervin and Lion, who include assaultive or destructive *ideations* as well as acts in their definition of violence. From the standpoint of dangerousness these two additional conceptualizations are most significant in that they represent the thinking reflected in statutes and sentencing practices which grow from attempts to designate *potentially* violent individuals.

To link the concept of dangerousness to aggression and violence is a step not usually taken in the literature, partly, it seems, because of a gulf which appears to exist between the academic and clinical disciplines involved in conceptualizing, measuring and discussing violence and aggression and the agents of legislation and social control who have increasingly depended on the idea of dangerousness.

An interesting example of the close but often unackowledged link between violence and dangerousness is the counterpoint produced by consecutive articles in the October 1972 issues of the journal *Crime and Delinquency*. The first article was entitled "The Diagnosis and Treatment of Dangerousness." The article immediately following was called "Can Violence Be Predicted?" The first study dealt with a group of individuals evaluated in the Massachusetts Center for the Diagnosis of Dangerous Persons as convicted offenders, mostly sex offenders. In this study, dangerousness was operationalized as rearrest for "serious assaultive crimes." The subsequent report on predicting violence dealt with a follow-up of California Youth Authority wards and measured violence by rearrest for violent crimes. Thus, here are two articles that deal respectively, according to their titles, with dangerousness and violence, but which both use precisely the same indicator for their differing terms.

On this note, it is not surprising to find that the same controversy and imprecision that characterize much of the work on aggression and violence also dominate the literature on dangerousness. A basic problem in conceptualizing dangerousness is the inability of many people to recognize that dangerousness is essentially a prediction, an estimation. Dangerousness is not dangerous behavior.

Aggression is assertive behavior. Violence is destructive aggression, and *dangerousness is an estimation of the probability of dangerous behavior*, which usually refers to violent physical assault against another, or sometimes to self. However, the question of what is dangerous behavior is separate from what is dangerousness. There should be no doubt, no controversy, about dangerousness being a prediction as there is with many of the questions about what aggression is. When we use "dangerousness," we are referring to someone's or some group's estimation of how probable he/she/they believe a given person is apt to perform an act which is seen as dangerous. Dangerousness, like beauty, is in the eye of the beholder, i.e., dangerousness is a perception, a definition of a person or situation by the perceiver. Dangerousness, as a perception, is a quality of the perceiver more than it is a characteristic of the one perceived as dangerous.

As clear, as important, and as frequently noted (1, 4, 5) as is this predictive, perceptual essence of dangerousness, one is continually confronted by definitions similar to that recently offered by Goldzband (6), who defined dangerousness as "a quality of an individual or situation leading to the potential or actualization of harm to an individual, a community, or to a social order." It cannot be overemphasized that dangerousness is not inherent in a person or situation. Dangerousness is the estimation of someone of the probability that something "dangerous" will occur. It is an inclination to attribute dangerousness to an individual and to define it so broadly that it is of little use that returns us to the two "variant" definitions of violence to which I alluded earlier. When violence is conceptualized to refer to *threats* of the application of force or as the *ideation* of assaultive or destructive acts, it too moves into the area of prediction. No longer is the concept necessarily referring to observed behavioral acts. No longer does violence have much practical legal meaning. From the standpoint of social control, such conceptualizations confound the distinction between penalizing (detaining) for predicted rather than actual behavior.

STATUTORY USES OF DANGEROUSNESS

Under various state civil involuntary mental commitment laws there are an estimated 50,000 persons per year committed because of estimations of dangerousness (1). In addition, there are approximately 60,000 individuals per year arrested and evaluated for dangerousness, the determination of which will determine lengths and/or types of incarceration or hospitalization.

Despite the rapidly growing importance of dangerousness in a variety of legal situations, very few practical explications of it and its direct, important links with violence and aggression have been attempted. Two of the most helpful elaborations of the legal difficulties and complexities of dangerousness are found in two decisions of Judge David Bazelon in the Washington, D.C. Court of Appeals: *Millard v. Harris* 406 F. 2nd 964 (1968) and *Cross v. Harris* 418 F. 2nd 1095. In the second of these cases, Bazelon limited dangerousness to "likely to attack or otherwise inflict injury, loss, pain, or other evil." In specifying the criteria of dangerousness to be required in testimony, he mentioned the likelihood of recurrence of the crime, the likely frequency of such behavior, and the magnitude of harm. The latter must be "substantial."

Even these criteria are nowhere near sufficient for actual judicial application. In fact, rarely do the courts press expert witnesses on the time frame of their predictions, precisely what the expected behavior is, and why they are inferring links between the cited criteria for dangerousness and the likelihood of the predicted behavior. Nevertheless, under the auspices of dangerousness, clinicians are frequently asked by the court to predict violent behavior among both civil and criminal patients.

While the situations that involve psychiatrists as estimators of dangerousness may be the most frequent, there are many other circumstances in which predictions of dangerousness are made. These latter circumstances take place in both the criminal justice and mental health systems and involve psychologists, judges, and parole boards in addition to psychiatrists.

In most instances the use of dangerousness involves both

correctional and mental health institutions. On the primarily criminal level, dangerousness is related to the sentencing process and to parole decisions. In the other circumstances, dangerousness is a crucial concept in statutes dealing with defective delinquents, sexual psychopaths, defendants not guilty by reason of insanity (NGRI), and incompetent defendants.

Let us first turn to the uses of dangerousness in the primarily criminal situation of sentencing and parole decision-making. An excellent example of the former is a very significant section of the 1972 revision of the Model Sentencing Act. This section proposed some specific criteria and procedures for sentencing the dangerousness offender who was defined as an offender:

> ... being sentenced for a felony in which he (a) inflicted or attempted to inflict serious bodily harm or (b) seriously endangered the life or safety of another and he was previously convicted of one or more felonies not related to the instant crime as a single criminal episode, and (c) the court finds that he is suffering from a severe mental or emotional disorder indicating a propensity toward continuing dangerousness activity. (emphasis added)

An example of this proposal being effected is the bill coming before the 1975 legislature in the State of Washington to review sentencing practices (7). Such criminal dispositions usually involve the mental health system only through mental health professionals' participation in the evaluation process preceding sentencing. Subsequently, regular criminal processing occurs, although the "dangerous offender" may ultimately be placed in a mental health facility.

Another predominantly criminal justice system decision related to dangerousness, but considerably more covert than the recommendations of the Model Sentencing Act, is that of parole. In a study of two Midwestern parole boards, Scott (1973) found that the single most important factor in the board's decisions was the inmate's current offense. Regardless of the institutional adjustment or sociodemographic characteristics of the inmate, the most significant factor for the parole boards he studied was the seriousness of the inmate's current charge. Scott does not put his findings into the context of dangerousness. However, since the seriousness of offense is a good indicator of how dangerous certain behaviors are viewed by society, the use of current offense and the estimates of the potential for its reoccurrence are in fact one type of prediction of dangerousness employed in the criminal justice system.

When we talk of sexual psychopath laws and defective delinquent statutes, we move into areas which increasingly overlap and confuse questions of criminal justice and mental health. These overlaps occur both through the agents involved in the decision-making and in the institutions to which individuals may be committed. Kittrie (8) has pointed out that from the first psychopathy law enacted in Massachusetts in 1911, the Briggs Act, through the second flood of such legislation in the late 1930's and 1940's to the latest phase typified by Maryland's 1951 defective delinquent statute, such laws have often encompassed a very wide range of criminal behaviors beyond sexual offenses. Allen and colleagues (9) noted that in Ohio approximately three-fourths of offenders committed under a sexual psychopath law were convicted of non-sex-related crimes.

Although it is not discussed by Kittrie, one especially significant feature of these psychopathy laws is that in every case he cites, and in the Ohio statute discussed by Allen et al., commitment depends on conviction, mental disability of some sort, and some demonstration of danger to society. In all twenty-nine states and the District of Columbia which currently have special legislation for psychopathic offenders and defective delinquents (7), the estimation of the probability that the individual will engage in some type of conduct which is defined as dangerous is central to the dispositional process.

The final two areas of criminal justice dispositions utilizing estimations of dangerousness for direct diversion into the mental health system are the judicial findings that a defendant is NGRI or incompetent to stand trial. The NGRI determination in most jurisdictions does not necessarily imply any decision involving dangerousness.* Instead, one detects the covert use of dangerousness to detain patients in civil mental hospitals, after the involuntary commitment which necessarily follows an NGRI finding in most states.

A recent example of these uses of dangerousness is the case of Bruce Sherman who, in May 1972 in Rochester, New York, was found NGRI in the shooting death of his wife. Less than three months after this trial, the civil hospital's release committee concluded that Sherman showed "no evidence of being mentally ill or in need of continued hospital care." Although he had an "explosive personality" that could be set off by his drinking, he had no treatable mental illness. Regardless, the trial judge refused to approve his release from the civil hospital because he felt Sherman was dangerous. The judge decided it

---

*An exception is the District of Columbia, where after the criminal court arrives at an NGRI verdict, there is a special hearing to determine whether the individual is mentally ill and dangerous and therefore requires mental hospitalization. The theory behind these "Bolton" hearings is that although an offender may not be criminally responsible at the time of offense, it does not necessarily follow that he is currently either mentally ill or dangerous, and only if both conditions are present is involuntary civil commitment permissible.

was the hospital's obligation to protect the community from this dangerous person, even if he did not have a treatable mental illness. So, although a determination of dangerousness had no part whatsoever to play in Sherman's criminal disposition, his continued criminal court-ordered detention was quite dependent on the court's estimation of the danger he posed to the community. It is this covert use of estimations of dangerousness that most typify the NGRI situaiton.

The second direct diversion to the mental health system from the criminal justice system involves incompetent defendants. This latter group is about ten to fifteen times larger than defendants found NGRI. The common law standards for competency deal with the defendant's ability to understand both the charges against him and the court process and to cooperate with an attorney in his own defense. So no question of dangerousness is directly involved in a judicial determination of fitness to proceed with a trial. However, in New York from 1971 through 1974, when the procedures were declared unconstitutional by the State Court of Appeals, the location to which the indicted felony defendant found incompetent was sent depended on the court's determination of dangerousness. This was accomplished in the absence of a statutory definition, established criteria or documentable expertise on the part of the two psychiatrists who were mandated to report their predictions to the court.

The undocumentable assumptions about predictive expertise at the core of both the New York State incompetency procedures and all other uses of dangerousness discussed become disconcertingly evident when one examines the existing empirical facts.

EVALUATING PREDICITONS OF DANGEROUSNESS

Perhaps the most difficult problem in assessing the accuracy of dangerousness predictions by the various professionals in the sundry locations just discussed is the infrequency with which anyone has collected data on these questions. In addition, there is practically no consensus on the meaning or operationalization of dangerousness.

As far back as 1960 in an important article, Katz and Goldstein (10) indicated that dangerousness was used to mean any one or a combination of ten things, from all crimes to any physical violence toward oneself. Among recent operationalizations of dangerousness have been arrest rates of ex-mental patients for violent crimes against person (11, 12), likelihood of released mental patients harming themselves or others (13), probability of committing any criminal act (14), "unwanted harm" primarily "as it might befall one of us" (15), actual injury and destruction of property (1), and potential for inflicting serious bodily harm on another (16). There remains little consensus on the meaning of dangerousness and there is considerable muddling of it with aggressive/violent/dangerous behavior.

With conceptualizations of dangerousness so confused, it is not surprising that there have been few attempts to actually distinguish criteria for predicting it. In all the research literature, there are only five studies we could discover that offer defined criteria for predicting dangerous behavior. Marcus (17) offers 14 factors inferred from the records of dangerous sex offenders. He proposed taking each factor, such as brutality sustained in childhood, low IQ, and lack of human warmth, arbitrarily assigning it a value between 1 and 10, summing for a dangerousness score. Bach-Y-Rita et al. (18) inferred 12 factors associated with dangerousness in a population of 130 violent patients. Ordway (19) presents a set of factors involving such psychiatric criteria as faulty reality testing and ego control. However, its use is not discussed outside a diagnostic case conference setting. None of these three sets of factors has been used predictively, and none adequately defines its components, their measurement or criterion variables. McGarry (20) reviewed the clinical, sociodemographic and criminal criteria that he felt, on reflection, he actually employed in arriving at estimations of dangerousness. Further, he also weighed each of these 14 factors so that a score could be determined between 36 and 360. These criteria were offered in a very preliminary fashion and were not purported to have internal reliability or predictive validity. It remains for this scale to be empirically tested and refined.

The fifth study is a notable, recent addition to this literature. It is also the most startling. This piece by Kozol and co-workers (16) concluded: "It appears that dangerousness can be reliably diagnosed and effectively treated." This assertion of Kozol and staff and its ensuing coverage raise some very serious questions in the light of the data they presented and the strikingly different findings reported in the very next article by Wenk et al (25) in the same journal in which the Kozol piece was published.

The Kozol study reports that of those sex offenders who underwent treatment at their facility and were discharged on the recommendation of the clinical staff, only 6.1 percent (5 of 82) subsequently committed serious assaultive crimes (their indicator of dangerousness). On the other hand, of those released by court order *against the advice of the clinical staff*, 34.7 percent (17 of 49) subsequently committed serious assaultive crimes. These reported results, while initially both impressive and exciting, become questionable upon closer examination of the reported research (21, 22). The most serious problem is the failure to control for length of time at risk in the community.

As discussed by Cocozza (21), 82 of the 386 patients recommended for release were so approved after an average of 43 months of treatment, giving them from 5 to 11 months at risk during the 48- to 54-month follow-up period. The data on the comparison group of 49 patients included 18 patients who were also treated, but who were at risk from 18 to 24 months—13 months longer. Thus the group released against psychiatric advice could have been at risk as much as four years longer than the treated lower-recidivism group. In addition, there is no way to tell what the period of risk was for the other 304 "non-dangerous" or the other 31 "dangerous" patients. Thus, without proper controls for length of time at risk by the patients in each group, it is impossible—from the data Kozol and colleagues presented in their original piece, as well as in a subsequent rejoinder (23) and news report (24)—to validly conclude that dangerousness can be predicted.

The findings of Wenk et al. (25), although not reported under the heading of dangerousness, are much more in agreement with almost all other research. They found that in attempting to predict violent recidivism, Kozol's indicator of dangerousness, among a sample of 4,146 California Youth Authority wards, the most efficient variable was a history of actual violence. This one category of individuals contained half the subjects who later became violent and had a violent recidivism rate three times greater than that of the remainder. The difficulty they encountered in their attempts to predict violence is the common one of excessive false positives. Only 52 of the 1,006 subjects who had a history of violence actually repeated. Thus, despite the fact that this characteristic was the best predictor, one would still be sounding a false alarm nineteen times in twenty and wasting 95 percent of any resources expended. They conclude that:

> Confidence in the ability to predict violence serves to legitimate intrusive types of social control. Our demonstration of the futility of such prediction should have consequences as great for the protection of individual liberty as a demonstration of the utility of violence prediction would have for the protection of society.

The findings and conclusion of the Wenk group are very similar to our previous work on the Baxstrom patients. These 967 patients were transferred from New York's two hospitals for the criminally insane against psychiatric advice to civil mental facilities after a 1966 U.S. Supreme Court decision.

This group presents a case of implicit psychiatric predictions of dangerousness in that a major reason for their prior detention in correctional, maximum security hospitals was the danger they would pose to staff and other patients in civil hospitals (cf. *Baxstrom v. Herold* 383 U.S. 107). Our retrospective research (26) was an attempt to find out what had happened to this group of patients who were widely feared by the hospital staffs that were forced to accept them. How much trouble (i.e., danger) had they caused and encountered in the civil hospitals and the community after release?

To answer such questions, we gathered information from hospital and correctional records and from a community follow-up of 85 patients. The Baxstrom patients were predominantly nonwhite, middle-aged ($\bar{x} = 47$ at transfer) individuals who were marginal in terms of education, work skills and marital stability. Most had previously been arrested and many had previous convictions. Contrary to the stereotypes of the criminally insane, very few had any sex crime convictions and 42 percent had never been convicted of a violent crime.

Of all these allegedly dangerous people, 15 percent were assaultive while hospitalized prior to any releases, and 49 percent were released at some time between 1966 and 1970. Of those released, 20 percent were rearrested, but only 7 percent were convicted of any offenses, and the vast majority of their convictions were for minor offenses, such as vagrancy and intoxication. Looking at both in-hospital and community behaviors, 20 percent were assaultive toward others during our four-year follow-up period.

Examining some of the more intriguing relationships between the variables we studied, it was apparent that while assaultive behavior in the hospitals can certainly be seen as negative behavior, such behavior was not associated with either release to the community or assaultive behavior in the community. Assaultive behavior *was* associated with being younger, and this variable (age) and the availability of family or friends in the community were the main determinants of who got out.

The major relationship we found relating prior factors to community assaultive behavior was between age and our Legal Dangerousness Scale (26, 27), which is a summary measure of four criminal background characteristics. However, while statistically significant relationship were obtainable, the level of false positives remained 2 to 1, thus severely limiting any clinical usefulness.

In sum, the implicit psychiatric predictions of the danger posed by the Baxstrom patients were vast overpredictions. The retrospective, statistical estimations from our research also concluded with a false positive rate double the number of accurate predictions on which individuals would exhibit assaultive, nondefensive behavior toward others. No place in the research literature is there any indication of proven psychiatric accuracy in making clinical judgments of dangerousness. In no research study has the level of false positives been sufficiently low for a generalizable patient group (the Baxstrom patients averaged 47 years of age and had been institutionalized continuously for an average of 14 years) to have substantial evaluative utility.

At no time in this section assessing predictive capabilities have we discussed data on the predictions of groups other than psychiatrists in the criminal justice and mental health systems, although such predictions of dangerousness are critical in many dispositional, treatment and custodial decisions. We have not discussed judges, parole boards, psychologists and others because there are no data available that allow such evaluations specifically for these groups. It is only recently that people have become aware of the centrality of the concept of dangerousness to such decision-making, and as yet there are no data that permit systematic assessment of predictions in these spheres. Certainly, one can examine recidivism records of parolees, subsequent behavior of probationers, and the arrest records of ex-mental patients to discuss the level of aggressive or violent behavior that such groups have exhibited, and from these data make some inferences concerning implicit, covert uses of predictions of dangerousness. However, until the role of this concept is more clearly perceived and parsed from the other factors involved in criminal justice and mental health processing, it is impossible to provide any empirical assesments of predictions of dangerousness in these contexts.

Having examined the data on psychiatric predictions of dangerousness which indicate disturbing levels of unproven expertise, let us turn to two pervasive statistical obstacles facing the predictors of dangerousness.

GENERAL PREDICTION PROBLEMS RELATED TO DANGEROUSNESS

There are two general difficulties in predicting dangerousness that are closely interrelated. They are the problems of trying to predict low-base-rate behavior and the accompanying problem of excessive numbers of false positives—i.e., identifying individuals as dangerous who are not, far in excess of correctly identifying those who are actually dangerous.

Both of these problems have been recognized for some time, but recently have not received the attention due them. In the mid-1950's

Paul Meehl (28) and Albert Rosen (29) systematically and thoroughly analyzed the associated problems of low-base-rate behaviors and excessive false positives. Rosen's work is particularly illustrative of the problems besetting the clinician, judge and parole board officer, who are asked to make estimations of dangerousness. He develops a theoretical discussion on low-base-rate behavior in the context of the event which he sees as the most infrequent one that clinicians are regularly asked to predict, suicide.

From previous studies, Rosen determined that there was a suicide rate of about .0033 among psychiatric inpatients. So among 12,000 hypothetical patients there would be approximately 40 suicides. Assuming that a suicide index could be developed to correctly predict 75 percent of both the suicide and non-suicide groups—i.e., 30 of the 40 suicidal patients could correctly be identified in advance of their attempt—there would be 2,990 patients in the non-suicide group *incorrectly* identified. To reduce these false positives on the non-suicidal group to 10 percent—still 1,200 patients—would decrease to 24 the number of the 40 suicidal patients who would be identified. Further reducing the incorrectly identified non-suicidal patients to .5% (60) would then correctly identify only 1 of the 40 suicidal patients. Thus, if one wishes to avoid incorrectly labeling many patients (false positives), it is not possible with this hypothetical tool, whose accuracy vastly exceeds anything actually available, to specify those individuals who will display the low-base-rate behavior, suicide.

A similar set of problems surrounds dangerous behavior, defined as assaultive, nondefensive actions directed against another. Given that this is the behavior that the predictors of dangerousness are most often expected to accurately predict, dangerous behavior in most groups is a very infrequent event. Nevertheless, one of the problems of elucidating the clinical and policy implications of these predictions is that there is the false assumption that in the groups to whom these predictions are applied, dangerous behavior is a frequent event. This assumption leads to the expectation that these are high-risk groups for future dangerous behavior and as a result they are susceptible to accurate predictions of dangerousness. This is in fact not the case.

Our Baxstrom research discussed above (26) and the works of Rappeport and Lassen (11, 12) and Giovannoni and Gurel (30) on former mental patients are excellent cases in point. It is the stereotype of the mental patient that he is dangerous and threatening (31). Following from this erroneous assumption is the acceptability of employing predictions of future dangerous behavior as a primary rationale for the involuntary hospitalization. Using the arrest rates of ex-mental patients and comparing them to base rates for the population at large, Rappeport and Lassen and Giovannoni and Gurel all concluded that for most offense categories, former mental patients are significantly *less* apt to be arrested than the public at large. In both studies, ex-patients were more often arrested for robbery, and in the Rappeport and Lassen data, more often for assaults. However, two points must be recognized. First, even in the robbery category where former patients were overrepresented, the annual arrest rate in the Rappeport and Lassen male data was 371/100,000, meaning that 99,629 of every 100,000 would *not* be arrested in a given year. Second, for the vast majority of offenses, this supposedly high-risk group is in fact a lower-risk group than the public at large. Therefore, the problems of incorrect predictions which necessarily follow from low-base-rate behavior are accentuated rather than diminished.

Thus it is imperative that it be recognized that for most groups in the criminal justice and mental health systems, or some combination thereof, the dangerous behavior being predicted remains low-base-rate behavior. Noting this, we may now properly move to consider three major themes that permeate current developments surrounding the use of dangerousness.

FUTURE DIRECTIONS

In this section I want to discuss three major directions, one suggested and two in progress, in the area of dangerousness. The suggested direction, reflected in the first section of this chapter, is the need for giving more attention to the conceptual links between aggression, violence and dangerousness so that some conceptual precision may develop. The two trends in progress are (1) the movement toward interdisciplinary approaches to estimating dangerousness which more carefully consider situational factors, and (2) the steady flow of legislation employing predictions of dangerousness, despite the inability of anyone to accurately predict it.

Unquestionably the most basic difficulty in dealing with the clinical and policy issues inherently surrounding dangerousness is its vague definitions. As discussed in great detail earlier, dangerousness has a multitude of meanings, most of which overlook its perceptual, predictive essence. If more consideration in law and clinical practice were given to elaborating the connections between dangerousness and the concepts of aggression and violence, this essence of dangerousness would become clearer.

Turning to trends in progress, first let us examine the growing awareness that if society remains committed to utilizing predictions of future dangerous behavior to detain certain classes of individuals, some tools for prediction must be developed that radically go beyond the fruitless attempts at individual clinical judgments. An outstanding example of the evolving, interdisciplinary approach to the issue of dangerousness, with a vigorous interest in the pertinent situational factors, is seen in the description of the clinical workups described in the work of Kozol and colleagues discussed earlier (16). While the data this group presented cannot validly lead to the claims they asserted, these questions do not detract from their potentially valuable evaluation procedures.

As described by Kozol, "each diagnostic study is based on clinical examinations, psychological tests, and a meticulous reconstruction of the life history elicited from multiple sources—the patient himself; his family, friends, neighbors, teachers, and employers; and court, correctional, and mental hospital records. . . . The clinical examinations are made independently by at least two psychiatrists, two psychologists, a social worker, and others." These procedures are very much in line with the recommendations of the excellent overview on preventing violence by Monahan (32), which concluded:

> What I am suggesting is that social scientists divert at least a part of their energies from studying violent persons to studying and predicting violent situations. Such a chance in tack might lead to appreciable gains in preventive efficiency (it could hardly do worse than current efforts at person identification), and would obviate the seemingly insurmountable problem of unjustly intervening in the lives of innumerable false positives.

It appears very certain that for the foreseeable future, society is not about to diminish its demand for preventive detention of those that it feels are dangerous. Based on this assumption, on scientific interest in these issues, and on the barrenness of the personal identification approach for accurate estimations of dangerousness, the situational approach, which is inherently a multidisciplinary approach, is one direction that must be followed. However, it must always be recognized that dangerous behavior is low-base-rate behavior, and that, as yet, no method clinical or statistical has been able to accurately predict such behavior.

A second current development in the area of predicting dangerousness is the ever-broadening uses of these predictions. It is an astounding paradox to see the steady publication of research data over the past five to ten years showing the inabilities of predictors of dangerousness to make accurate estimations and simultaneously to oberve state legislators and groups producing or recommending criminal and mental health codes and procedures which rely so heavily on the predictive concept. It is because of this state of affairs that the notion of dangerousness, as the policy application of the more fundatmental ideas of aggression and violence, is such a crucial concept. It is because of these statutory developments that it is important for the policy maker and clinician to recognize the predictive essence of dangerousness. Equally important is the need for the researchers in the area of aggression and violence to recognize that their work tends to take on its major public significance from the transition of findings and theories into legislation under the guise of dangerousness. As such, it is appropriate and important for the topic of predicting dangerousness to be part of this review of aggression, and work in this area must grow in its awareness of the significance of the concept of dangerousness and its very direct relevancy for the concepts and research on aggression and violence.

REFERENCES

1. Rubins B: Prediction of dangerousness in mentally ill criminals. *Arch Gen Psychiatry 27*:397–407, 1972.
2. Ervin FR, Lion JR: Clinical evaluation of the violent patient. In *Crimes of Violence*, National Commission on the Causes and Prevention of Violence Staff Study Series Vol. 13, US Gov't Print Office, Washington, 1969.
3. Gilula MF, Daniels DN: Violence and man's struggle to adapt. *Science 164*:396–405, 1969.
4. Morris N: Psychiatry and the dangerous criminal. *Southern California Law Review 41*:514–547, 1968.
5. Halleck S: *Psychiatry and the Dilemmas of Crime.* New York: Harper and Row, 1967.
6. Goldzband M: Prediction of dangerousness. Paper read at the American Academy of Psychiatry and the Law Annual Meeting, Pittsburgh, October, 1973.
7. Gardner, OM: Sentencing act: Final interim draft. Prepared for The Governor's Task Force on Decision-Making Models in Corrections, Olympia, Washington, November 25, 1974.
8. Kittrie, NN: *The Right to be Different: Deviance and Enforced Therapy.* Baltimore: The Johns Hopkins Press, 1972.
9. Allen HE, Simmonsen, CF, Gordon MS: Operational research in criminology: An examination of the decision-making process for commitment under sexual psychopath statute for apparently unrelated offenses. Paper presented at Annual Meeting of the American Society of Criminology. New York, 1973.
10. Katz J, Goldstein J: Dangerousness and mental illness. *J Nervous and Mental Disease 131*:404–13, 1960.
11. Rappeport J, Lassen G: Dangerous—Arrest rate comparisons of discharged patients and the general population. *Amer J Psychiatry 121*:776–783, 1965.
12. Rappeport J, Lassen G: The dangerousness of female patients: A comparison of the arrest rates of discharged psychiatric patients and the general population. *Amer J Psychiatry 123*:413–419, 1966.
13. Scheff TJ: The societal reaction to deviance: Ascriptive elements in the psychiatric screening of mental patients in a mid-western state. *Social Problems (Spring)*:401–13, 1964.

14. Greenwald R: Disposition of the insane defendant after 'Acquittal' — The long road from committment to release. *J Criminal Law, Criminology and Police Science* 59:583–594, 1968.

15. Schulman, RE: Dangerousness behavior and social policy: A model for intervention. Paper read at American Psychological Association Annual Meeting, 1970.

16. Kozol HL, Boucher RJ, Garofalo, RF: The diagnosis and treatment of dangerousness. *Crime and Delinquency.* 18:371–392, 1972.

17. Marcus, AM: Encounters with the dangerous sexual offender. *Canada's Mental Health,* 18:5–12, 1970.

18. Bach-Y-Rita G, Lion JR, Climent CE, Ervin FR: Episode dyscontrol: A study of 130 violent patients. *Amer J Psychiatry* 127:1473–1478, 1971.

19. Ordway J: Experiences in evaluating dangerousness in private. in *The Clinical Evaluation of the Mentally Ill.* Jonas Rappeport (ed) Amer Psychiatric Association, 1967.

20. McGarry, AL: Dangerousness and civil commitment in Massachusetts. Paper read at Amer Psychiatric Association Annual Meetings, Detroit, Michigan, May, 1974.

21. Cocozza JJ: Dangerousness. *Psychiatric News,* Washington, D.C.: Amer Psychiatric Association, August 15:2, 1973.

22. Monahan J: Dangerous offenders: A critique of Kozol et al. *Crime and Delinquency* 19:418–420, 1973.

23. Kozol HL, Boucher RJ, Garofalo, RF: Dangerousness. *Crime and Delinquency* 19:554–5, 1973.

24. *Psychiatric News.* Dangerousness said predictable by new diagnostic criteria. 8:1, 32, 1973.

25. Wenk E, Robinson JO, Smith GW: Can violence be predicted? *Crime and Delinquency* 18:393–402, 1972.

26. Steadman HJ, Cocozza JJ: Careers of the Criminally Insane: Excessive Social Control of Deviance. Lexington, Mass.: D.C. Heath and Company (Lexington Books), 1974.

27. Cocozza JJ, Steadman HJ: Some refinements in the measurement and prediction of dangerous behavior. *Amer J of Psychiatry* 131:9, 1974.

28. Meehl RE, Rosen A: Antecedent probability and the efficiency of psychomatric signs, patterns, or cutting scores. *Psychol Bull* 52:194–216, 1955.

29. Rosen A: Detection of suicidal patients: an example of some limitations in the prediction of infrequent events. *J Consult Psychol* 18:397–403, 1954.

30. Giovannoni JM, Gurel L: Socially disruptive behavior of exmental patients. *Arch Gen Psychiat* 17:146–53, 1967.

31. Nunnally JC: *Popular Conceptions of Mental Health.* New York: Holt, Rinehart, and Winston, 1961.

32. Monahan J: The prediction of violence. Proceedings of the Pacific Northwest Conference on Violence and Criminal Justice. Issaquah, Washington, December 6–8, 1973.

National and International Violence

MANOEL W. PENNA

The Research Institute of America reported that in the twenty-two years following the end of World War II 7,480,000 persons were killed by other human beings in tribal-type acts of violence occurring all over the world (20). By any standards this is a staggering figure which unmistakably points to the magnitude of the problem. Nevertheless, this is the kind of statistics which may cause surprise but remains doomed to be bound between the covers of a volume, occasionally quoted in a report of world records, sundry aberrations or incredible achievements of mankind. It would be a mistake to interpret this as an argument to demonstrate a lack of interest in the problem of violence. On the contrary, violence has become a common theme both in the technical literature and in the lay press. What we have is a contradiction: on the one hand, a variable degree of arousal and interest in the problem by prefessionals and the public; on the other hand a de facto acceptance of violence as a fact of life. Such a paradox is intriguing and deserves an explanation for one would suspect that it would illuminate the nature of the processes which perpetuate violence despite the progress of civilization.

The most astonishing fact about violence is its banality. This, however, is not a unique characteristic of violence per se, but one that is shared by other endemic plights of mankind. Starvation is one such example, a problem for which we have the potential technological solution but are unable to use it because of an inability to overcome obstacles lying in political and socioeconomic processes. Despite its intrusion in the average home through the cogent plastic representation of the media we maintain our habits and customs and manage to subdue the alarm. Perhaps the common ground is the banality of death itself, the most common, predictable and inevitable of the human predicaments and yet one that we very energetically avoid and deny for ourselves. The need to understand the psychological mechanisms involved in this process is immediate and urgent, for they have proved to possess a high degree of resilience and unresponsiveness to the educational methods we have available.

It seems that in order to break through such massive resistance so that a common concern is generated and expressed, violent acts need to fulfill one or more of three conditions which bring them into the proximity of the individual or the group: to embody an immediate personal threat, to become a concrete possibility of economic loss, or to represent a serious political challenge for a ruling class. Short of these attributes, social groups have generally developed a machinery to deal with violence and maintain the status quo. Because these mechanisms can be equally violent, Frank has pointed out the often forgotten fact that obedience to legitimate authority can be an instigator of violence (10).

Since acts of violence are so common and pervasive a phenomenon, a review of its manifestations on a national and international scale would be a formidable undertaking. Given the present state of our knowledge on the subject matter, a detailed discussion—even if practically feasible—would hardly be useful or necessry. Nevertheless, a review of selected aspects of the problem can delineate major parameters involved and put in perspective certain significant theoretical and methodological difficulties encountered in the study of the matter.

The decision as to which manifestations of violence are relevant for consideration is made difficult by the fact that the particular one on focus at a given period of time is largely determined by the whims of fashion. What makes it a fashionable subject? First of all, it needs to fulfill the conditions mentioned above; in addition, it needs to gain a large enough exposure in the news media to become an object of public concern. The main drawback is that irrespective of the seriousness of the matter, it is subject to the vicissitudes suffered by all fads, waxing and waning over a period of time.

One remarkable example was the racial riots of the sixties. As they menacingly spread over the country they became a focal point of concern which mobilized a good amount of energy and financial resources in an attempt at finding a solution for the problem. Institutions were created, centered mainly around the study of racial violence; old words acquired new importance in the everyday vocabulary—protests, grievance, confrontation; problem-solving techniques, such as third-party mediation, were proposed with renewed fervor. The emotional arousal and the activism generated by the mood of the time seem to have been instrumental in implementing the correction of some of the inequalities as well as giving some segments of the oppressed a new sense of dignity. However, as in many similar situations, a certain kind of puritanical zeal forcefully pushed in the direction of developing "therapeutic" approaches to what in reality was a large and difficult socioeconomic and political problem. As an example, Community Mental Health, both as an idea and as a program, was swept along in this tide of uncritical enthusiasm, a phenomenon which has gained very little recognition despite being one of the most important foundations of its difficulties.

Regardless of these shortcomings, substantial studies were carried out in an attempt to understand the complexity of the rioting phenomenon. The conflicting ethical and scientific attitudes that we have toward violence as manifested in civil disorders and the manner in which they influence our perceptions and reactions to the latter was discussed by Spiegel (22). He presents us with one of our first problems in understanding large-scale manifestations of violence: how does one account for their occurrence in a particular historical movement at a given place? The preconditions underlying the outbreak of a civil disorder which have been put forth basically relate to an unequal distribution of goods and privileges. Obviously, these are hardly headline items: they have had a ubiquitous existence and a long life, and are far from being extinct. In fact, they are common to the point of being banal, in the sense discussed earlier. On the other hand, civil disorders are intermittent, and therefore need additional elements to come into existence. One of them, proposes Spiegel, is the presence of a "hostile belief system," a complex combination of projection and distorted perception and interpretation which leads groups of both blacks and whites to see each other's behavior as being "beyond the pale of accepted norms" (22). Thus making it unfair, provocative and calling for retaliation. The explanatory value of the concept is weakened when one considers that it can be both a cause and a consequence of the inequalities mentioned above. Two other elements advanced by Spiegel, inadequate communication and social control, could be subsumed under the former or represent a larger, economic-political process, determining the extent of negotiation and compromise between two groups with a differential access to power.

Rioting as a process per se has also been the subject of controversy.

Spiegel is well known for proposing what has come to be called the stage theory of riots. He recognizes four phases in their development (22). In the first the preexisting hostile belief system is materialized in a concrete behavioral event which is perceived as a confirmation of those beliefs and involves some sort of clash between blacks and whites. This precipitating event leads to the second stage of confrontation, brought about by the invasion of the streets by a crowd and the mobilization of law enforcements agents to restore and maintain order. Most civil disturbances meet their resolution at this point. When certain nonspecified conditions are present the crowd becomes unruly, and there is a spree of looting and violence characterizing the third stage of "Roman Holiday." This launches the final phase, where the law enforcement officers besiege the conflicted area, and the conflict eventually comes to a resolution. In the wake of the disturbance, measures may be taken that will relieve the preconditions of the conflict; or denial may gain the upper hand, thus perpetuating the state of dissatisfaction which may lead to further disturbances.

Spiegel's approach leaves many questions unanswered—a not unexpected result, considering the limitation of a rather simple method applied to a complex social phenomenon. Social scientists expanded the analysis of the problem by bringing into focus other aspects of the matter combined with a more varied methodology. Three major contributions stand out, all published since 1970, and containing critical reviews of the relevant literature.

In examining a series of hypothesis which have been proposed as an explanation for the localization of the racial riots of the sixties, Spilerman (24) emphasizes the need to distinguish between the underlying causes and the immediate precipitants. The latter are of a more incidental nature, comprising events which occur with high frequency but at random, and presumably capable of escalating into a major disturbance only where certain conditions preexist. Therefore it is of the utmost importance to try and clarify what are these conditions which have been, either theoretically or empirically, correlated with the "disorder-proneness" of a given community being afflicted by a racial disorder. This is exactly what Spilerman determines through the construction of mathematical models reflecting the most common conditions which have been advanced as possible causes of these disorders. He then compares the predictions achieved through this method with the actual empirical data. What were his results? Many prevalent hypothesis—such as that the occurrence of a racial disorder would reinforce, positively or negatively, the outbreak of subsequent disturbances, or that these disorders could spread out through geographic contagion—were not supported by his data. In fact, the only assumption substantiated by his data was that communities were heterogeneous as far as the probability of experiencing a racial disorder was concerned. This immediately raises the question as to which characteristics are significant in determining the likelihood of a community being victimized by a racial disturbance. Spilerman studies several which have been proposed in the literature, such as social disorganization, absolute or relative deprivation, discrepancies between one's condition and one's expectation, and unresponsive municipal political structure; he comes to the conclusion that, except for the size of the black population, none of these structural characteristics help in predicting the distribution of the racial disorders. He proposes, instead, that this can be better understood in terms of individual characteristics in that all blacks have uniformly experienced frustrations which, dramatized through television, have fostered the development of a racial consciousness or identity. In summary, his contention is that the major question to be answered concerns the relationship between the underlying structured preconditions and the expression of collective disorder; he proposes that these conditions were prelavent in large scale but only led to outbreaks of civil disturbances where they were accentuated by the uniformly colored perception of blacks (24).

With Firestone we return to a theoretical analysis of the riot process per se. His contribution lies in examining a variety of the theories proposed and attempting to integrate them in a larger synthesis (8). He starts off by scrutinizing Spiegel's stage theory of riots in an attempt to refine certain aspects which were not clearly defined, despite their crucial importance, by augmenting or decreasing its intensity, in the determination of the direction followed by the process. He pursues his goal primarily through an analysis of the interaction between the situational and the psychological aspects of the disturbance. The latter has been a subject of debate between proponents of the rationality and defenders of the irrationality of the motivation which leads from hostility to violence, in the development of a riot. Firestone suggests that both types can be present. Irrational motivation would be related to the expression of anger in which violence, in a cathartic manner, becomes a goal in itself. On the other hand, if the situation is perceived as an opportunity to make a strong protest against a state of affairs in need of correction, the motivation for rioting would be a rational one. How does this proposition help clarify the dynamic sequence of events in Spiegel's theory? It suggests that the interaction between rioters and law enforcement officers throughout the development of the different stages of the disturbance can be better understood in terms of the type or combination of motivations underlying the escalation of the violent response which was initially triggered by feelings of hostility and grievance aroused by the precipitating event. Thus, at the stage of street confrontation it would be expected that appeals to the rational motivation of the rioters — pointing out the ineffectiveness of the protest, its destructiveness to the community, or even its lack of purpose once early concessions have been made — would have a calming effect on the disturbance. At the same time, riot promoters, independent from or in accord with their rational arguments, would be stimulating the arousal of feelings of anger that would only be discharged through violent means (irrational motivation). Under these circumstances the response of law enforcement agents acquires clear relevance: undercontrol many encourage the belief that there is indeed a good opportunity for violent protest, while overcontrol may generate more intense feelings of anger that can submerge rational consideration under the waves of violence "as consummation rather than instrument" (8), which characterizes Spiegel's phase of Roman Holiday. When this stage is reached, overcontrol can only aggravate the situation — and lead to the stage of siege — since by then both the ones who wanted to protest and those who wanted to express their anger would have attained their objectives.

Firestone disposes of alternative theories of the riot process rather quickly because he believes that in some way they can be subsumed in his scheme. He also emphasizes the need for a transactional model if a comprehensive description of the process is to be undertaken, but believes that his propostions apply not only to the rioters but to the dominant group as well.

Firestone acknowledges the methodological limitations of verbal descriptions of riot processes in terms of future research, and proposes a mathematical model to be considered in further studies; however, this model remains what the author calls it: a loose translation.

With Morgan and Clark we return to the causal analysis of racial disorders (17). In contrast to Spilerman's contention that the size of the nonwhite population was the most significant element Morgan and Clark point to other factors as being relevant in determining the likelihood of a community suffering a racial disturbance. Although their operational definition of a racial disorder is broader than Spilerman's, they limited themselves only to those occurring in 1967. Of the nine disorder variables analyzed, city size proved to be significant. Their data also indicated that the size of the police force was an important element, not in generating an atmosphere inducing resentment and hostility among the black population, but in relation to increasing the occurrence of potential situations of confrontation.

In addition, they argue that we need two different sets of variables to account for the frequency and for the severity of racial disorders. Thus, while in their analysis they were able to explain 34 percent of the occurrence of disorders on the basis of the size of the black population and of the police force, only 11 percent of the variation could be accounted for when the severity of the disorder was included in the equation, therefore suggesting that different dynamic factors are relevant to the processes of initiating as against escalating the disorder.

These findings notwithstanding, it remains that the crucial process to be understood is how the underlying social conditions prevalent in the riot-affected cities relate to the individual decision to participate in the disorder. The authors propose that the level of frustration — which they call grievance level — is just such a link. Conditions that lead to dissatisfaction with a person's life-style as well as those that perpetuate racial discrimination have a tendency to increase the grievance level. Interestingly, two variables significantly influencing the degree of dissatisfaction with one's life-style seem to have opposite effects on the severity of the disorder: inequality in housing increases it, while inequality in jobs decreases it. In support of their findings, the authors call attention to national Gallup polls which have shown that between 1949 and 1969 blacks' satisfaction with their jobs increased by 21 percent while satisfaction with their housing decreased 9 percent.

As we close our review of the literature on racial disorders we are left with some understanding of the underlying conditions and the operation of the dynamic forces which govern the development of the disturbance; but we are also left with many unanswered questions about the subtleties of their interaction — a state of affairs far from being alien to the clinician who engages in the individual evaluation and treatment of the violent patient. Similarly, we need to be reminded that dynamics does not necessarily imply causation. The racial disturbances have their root in social, cultural, economic and political processes, about which we have a good deal of knowledge. Furthermore, they are amenable to change. What corrective measures have been or need to be applied, and how thoroughly, still remain a contemporary problem which affects the common man.

General concerns change over time, and other matters involving acts of violence move to the center of attention. Periodically an interest in mass murder surfaces; recently the problem of skyjacking seemed to capture most of the interest. These are obviously dramatic events which the news media seize upon, but their social significance is rather limited. Perhaps for this reason they have generated mainly anecdotal accounts of a particular experience (13), but a search of the major medical, sociological and psychological indexes and abstracts of the last years fails to reveal anything of real substance. Regardless, skyjacking's appeal to fantasy gives it attractiveness as a new event which could have contributed to the perpetuation of the problem. Besides, the possible economic repercussions in terms of airlines' loss of passengers are certainly significant in the development of a policy of prevention at considerable financial cost. Initial attempts at developing profiles that would identify potential culprits were not successful. The apparent effective measure that brought skyjacking under control was the instrumental surveillance that made if difficult for a weapon to be carried into an airplane, once again emphasizing the role of the availability of a weapon in bringing about an act of violence. As to the role of information in stimulating a repetition of violent behavior, it is noteworthy that the increase in reports of violent crimes following President Kennedy's assassination led to the proposal of a theory of contagion in criminal violence (2). Following the epidemiological metaphor we could wonder whether the vector would be the news media.

In terms of human suffering, other manifestations of violence unquestionably have greater significance. Torture of other human beings in the service of political goals had its best-known institutionalized example in the Nazi state, but, unfortunately, it still continues to be practiced on a much larger scale than we care to knowledge. In terms of the toll in human lives and sheer destructiveness, no other form of collective violence surpasses the magnitude of war. However, in the contemporary world we see an increasing blurring of the distinctions between war, revolutionary movements and acts of terrorism. Often it becomes a question of legitimacy or effectiveness in accomplishing goals. Thus acts of terrorism may be carried out in the process of waging war, or because they have strategic or symbolic value in the development of a revolutionary movement. But because of an ethical double-standard in judging acts of violence, when people refer to terrorism they usually mean actions carried out against the social system with which they are aligned. Their concern then is to identify and control potential terrorists, thus preventing destruction of property or loss of lives—in other words, the type of concern usually identified with law-enforcement activities. On the other end of the spectrum, terrorism is perceived as a manifestation of political activity; the concern here is the identification and correction of serious sources of dissatisfaction, and the provision of alternative means for dissenters to express their protest and effectively influence a more equitable balance of power.

Once again, in the course of this brief discussion of collective violence, we are confronted with the question of what leads men to revolt. Despite being an old question, there is widespread disagreement in the answer. Furthermore, the issue not only has been a subject of scientific investigation but also involves obvious but nonetheless complex social, cultural and political considerations (3,4). Most theories seem to focus on underlying causes related to an unequal distribution of goods, priviliges or power, a condition evidently prevalent in many societies whether or not they are affected by a revolutionary process. As an explanation, Davies suggests that for a revolution to occur, rising expectations need to be followed by their effective frustration in an S-shaped curve (5). The similarity between this idea and the explanations proposed for the racial disturbances once again points to the common trends weaving the diverse expressions of collective violence.

To avoid misunderstanding it is necessary to emphasize that the above considerations are not intended to imply that crucial gaps do not exist in our understanding of the process involved in a revolutionary movement. An even more important warning needs to be sounded against the unwarranted exclusive use of the clinical method in the study of large-scale manifestations of violence. As Bienen (3) suggests, to look at this type of violence as a pathological process does not seem to add anything of significance to our knowledge. Furthermore, this attitude has the potential of becoming a large defensive operation through which we rationalize away the whole problem in terms of psychopathology, thus protecting ourselves from being confronted with much larger and many times more uncomfortable social issues. To quote Bienen: "The language of 'sickness' and 'therapy' may well turn out to be another set of clichés for obfuscating understanding, another way, to paraphrase Clifford Guertz, of not wanting to learn too much about ourselves too quickly" (3 p. 11). The problem is that we are left with the innumerable variables which have been proposed in the literature as causes of violence, and, unfortunately, they are often mutually contradictory. Bienen also correctly points out the move from a structural to a behavioral approach in the study of violence, a theoretical but not a methodological change, since the behavioral variables have not been directly measured but rather deduced from the former.

The alarm having sounded, the fact remains that many clinicians in their everyday work with individual patients are often confronted with the tasks of disentangling dynamic and other factors associated with the display of violent behavior. On occasion this behavior transcends the traditionally recognized arena of clinical expertise and spreads into more unfamiliar territory. As an example, amok has recently been shown to manifest epidemic fluctuations which are related to certain politicoeconomic and cultural factors (26). It is therefore understandable that many clinicians have addressed themselves to the problems of collective violence even while recognizing the limitations of their knowledge when applied to large groups of people. After all, it has already been said that violence is literally a matter of life or death, and, as such, it is everybody's concern. The problem is that our knowledge has not advanced as fast as our concern (with the qualifications previously made), and no matter whether we study racial riots, terrorism, revolution or wars we are always left with some basic general problems that we will proceed to review.

An elementary source of controversy permeating the numerous theories of aggression has been postulated as a question as to whether aggression is genetically determined or culturally learned. While a serious argument could be made even against wording the question in such a manner, it is noteworthy that the debate is an old one, with ancient roots in philosophical thought (27). It seems that what gives this debate its aura of contemporary urgency is the optimistic attitude fostered by technological developments which appear always to be widening the horizon of the possible and which, in a magical way, encourage the hope for a technological resolution of the problems of living and improvement of the human condition.

Since Freud (11), psychoanalysis has been concerned with the problem of aggression and its relationship to human destructiveness. In contrast to what was said above, there seems to be some disillustionment with the psychoanalytic theory of aggression. Parin (19) attributes this to feelings of helplessness elicited by postulates which offer no tangible ways for controlling human destructiveness. In addition, psychoanalysis brings another level of complexity with the study of the role of aggressive drives in normal development, thereby treating them as necessary factors for psychological growth to occur. A thoughtful discussion of their importance in human adaption was presented by Spitz (25). He accepts the notion that animals develop phylogenetically determined behavior patterns which are regulated in a relatively rigid way through natural selection. This works for animals because they live in a nonchanging or slowly changing environment. The situation is markedly different for man, who is constantly confronted with changes both in available weapons and in social organization. Thus, man has to adapt to a changing environment even in the course of ontogenesis. Successful adaptation requires a new form of regulation of the aggressive drives, and Spitz proposes that this is accomplished through the development of the psychic apparatus, a feat made possible by the prolonged period of helplessness and dependency of the infant, a condition which, though increasing his vulnerability, allows for unlimited opportunities to learn.

After studying two African cultures, and comparing them with Western culture, Parin also concludes in favor of the adaptational value of the aggressive drive, "the force that makes coexistence possible and enduring, lends order to personal contacts, guarantees the preservation of life and self-assertion, and sustains social structures and changes them" (19). He concludes that the expression of the aggressive drive is regulated and shaped by the ego relecting specific signs of its development within the culture. On this basis it follows that the increasing similarity of pathological expressions of aggression the further we move from the health norm of the culture would be explained as a result of ego impairment.

Animal studies have been an important paradigm for the continuous exploration of aggressive behavior, but the contribution of the ethologist has become more well known primarily due to the popularization of their studies by Lorenz (15). Some of the limitations in translating these findings in terms of human behavior have discussed by Spitz (25). More complex approaches, within an evolutionary and developmental framework, have been proposed to study aggressive behavior in their natural habitat (12), but methodological difficulties are likely to limit their scope.

As far as aggression constitutes a retaliatory response to frustration, an important aspect to be investigated deals with the question of response generalization, i.e., how similar or associationally close the aggressive response is to the aggression suffered. While a tendency for the response to approximate the directness of the frustration has been reported (9), there was a suggestion that the situation was an important variable in determining the selection of the response. The relevance of the problem can be seen in the conflict between blacks and whites: considering that blacks were responding to deprivation, rioting would not be as direct a response as action aimed at improving their status.

From a cross-cultural perspective, Allen studied fifty-eight cultures in trying to identify variables of social structure, along with childhood and adulthood experiences related to the expression of aggression (1). He considered two forms of aggression: direct, aimed at the source of frustration; and indirect, which, by being displaced to another person or an object, allows additional increase of tension. He finds highly significant the correlation indicating that the more direct and appropriate the expression of aggression is, the lower is the incidence of crime as defined by the culture. His data do not support the hypothesis of an inverse relationship between suicide and homicide, but they suggest a positive relationship between crime and suicide. He found that direct aggression correlated negatively with childhood frustration and anxiety and positively with infant and childhood indulgence. On the other hand, he believes that the finding of a negative correlation between crime and childhood indulgence supports "the psychoanalytic theory that stealing is an attempt to seize symbols of security and affection" (1). Allen also reported that social stratification and political integration were associated with crime but not with aggression, that greater erogenous satisfaction in childhood was associated with lower incidence of crime, and that the crime increased as the society showed a gap between the levels of aspiration and the actual possibilities of achieving them.

In a different vein, a clear example of the difficulties encountered by clinicians when dealing with large-group phenomena, encompassing a range of variables extending beyond the limits of the clinical field, can be found in Spiegel on the subject of violent confrontation (23). Initially, he acknowledges that there are much larger socioeconomic and political issues when he states that "there is very little evidence that social change involving a redistribution of power has ever taken place, anywhere, without confrontation and the possibility of violence" (23). One could assume that violence in such a context is motivated by a rational aim—redistribution of power—and determined by the unavailability or ineffectiveness of other channels for protesting and promoting change. Nevertheless, he maintains further on that the issue to be clarified is "the occurrence and persistence of violent confrontations." He proposes to investigate the problem through a three-way strategy that focuses on dynamic processes at the intrapsychic (both conscious and unconscious), socio-psychological (group phenomena), and cultural (value orientation) levels. It all adds up to quite a comprehensive approach, but the synthesis remains elusive.

Another example of the perils of straddling the clinical and social approaches is offered by Pinderhughes (20). He starts with the assumption that normal individuals in the course of their lives use paranoid patterns to resolve ambivalence. In this process they end up relating to their own group through introjection, which aggrandizes their side, and to outsiders through projection, which devaluates them. Eventually these projects and introjects are translated into cultural values to which adults cling with the same tenacity and irrationality with which children cling to their parents and their toys. This "paranoia" is proposed as a universal mechanism which underlies most if not all conflicts between social groups; as an example, the conflict between blacks and whites is explained in terms of "grouprelated paranoia." Pinderhughes emphasizes the importance of this process by claiming that "one of the reasons why we have made so little progress in curbing and eliminating discrimination, exploitation, violence and war lies in our refusal to recognize and acknowledge that all human beings depend heavily upon paranoid processes throughout their lives" (20). He further believes that "it is not possible to do violence without projecting evil into the person, group, or other object of violence" (24). At best he seems to be stretching the concept of paranoia to a point which most clinicians would find unwise if not clearly unwarranted.

Two crucial aspects in the study of aggression and violence is that it encompasses a wide variety of behaviors and calls for a highly complex range of ethical evaluations. Few would argue against the idea that aggression is related to normal, self-assertive activity, which may be pathologically inhibited and calls for therapy directed toward freeing its expression (14). Or that aggression underlies a full spectrum of activities ranging from curiosity, then through self-assertion and dominance, to hatred, and because of its close ties to "libidinal gratification, mastery and learning," cannot be eliminated from human behavior (16). It is probably equally wise to recognize that both aggression and social conflict are real and "necessary forces, and move on to consideration of how one can structure the goals and modalities of their expression in society, and with what consequences" (18). However, as Feshback (7) points out, since Freud we have been conceptualizing all forms of aggression as manifestations of the aggressive drive, including forms of collective aggression such as wars and riots. A good deal could be lost with this approach, since what seems innate in aggressive behavior is the capacity for such response, while its actual translation in behavioral acts appears to be regulated by a variety of psychological, social and cultural mechanisms. The importance of studying and isolating them lies both in their actual roles as instigators of violence (10) and in their potential usefulness in developing a public policy to regulate expressions of violence.

It must be understood that violence may involve direct or psychological injury (10). This is an obvious consequence of the widespread role symbols play in the lives of human beings. Therefore, it is not surprising that a close relationship exists between aggression and self-esteem and status (7); consequently, inequitable distribution of justice, deprivations, humiliations and frustrations, whether real or symbolic, may and have led to serious outbreak of collective violence (10). In this regard, violence has been advocated not only as an instrument of liberation and social change but also as necessary action to give the oppressed a new sense of dignity (6). Others have argued that "it is the power to retaliate rather than the retaliatory act itself and the expression of one's rage rather than the destruction of the humiliating agent that are the critical factors" (7).

The relationship between violence and sex is another area of interest. As Frank points out (10): "sexual activity and fighting are the two most intimate forms of human interaction. Both involve exclusive attention to the other person, close bodily contact, and strong emotional arousal." As he also observes, both violent and sexual behavior are responsive to cultural and environmental cues, they seem to have an antagonistic relationship, and the expressions of both is mostly regulated by norms, customs and traditions. In this regard it is of interest that we seem to have spent considerably more energy controlling or suppressing sexuality than aggression, a process which extends all the way from child rearing to the censorship of objects of art, movies and television. It is possible that we have reversed our priorities and ought to scrutinize our rationale for doing so.

With all these considerations, Frank's appeal sounds cogent and reasonable when he claims that "our main hope to reduce expressive violence lies in decreasing its psychological and socio-economic instigators and creating more effective institutions for its control" (10). This task is a formidable one, considering the fact that we use different ethical standards when we evaluate a violent act according to the circumstances surrounding them. This is clearly illustrated by Feshback (7): tendency to approve violence committed in obedience to the law or in the service of a social interest while disapproving unlawful violence, or violence in the service of a personal interest. An even more serious ethical dilemna is created when violence that successfully accomplishes its objectives is perceived as good. It seems inevitable that violence will stay with us as long as we adhere to norms and values that not only condone but encourage it.

REFERENCES

1. Allen MG: A cross-cultural study of aggression and crime. *J of Cross-Cultural Psychology* 2:259–271, 1972.
2. Berkowitz L and Macaulay J: The contagion of criminal violence. *Sociometry* 34:238–260, 1971.
3. Bienen H: *Violence and Social Change*. Chicago, University of Chicago Press, 1968.
4. Davies JC (ed): *When Men Revolt and Why*. New York, The Free Press, 1971.
5. Davies JC: Toward a theory of revolution. *American Soc. Review* 6:5–19, 1962.
6. Fanon F: *The Wretched of the Earth*. New York, Grove Press, 1963.
7. Feshback S: Dynamics and morality of violence and aggression: Some psychological considerations. *American Psychologist* 26:281–292, 1971.

8. Firestone JM: Theory of the riot process. *American Behavioral Scientist.* 15:859–882, 1972.
9. Foa EB, Turner JL, Foa UG: Response generalization in aggression. *Human Relations* 25:337–350, 1972.
10. Frank JD: Some psychological determinants of violence and its control. *Aust. N.Z. J. Psychiatry.* 6:158–164, 1972.
11. Freud S: *Why War?* Standard Edition of the Complete Psychological Works of Sigmund Freud. J Strachey, (ed.) London, Hogarth Press, 1933.
12. Hambug DA: An evolutionary and developmental approach to human aggressiveness. *Psychoanalytic Quart.* 42:185–196, 1973.
13. Jacobson SR: Individual and group responses to confinement in a skyjacked plane. *Amer. J. Orthopsychiat.* 43:459–469, 1973.
14. Joseph ED: Aggression redefined—Its adaptational aspects. Psychoanalytic Quart. 42:197–213, 1973.
15. Lorenz K: *On Aggression.* New York, Harcourt Brace Jovanovich, 1966.
16. Marcovitz E: Aggression in human adaptation. *Psychoanalytic Quart.* 42:226–233, 1973.
17. Morgan WR, Clark TN: The causes of racial disorders: A grievance-level explanation. *Amer. Soc. Review.* 38:611–624, 1973.
18. Mumford E: Sociology and aggression. *Psychoanalytic Quart.* 42:234–238, 1973.
19. Parin P: A contribution of ethno-psychoanalytic investigation to the theory of aggression, *Int. J. Psychoanalysis* 53:251–257, 1972.
20. Pinderhughes CA: The universal resolution of ambivalence by paranoia with an example by black and white. *Amer. J. Psychotherapy* 24:597–610, 1970.
21. Pinderhughes CA: Managing paranoia in violent relationships. In G. Usdin, (ed.), *Perspectives on Violence.* New York, Brunner/Mazer, 1972.
22. Spiegel JP: Social and psychological factors in civil disorders. Address Presented for the Stanton Evening Lecture at the Health Sciences Auditorium, University of Maryland School of Medicine, March 18, 1968.
23. Spiegel JP: The dynamics of violent confrontation. *Int. J. Psychiatry* 10:93–108, 1972.
24. Spilerman S: The causes of racial disturbances: A comparison of alternative explanations, *Amer. Soc. Review* 35:627–649, 1970.
25. Spitz RA: Aggression and adaptation. *J. Nervous and Mental Diseases* 149:81–90, 1969.
26. Westermeyer J: On the Epidemicity of amok violence. *Arch. Gen. Psychiat* 28:873–876, 1973.
27. Zegans LS: Philosophical antecedents to modern theories of human aggressive instinct. *Psychoanalytic Quart.* 42:239–266, 1973.

The Violent Offender
in the Court

BOYLSTON D. SMITH
HENRY MUSK

An annual report is purported to present a survey of what is new and relevant in a certain field of study. the pertinent issues which have been identified and debated are discussed and evaluated by known workers in the particular field. For those who wish to consider forensic psychiatry as a science, progress seems intolerably slow. The issues discovered and written about do not change rapidly, and new scientific discoveries are urgently sought but rarely come forth. Those data presented for the court's use do not seem to adequately answer the needs of the individuals charged with a crime, the prosecutor's office, the defense counsel, the judges or the juries. Judge David Bazelon once commented that his is experience with expert psychiatric opinion in the courts led him to conclude that most psychiatrists give the right answers to the wrong questions. In a very recent article, he writes, "First of all, psychiatrists did not acknowledge the limits of their expertise. Secondly, they failed to confront honestly and openly the conflicts that impaired their competence even when their expertise was sufficient and relevant. When expertise was not an issue, psychiatrists failed to make it clear to the court how a lack of resources compromised their examination of a patient" (1).

It seems certain that the past few years will be remembered as the period in which forensic psychiatry was challenged to scientifically identify what it does know. The forensic psychiatrist is being challenged to reveal to the court what he does know about human behavior and stop allowing himself to be pressured into presenting as fact his conclusions which rest on ethical, moral and legal considerations beyond his expertise.

Recently Louis McGarry, working in Massachusetts, has attempted to devise a method for allowing psychiatrists who are asked to determine an offender's competency to stand trial to comment only upon behavioral issues on which they have some expertise and leave the final decision-making as to competency firmly in the hands of the court (2). Whether the Massachusetts courts will, in the long run, go along with such a system is debatable. There is always a tendency for the courts to push the psychiatrist into giving opinions and to subtly use these opinions as a major justification for legal decisions. If there is to be more rational use of psychiatric expertise, psychiatrists will have to develop more candor in defining their limitations, and judges and attorneys will have to concede that the court alone must make legal decisions (3).

Zusman and Carnahan suggest that the system is at fault. They say that major legal decisions rely (often inappropriately) upon psychiatric participation. The law's concern has not focused upon the potentially rich therapeutic contributions of psychiatry, but rather has emphasized the assumed predictive powers of individual psychiatrists to evaluate individuals' state of mind and estimate tendencies to act in undesirable ways. Thus, psychiatry has been relatively content to accommodate itself to the rules of the legal games. What is needed is a method to convince both disciplines (law and psychiatry) of the failure of such rules and the need for alternatives. One answer seems to be in changing the training of those who are being prepared to become major participants. A one-year graduate program beyond the present training program is being proposed for psychiatrists, lawyers and graduates of doctoral programs in the behavioral sciences (4).

The first requirement for adequate patient advocacy is clinical training. The need for members of the legal profession to have a greater understanding of psychological phenomena and psychiatric resources has found increasing response in the curriculae of our law schools and the growing number.of source materials. But lectures and books are not enough. The problem here is not simply that of cold assimilation of abstract scientific facts and theories. On the contrary, only through the personal experience of relating with disabled persons and with their doctors can the specialist lawyer acquire that kind of full understanding and empathy which is so essential to his acceptance of his client with the confidence needed to assist him (5).

Some psychiatrists with years of experience in the courts and who are teachers of law and psychiatry would like to see forensic psychiatry become a formally accredited subspecialty in medicine with its own specialty board. According to Seymour Pollack, M.D., "What must develop is a special course of advanced study, education, training, and supervised experience, with the advanced student ending as an accredited authority and skilled technician in dealing with this particular subject. Also, both public acceptance and professional accreditation of specialty status are requisite. Public acceptance of the need for the specialty is important, but even more important is the need for the specialty to have practical value to the practitioner" (6).

Psychiatric leaders like Menninger and Roche have put forth cogent arguments for keeping psychiatrists out of the courtroom at all costs. In recent years the number of prominent jurists and psychiatrists who recommend the abolition of the insanity defense has been growing. Of course, the proposal that the defense of insanity be abolished is not original. Lady Barbara Wooton, Professor H.L.A. Hart, Chief Justice Weintraub of New Jersey, Joel Feinberg, Dr. Thomas S. Szasz and Dr. S. L. Halleck have all advocated its abolition, though for diverse reasons and with diverse substitutes for it (7).

A major complaint about the insanity defense in determining criminal responsibility can be summed up in the primary question: Is it ever valid to make a diagnosis and an estimate of psychic causation based on an examination months to years after the period of time in question and based mainly on the report of the only observer usually present throughout the commission of the crime—the supposedly irrational, mentally ill defendant? (8).

A second complaint challenges the concept of the impartial expert's role, especailly regarding the testimony of the so-called state psychiatrist or the court-employed psychiatrist. Judge Bazelon reminds psychiatrists that the rules of the court presuppose that people are biased—that their testimony and opinions are inevitably shaped by their backgrounds, personalities, interests and values (9).

Still other abolitionists point out that most psychiatrists identify with their patient and want to help him avoid what both parties consider to be an overwhelming or unjust obligation, but strong partisanship destroys the psychiatrist's objectivity (10).

When most states had a death penalty, the insanity defense had more importance. Some who have studied the consequences of the insanity defense feel there is only a marginal difference between the peno-correctional and the psychiatric-custodial processes if one is found not guilty on grounds of insanity. According to Norval Morris, the defense of insanity could be eliminated. Evidence of mental illness would be admissible as to the mens rea issue to the same limited extent that deafness, blindness, a heart condition, stomach cramps, illiteracy, stupidity, lack of education, "foreignness," drunkenness, and drug addiction are admissible. If convicted, the accused's mental condition would, of course, be highly relevant to his sentence and to his correctional treatment. Also, there is double stigmatization, since prison authorities regard their inmates in the facilities for the psychologically disturbed as both criminal and insane, bad and mad; mental hospital authorities regard their inmates who have been convicted—or even only arrested and charged with crime—as both insane and criminal, mad and bad (11).

When one considers the innerconnection between the insanity defense, dangerousness and treatment resources, it should be kept in mind that most dangerous criminals are never referred for psychiatric evaluation. For instance, at present in New York City only 1 percent of individuals charged with felonies have their cases settled by a trial. The other 99 percent have their cases settled by the inequitable system of plea bargaining (12). In other jurisdictions only the exceptional case goes to the jury, and of these, only in 2 percent of the cases is the insanity defense raised (13).

Since there are so many reported violent crimes, and a fairly high percentage of mentally disturbed inmates in every penitentiary, why do so few defendants accused of violent crimes plead not guilty by reason of insanity? Seymour Halleck offers some of the reasons that to us seem valid. He says that only certain individuals have the opportunity to obtain a psychiatric excuse, and it is seldom even considered unless the patient complains vehemently about his suffering or behaves in a bizarre or unreasonable manner. The person who suffers quietly or the person who harbors bizarre thoughts but keeps them to himself will probably not be considered eligible for a psychiatric excuse. The very act of requesting preferential treatment requires a certain degree of aggressiveness on the part of the patient or perhaps on the part of his attorney. Those who know the laws and are aware that an excuse is available are most likely to request and to receive one. A prestigious social position and lots of money help. Psychiatric excuses are rarely given to members of lower socioeconomic groups (14).

The latest complaint about the insanity defense is directed toward the American Law Institute Test for criminal responsibilty. Both Pugh and Rappeport have reported that in their experience the testifying psychiatrist is rarely asked about such matters as what he believes such words as "substantial capacity," "appreciate," etc., mean to him. There is no clear indication that the meaning attributed by any one psychiatrist in a given case is consistent with the meaning attributed by any other psychiatrist in that case (15).

Not all lawyers or psychiatrists desire the abolition of the insanity defense. Many like Richard Arens are advocating a reform of the criminal justice system, especially in dealing with the mentally and emotionally ill. He remarks that the new abolitionists invoke the spirit of liberty. They do so, however, under circumstances painfully reminiscent of the adage that some of the greatest crimes are committed in its name. Inevitably the abolitionist proposal will meet with almost uniform revulsion on the part of any lawyer conversant with criminal practice and committed to the ideology of the Bill of Rights. Arens recommends improving the concepts put forth in the Durham rule.

Although Arens is for retaining the insanity defense, he refers to the fact that most pretrial psychiatric evaluations are done in hospitals where the environment is inappropriate and often hostile (16).

THE LAWMAKERS AND THE INSANITY DEFENSE

"Law does not provide a wisdom unto itself; it only suggests a method for seeking wisdom. It ensures that conflicts and competing values are honestly aired rather than covered up. The court's proper role is not to determine whether a decision is correct or wise but whether there has been a full exploration of all relevant facts and possible alternatives: Who can be held morally responsible for a crime? Who can be ordered into a hospital for compulsory treatment? What kinds of treatment can be imposed involuntarily and for how long? What standards should govern the imposition of solitary confinement and other restrictive measures? Such questions pose issues that require a delicate balancing of power between the state and the individual; the stakes are the highest when human and personal rights are involved (17)."

In finding answers to the above posed questions, the importance of tests for criminal responsibility has been strongly emphasized. The traditional American test for the defense of insanity is the M'Naghten rule, the by-product of an 1843 English murder case. As a result of M'Naghten's being found not guilty by reason of insanity and the ensuing debate in the House of Lords, the M'Naghten rule came into use. The most important opinion handed down by the judges states: "To establish a defense on the ground of insanity, it must be clearly proved that, at the time of the committing of the act, the party accused was laboring under such a defect of reason, from disease of the mind, as not to know the nature and quality of the act he was doing, or if he did know it, that he did not know he was doing what was wrong."

The M'Naghten Rule was adopted and later modified by the federal courts and all state courts with the exception of New Hampshire. The supreme court of New Hampshire in the Jones case threw over all of the so-called "tests," declaring that whether or not any alleged criminal act was the outgrowth of mental disease was a question not of law but of fact for the jury. The court said in the Jones case: "Enough has already been said as to the use of symptoms, phases, or manifestations of mental disease as legal tests of capacity to entertain a criminal intent. They are all clearly matters of evidence to be weighed by the jury upon the question whether the act was the offspring of insanity. If it was, a criminal intent did not produce it. If it was not, a criminal intent did produce it and it was crime."

In 1954 the United States Court of Appeals for the District of Columbia, speaking through Judge David L. Bazelon in the case of *Durham v. U.S.*, adopted what is essentially the New Hampshire Rule. It simply states, "an accused is not criminally responsible if his unlawful act was the product of mental illness or mental defect (18)." The Durham rule was criticized as being too broad in scope, too vague in meaning, and as being without any real standards for application in any given case. Although the Durham rule was accepted by some of the federal jurisdictions, acceptance by state courts was quite limited.

On June 23, 1972, the Court of Appeals declared in *U.S. v. Brawner* that the Durham rule was superseded by a new rule: "A person is not responsible for criminal conduct if at the time of such conduct as a result of mental disease or defect he lacks substantial capacity either to appreciate the criminality (wrongfulness) of his conduct or to conform his conduct to the requirements of the law" (19).

In the Brawner decision the court accepted the American Law Institute's Model Penal Code recommendation for a new test of criminal responsibility. Since the Brawner decision, the A.L.I. Test has been adopted in various versions by nine federal ciruits, the District of Columbia and twelve states. The remaining states and other federal jurisdictions still use some variation of the M'Naghten Rule.

Following the Brawner decision, Judge Bazelon commented as follows: "The purpose of the Durham decision was not fulfilled. Psychiatrists continued adamantly to cling to conclusory labels without explaining the origin, development, or manifestations of a disease in terms meaningful to a jury. The jury was confronted with a welter of confusing terms such as personality defect, sociopathy, and personality disorder. What became more and more apparent was that these terms did not rest on disciplined investigation based on facts and reasoning, as was required for the fulfillment of the Durham decision (20)."

In 1970, Congress, apparently concerned about the permissiveness of the Durham rule, enacted a statute requiring the defendant to establish his insanity by a preponderance of evidence in insanity cases in the District of Columbia. Half of the states place the burden of proof on the defendant, most of them requiring him to establish his insanity by a preponderance of evidence. Oregon used to require the defendant to prove his insanity beyond a reasonable doubt. That statute has since been repealed.

That the placing of the burden is thought by courts to be critical is borne out by the approach adopted several years ago in Wisconsin, where the defendant was given the usual option of choosing either the M'Naghten test, in which case the prosecution had to bear the burden of establishing the defendant's sanity beyond a reasonable doubt, or the more liberal Model Penal Code Test, in which case the defendant had to bear the burden of establishing his insanity by a preponderance of the evidence. See *State v. Shoffner*, 31 Wis. 2d 412, 143 N.W. 2d 458 (1966), now changed by statute. Would it be a reasonable compromise to place the burden of proof on the prosecution but to lessen it to a preponderance of the evidence, as has been proposed by the American Bar Association? Would this be acceptable under the due process clause?

Advocates of both positions appear to be largely motivated by considerations of public policy and by their attitudes toward the insanity defense.

Supporters for placing the burden on the prosecution argue that the insanity defense is only a more precise formulation of the mental state or *mens rea* requirement, which is traditionally an essential element of the crime for the prosecution to prove. A further practical argument is that the prosecution has greater resources for the purpose of establishing sanity, has better access to and more money for psychiatric and psychological assistance, and other means for challenging the defendant's case.

The various formulae concerning how much evidence the defendant need produce in order to rebut the presumption reflect fundamental postures toward the insanity defense. Some jurisdictions require "any," "slight," "some," or a "scintila" of evidence of insanity. Others require "sufficient" or "substantial" evidence of insanity. These vague terms have been subject to considerable interpretation. What "some" evidence means in the District of Columbia was an issue in the Durham case.

The concept, as it has developed in Wisconsin, that a defendant, entering a plea of not guilty by reason of insanity, may request a two-stage trial, but must expect testimony as to his mental condition to be admissible only on the issue of insanity rests upon the separability of guilt and insanity as issues in the single trial.

Some states provide for bifurcated trials in which the insanity defense is presented in a hearing that is separate from the hearing whose function it is to determine guilt or innocence apart from the issue of insanity.

There seem to be several advantages in a bifurcated trial. First, it tends to provide a more clear-cut delineation of the issue, preventing jury confusion. Second, it may eliminate appeals to the jury's sympathy. Third, it tends to prevent compromise verdicts. Fourth, it can save time if the defendant is found not guilty at the guilt-innocence hearing. Fifth, it can prevent evidence relating to insanity from contaminating the guilt-innocence decision. Sixth, it can protect the defendant's self-incrimination right if he wishes to testify as to insanity but not on the issue of the act itself.

Recently, however, courts have been having second thoughts about the constitutional validity of bifurcated trials in the light of due process—especially where limitations are placed on receiving evidence of the defendant's mental state at the guilt-innocence hearing, on the assumption that such evidence would be presented at the insanity hearing. The California Supreme Court saved its bifurcated trial procedure by ruling that at the guilt-innocence hearing all evidence relating to the defendant's mental condition is admissible, provided the evidence does not relate specifically to the insanity defense itself.

In the law, the dividing line as to accountability or nonaccountability due to mental condition is the test of insanity, whatever the legal definition of these terms may be or come to be. The sane person is held accountable for his actions. The insane person is not. Personality disturbances or emotional disorders that fall short of insanity are not required areas of court inquiry and particularly not in that portion of a bifurcated trial on the issue of guilt (21).

WHO IS DANGEROUS?

The American Psychiatric Association Task Force on the Clinical Aspects of the Violent Individual says that for the purpose of their report, violence has been defined as acts that produce physical harm or destruction.

Some years ago the Maryland State Legislature defined by statute the term "defective delinquent." The statute reads: "We feel that a proper definition of defective delinquents would be those individuals who, by the demonstration of persistent aggravated anti-social or criminal behavior, evidence a propensity toward criminal activity and who, on the evidence of standard test and clinical procedures, reveal either intellectual deficiency or emotional disorder, or both." They went on to explain that the term "defective" is to be understood as applying in the two chief spheres of human behavior: the intellectual and the emotional (22).

The American Law Institute's Model Penal Code authorizes a trial judge, when sentencing a person convicted of a felony, to extend the term of imprisonment beyond the maximum provided for that category of felon when "the defendant is a dangerous, mentally abnormal person whose commitment for an extended term is necessary for protection of the public." As a precondition to judicial imposition of the extended sentence, there must be a psychiatric examination "resulting in the conclusion that his mental condition is gravely abnormal; that his criminal conduct has been characterized by a pattern of repetitive or compulsive behavior or by persistent aggressive behavior with heedless indifference to consequences; and that such condition makes him a serious danger to others" (23).

The Model Sentencing Act of the Advisory Council of Judges makes a pivotal distinction between dangerous offenders and all others. "Dangerous Offenders" are defined as those who have committed or attempted certain crimes of physical violence and who are found by the court to be "suffering from a severe personality disorder indicating a propensity toward criminal activity." (24).

The tendency to relate violence and sex offenses is probably exaggerated: however, the incidence of sexual attack is not known. Forcible rape and incestuous offenses are frequently not reported to law enforcement officers. Perhaps less than one in five sexual attacks involving force is ever reported. However, sexual offenses are but a small part of the crime scene, certainly less than 5 percent of all crimes. In addition, most prosecutions involving sex crimes reflect a desire to punish individuals for the breaking of laws governing morals or social customs rather than an attempt to protect people from actual attacks or from unwanted sexual behavior. The most prevalent sex offenses are exhibitionism, voyeurism and fetishism. These types of offenses have been referred to as "public nuisance offenses." Whether this type of sexual behavior does, in effect, any "harm" to the victims is open to question. One rarely sees cases of sadistic sexual attacks upon children; those are most frequently committed by adolescent offenders who are either severely retarded or psychotic or both. In sexual attacks against adults, likewise, most victims of rape are subjected to very little physical abuse (25).

The belief that all sexual offenders are dangerous has recently been described as a "myth," that is, "an erroneous popular belief." As reported by Kozol, "Not more than one in eighteen of all convicted sex offenders can be considered dangerous, and out of a group of 3,600 convicted sex offenders, only 700 actually committed sexual attacks" (26).

Nicholas N. Kittrie in his book, The Right to Be Different, in discussing deviance and enforced therapy devotes a chapter to the psychopath. He writes that the majority of the psychopathy laws have been enacted during the past thirty years and, like other state laws, do not have much uniformity. The procedures differ, the types of offenders included are varied. Generally, however, an emphasis upon the sexual offender is evident: an emphasis attributable to the fact that psychopathy legislation is often the result of similar public reactions to sensationally publicized sex crimes. The treatment programs provided vary, but all share a provision that prescribes an involuntary and continuous term of commitment until a cure (or at least a marked improvement) is achieved.

Two common denominators of the psychopathy laws are their asserted noncriminal nature and the illusive nature of their subject—a habitual delinquent not considered mentally ill, yet believed to suffer from a personality disorder because of his inability to conform his behavior to the minimum demands of society.

Dr. Kittrie reports that at present twenty-nine states and the District of Columbia have some special legislation for the treatment of the defective delinquent or psychopathic offender. Fewer than half of the statutes agree on the nomenclature for the individual subject to these special programs. Various state statutes make reference to "Sexually Dangerous Persons," "Mentally Disturbed Sex Offenders," "Psychopathic Offenders," and "Defective Delinquents." In twelve jurisdictions, he is some type of "psychopath," and seventeen jurisdictions include a sex element in their definition. Most commonly, a person subjected to these special laws must have been brought to the attention of the authorities by a prior charge of specified offense, frequently a sexual offense. This offense, however, may range from a passive act of genital exhibitionism or consenting homosexuality to forcible rape.

Another element of psychopathy is a behavioral irregularity, primarily a propensity to repeat the prohibited behavior, which may be demonstrated either through a positive finding of potential threat to the community, or through evidence of an individual's "lack of power to control his sexual impulses." Although some form of mental abnormality is usually required to establish psychopathy, many statutes state that the affected person does not have to be mentally ill, failing to specify, however, which test of insanity, criminal or civil, will negate psychopathy. Only a few states include mentally ill persons within their special psychopathy programs.

If limited experimentation is accepted as major justification of these special programs, their utility will never be determined without trained personnel and adequate facilities. State legislatures, however, frequently enact this new type of law without providing for the supportive hospital facilities and services required; instead they place the burden on the already overtaxed mental hospitals and correctional institutions.

Another of the problems of the psychopathy programs is the present inability of the medical profession to prescribe a generally effective treatment. Indeed, some authorities doubt altogether the ability of medical science to cure or improve substantially the condition of the vast majority of those designated psychopathic. There are no drugs or specific therapy known that benefit the condition of this morally or socially abnormal person. The only treatment for psychopathy known at present is essentailly nonmedical—a long-term program of total reeducation. For many of the psychopaths, however, such reeducation comes too late in life to be effective. Their institutional commitment is not therapeutic but simply an act of social defense, designed primarily to insulate the public from them (27).

According to Norval Morris, the variety of legal approaches to this task of distinguishing dangerous from less serious offenders pose the following challenges to the pscyhiatrist: (1) Habitual criminal laws are widespread and long-established. The consensus is that they are a failure, productive of chaotic and unjust results when they are used, and greatly nullified in practice. They have swept up the persistent social nuisances while leaving the dangerous and serious offenders untouched. (2) Sexual psychopath laws have spread like a rash of injustice across the country, unjustly failing to distinguish the inadequate and aberrant from the dangerous and brutal. Their social and legislative psychopathology is clear; their contribution to the problem of the dangerous offender is slight. (3) Wherever discretion in sentencing exists (and that is now ubiquitous) the judge may and frequently does fix the sentence at least partly in relation to his view, guided by such advice as he has received, of the future danger the criminal presents to the community. (4) Wherever discretion in paroling exists (also ubiquitous) the parole board may and frequently does defer the criminal's release if it regards him as a continuing and serious danger to the community. (5) Special quarantine-type legislation which protracts custodial banishment is frequently to be found for persistent petty offenders, professional criminals, multiple offenders, vagrants, prostitutes, alcoholics and narcotic addicts. None of these techniques has effectively brought us to grips with the variety of classifications we must have for dangerous offenders if our criminal justice system is to become socially protective (28).

The prediction of dangerousness will be taken up by other contributors to this volume, so we will restrict our contribution to a statement from Draft #2, October 1973, of the report of the APA Task Force on Clinical Aspects of the Violent Individual. The report reads, "With respect to the most predictions of violence, the likelihood of the expected behavior such as violation of parole by a released prisoner whose previous crime was one of violence or the possibility of serious assault being committed by a released mental patient would be slight. This means that even if the characteristics of such future violent patients could be specified with fairly great accuracy, predictions based upon such characteristics will identify far more "false positives" than "true positives." Even if an index of violence proneness could be developed so as to correctly identify prior to release 50 percent of those individuals who will violate parole by committing violent offenses, the actual employment of such an index would identify eight times as many "false positives" as "true positives." This means that seven of the eight persons retained in prison as a result of application of the index would not have committed such offenses if released. Statistically the greatest accuracy is achieved by designating the smallest number of persons dangerous (29).

Bruce Ennis's recent position paper representing views of the American Civil Liberties Union states that only the California and Massachusetts standards for mental hospital commitment would escape the allegation of being unconstitutional by reason of vagueness. Massachusets law elaborated the standards for "likelihood of: (1) a substantial risk of physical harm to the person himself as manifested by evidence of threat of, or attempts at, suicide or serious bodily harm; (2) a substantial risk of physical harm to other persons or manifested by evidence of homicidal or other violent behavior; or evidence that others are placed in reasonable fear of violent behavior or serious physical harm; (3) a very substantial risk of physical impairment or injury to the person himself as manifested by evidence that such person's judgment is so affected that he is unable to protect himself in the community and that reasonable provision for his protection is not available in the community (30).

The usefulness of categorizing persons accused of violent offenses in psychiatric terms may be of value to judges like Judge Miller who said in dissenting in the case of *Hough v. United States:* "It is, of course, much easier to believe that a sane man will not in the reasonable future be dangerous to himself or others than to believe that an insane person will not be" (31).

On Judge Miller's statement, Thomas Szasz commented: "Here is an ancient view, equating violence and insanity, dressed in slightly more modern garb. What is being asserted here, if anything? Both 'insanity' and 'dangerousness' are such vague terms that it is impossible to know what is being asserted by such a statement. But not only is this statement vague, worse, it is tautologous, for we habitually infer a condition of 'insanity' from acts of violence . . . But if we infer insanity from violence, naturally we shall always expect violence when we speak of insanity, even though,in everyday life, the latter term is often used quite independently of whether or not a person is considered 'dangerous'" (32).

ALCOHOL, DRUGS AND DANGEROUSNESS

For some years, Samuel Guze and his staff have studied the personal, family and social backgrounds of convicted male and female felons. In his earlier studies of the male felons, he reported that among convicted male felons, the prevalence of sociopathy, alcoholism and drug dependency is increased. An increased prevalence of these same conditions and of hysteria is found among the felons' first-degree relatives: hysteria in the female relatives, and the others predominantly in the male relatives. On the other hand, family studies of women with hysteria show an increased prevalence of hysteria in the female relatives, and of sociopathy and alcoholism in the male relatives (33).

L.N. Robins reported that 72 percent of a large group of men he diagnosed as having antisocial personalities also had a history of excessive habitual alcohol intake (34). In a study of a smaller group of antisocial female felons, Guze and his associates found that 67 percent had serious drinking problems (35).

"Alcohol is a common contributing factor to violence, both in crime and automobile fatalities. Alcohol may lead to what has been described as a state of 'pathological intoxication,' a transient psychotic-like condition often accompanied by violent behavior. Alcohol has been reportred to activate psychomotor epilepsy. Other work indicates the drug to have no activating EEG properties when administered in a laboratory setting to men who complained of such violent 'blackouts.' The interpretation of conflicting data of this type is perhaps one illustration of the importance of environmental setting in the pathophysiology of violence" (36).

MacAndrew and Edgerton have convincingly shown that drug effects on social behavior vary with prior social learning. Marshaling impressive sociological evidence, they show that ethanol use is associated with much violence in some societies, with no violence in some, with violence only under certain circumstances in others, and that the incidence of ethanol-related violence has changed in still other societies as social conditions have changed. They conclude that social factors are the major determinants of violence after drinking, and that the pharmacological contribution of ethanol is minimal. MacAndrew and Edgerton also find little evidence for an ethanol-induced release of sexual inhibitions. Thus, sociology more than pharmacology may color our commonly held views of social pharmacology (37).

"It is difficult, if not impossible, to establish a direct relationship between crime and the use of various drugs. There is no question, however, that the two are related. Which comes first, drug use or criminal behavior, is under debate; much evidence, however, has been accumulated by the Commission on Marihuana and Drug Abuse to indicate that criminal activity begins before involvement with drugs. After that, they reinforce one another. As a general rule, the ability of drugs to exacerbate existing psychopathology, delinquency and criminality is conditional upon the pre-existence of psychological and social maladjustment prior to the onset of drug use or dependency" (38).

"There is much public concern linking heroin to violence. Available data does not, however, show heroin users to be over-representative, and very probably they are under-represented, among those who accomplish violence. A difficulty in interpretation of studies depends upon whether or not the crime of robbery is included as a crime of violence. Including robbery as a crime of violence does increase the number of person crimes associated with heroin use" (39).

Chemical intoxication in individuals charged with violent crimes has been a difficult issue for the courts throughout history. As long as mens rea or intent has been viewed as an important element of a crime, intoxication and its relationship to criminal behavior has troubled jurists. The punishment of persons who are so disabled as the result of a mental aberration to not have the capacity to form intent would not set a reasonable example of deterrence to others.

Particularly difficult questions are raised by a crime committed during a period of pathologic intoxication. The patient has a complete amnesia for his behavior and will never remember having done what he is charged with. But within the framework of his pathologic intoxication he will have acted sanely. He will show premeditation, planning and an effort to escape, all of which suggests that he has full responsibility even though his amnesia is genuine. In delirium tremens, on the other hand, the patient is clearly in no condition to plan, deliberate, weigh consequences, evaluate the wrongfulness of the act or understand its quality (40).

In jurisdictions where the test for criminal responsibility and mental capacity is the A.L.I. Test, the narrow limitations of the wording of the M'Naghten Rule have been broadened so that the court is no longer confined to inquiring only about one's cognitive capacity, while ignoring the possibility of an impaired volitional capacity (the emotional capacity to control oneself). The terms "mental disease" and "mental defect" are being viewed from a broader base, supposedly more in line with the scientific advances made in the field of psychiatry.

In *Robinson v. California*, 370 U.S. 660 (1962), the Supreme Court held unconstitutional a California statute which made it a misdemeanor, punishable by imprisonment, for a person to "be addicted to the use of narcotics." Said the Court, the statute "makes the 'status' of narcotic addiction a criminal offense." Id. at 666. The court ruled that "a state law which imprisons a person thus afflicted as a criminal, even though he has never touched any narcotic drug within the State or been guilty of any irregular behavior there, inflicts a cruel and unusual punishment in violation of the Fourteenth Amendment." Id. at 667

The ruling immediately gave rise to the question of whether an addict could properly be punished for acts compelled by his addiction, such as purchase, possession and use of narcotics.

The first test of the impact of Robinson was in the area of alcoholism, and in connection with acts of a compulsive alcoholic. In *Driver v. Hinnant*, 356 F.2d, 761 (4th Cir. 1966), the Fourth Circuit Court of Appeals struck down a North Carolina public drunkenness statute partly on the basis of the rationale of Robinson. Said the court, the North Carolina statute punished an involuntary symptom of a status, namely, public intoxication. The court also held that the compulsive alcoholic lacked the evil intent or consciousness of wrongdoing which is an essential of mens rea.

In the same year the District of Columbia Circuit Court of Appeals, in *Easter v. District of Columbia*, 361 F.2d 50 (D.C. Cir. 1966), also found chronic alcoholism to be a defense to public drunkenness. But the court's decision was not based on Robinson or on constitutional requirements; it was rooted in a common-law "insanity defense" approach relating to the alcoholic's inability to conform his behavior to the requirements of the law.

The Supreme Court refused to apply the rationale of *Robinson v. California* to public drunkenness. In *Powell v. Texas*, 392 U.S. 514 (1968), a 5-to-4 decision, the court upheld the conviction of a chronic alcoholic for public drunkenness. Said the Court, it rejected the role of being "the ultimate arbiter of the standards of criminal responsibility, in diverse areas of the criminal law, throughout the country." Id. at 533. The majority of the Court refused to give a broad reading to the "cruel and unusual punishment" clause. The dissent, written by Justice Fortas, argued that a criminal penalty should not be inflicted on a person "for being in a condition he is powerless to change." Id. at 567.

The issue of the criminal responsibility of the nontrafficking drug addict for possession of narcotics was finally joined in *United States v. Moore*, 468 F.2d 1139 (D.C. Cir. 1973), cert. denied, 94 S. Ct. 298 (1973), where Moore made arguments substantially based on the approach earlier accepted by the District of Columbia Court of Appeals in the Easter case. Moore argued lack of free will; the fact that Congress had not intended, in the statute under which Moore was indicted, to punish the nontrafficking addict who possessed small amounts intended exclusively for his own use; and the rationale of Robinson. Moore did not invoke the insanity defense, although the court would have permitted testimony on that issue. The court in a 5-to-4 plurality opinion, rejected Moore's arguments and upheld his conviction. The question was the practicality of determining guilt or innocence on the basis of a finding of loss of self-control. Both Judge Wilkey, who wrote for the majority, and Judge Leventhal, who concurred, were convinced that it would be practically impossible for a jury to make such a determination rationally. The dissent argued that the jury should indeed be permitted to find whether, because of the compulsive character of his addiction, the addict (at the time) lacked substantial capacity to conform his conduct to the requirements of the law under the new Brawner rule (A.L.I.)—thus establishing, in effect, a new test of criminal responsibility for the narcotics addict.

A significant decision on insanity resulting from drug use is *People v. Kelly*,—Cal.—, 516 P.2d 875, 111 Cal. Rptr. 171 (1973), which concerned an eighteen-year-old girl who had been using drugs excessively for several years at the time she assaulted her mother. The police had found her wandering about an airport under the influence of drugs. They turned her over to her parents. The next day the defendant repeatedly stabbed her mother with a number of kitchen knives. A psychiatrist who examined her reported that the daughter thought her parents "were the devils." Defendant waived a jury trial and was convicted of assault with a deadly weapon. The trial judge found that the defendant had been insane at the time, but rejected the insanity defense on the basis that the insanity was not of a "settled or permanent nature," since there was evidence that the defendant would ultimately recover if she stopped using drugs.

In reversing, the California Supreme Court found that the

defendant's continued ingestion of drugs for two months prior to the event had triggered a "legitimate psychosis" which rendered her unable to distinguish right from wrong at the time, and ruled that in such a case it is not necessary to the defense that a finding of "permanence" be made, as long as the psychosis is of a "settled" nature. There had been testimony, which both courts accepted, that the defendant's "insanity" would last longer than the period of actual intoxication. One psychiatrist estimated that even if the defendant went off drugs she might be psychotic for another nine to ten months. Another psychiatrist, who testified that the psychosis represented an "organic disturbance of the brain cells," stated that the psychosis was "settled," but not permanent, in that it would eventually disappear (41).

In *Parker v. State of Maryland* (1969) the opinion of the Court is that regardless of what test is applicable to determining insanity, the majority distinguish between (1) the mental effect of voluntary intoxication which is the immediate result of a particular alcoholic bout and (2) an alcoholic psychosis resulting from long-continued habits of excessive drinking. The first does not excuse responsibility for a criminal act; the second may. In other words, if a person drinks intoxicating liquor and is sane both prior to drinking and after the influence of the intoxicant has worn off, but is insane by the applicable test while under the influence of intoxicant, he comes under the first category. If he is insane whether or not he is directly under the influence of an intoxicant, even though that insanity was caused by voluntary drinking, he comes under the second category. The cases usually refer to the first category as a "temporary" insanity and the second category as a "permanent," "fixed" or "settled" insanity (42).

DANGEROUSNESS AND DUE PROCESS

The overtones and implications of the putting on trial, for their freedom or for their lives, defendants who are "altered" by drugs so that they may achieve an "artificial competency" brings up serious questions concerning the Fourteenth, Fourth and Fifth Amemdments.

The United States Supreme Court has determined in the case of *Pate v. Robinson* 383 U.S. 375, 85 Sct. 836, 15L. Ed. (1966) that the trial and conviction of an incompetent defendant constitutes a denial of a fair trial and, further, that any indication to the trial court that for any reason the competence of the defendant may be called into question should impel the court, on its own motion, if necessary, to conduct an inquiry into the defendant's competence to stand trial. We would broaden this concept to make such an a priori determination of competence to stand trial a necessary court function in any case in which the defendant is on a regimen of state prescribed and administered drugs which affect the mind, the nervous system, the attitudes and the reflexes of the accused. This would not include, for example, insulin, antiflatulents, vitamins, respiratory stimulants and diuretics, but emphatically would include anticonvulsants, antidepressives, narcotics and tranquilizers of any kind, and psychostimulants and sedatives. Procedurally, as the Supreme Court indicated in *Pate*, the court should routinely inquire prior to commencing a criminal trial whether the defendant is on any kind of artificial sustenance.

An increasing number of cases deal with the tangential question of incapacity or incompetence to stand trial because of, not a state prescribed and administered regimen of drugs, but rather of a self-indulgence in drugs, e.g., heroin, cocaine, alcohol. There are also a goodly number of defendants who were previously addicted to narcotics who come for trial on maintenance doses of methadone ordered by legitimate treatment programs.

Ernest Wilkerson, staff attorney and program director for the Practising Law Institute, makes the following recommendations: (1) a compulsory and routine pretrial determination by a judge or the jury of competence to stand trial in the case of every defendant who is on a state prescribed and administered psychotropic regimen; (2) a compulsory and routine pre-return drug-free period in the observing institution before sending back for trial a criminal defendant committed for a determination of competency; (3) continual search between the medical and legal disciplines for common language and common concepts in the areas of drug administration by the former and competency determination by the latter so that the interests of due process, fair trial and justice may be ever better served.

Any accused, competent or incompetent, has rights guaranteed him by our Constitution and statutes. He is entitled to speedy trial and a fair trial; any unnecessary delays would violate these rights. Witnesses disappear or their memories become less reliable. Investigating officers and prosecutors may be replaced. Records may be lost or destroyed. If the court is insistent that the defendant not be considered competent to stand trial while on psychiatric medication, some trials would be delayed for months and even years, for apparently some defendants would not be able to function without drugs (43).

The right to treatment for all institutional mental patients, including so-called dangerous mentally ill offenders, began to be exerted in the last decade. In 1960 Morton Birnbaum proclaimed the advent of a new right to treatment for institutionalized citizens. As summarized in an editorial: "The fact that a person has a mental ailment is not a crime. Therefore, if anyone is involuntarily restrained of his liberty because of a mental ailment, that state owes a duty to provide him reasonable medical attention. If medical attention reasonably well adapted to his needs is not given, the victim is not a patient but virtually a prisoner."

In 1964, *Sas v. Maryland* was the first case to examine a treatment program to determine whether the involuntary confinement met constitutional requirements. Sas, who had been committed under Maryland's Defective Delinquent Act, asserted that his indeterminate sentence could not be justified because he was not receiving any treatment. The court remanded on constitutional issues such as whether the institution furnished treatment for the defective delinquents sufficient to distinguish their incarceration from the confinement of other law breakers. Although the Fourteenth Amendment issue was raised, the case was resolved on the point that Sas was not a defective delinquent, without further consideration of his right to treatment.

The first case to directly address itself to the right to treatment and arouse national interest was *Rouse v. Cameron* in 1966. The petitioner, Charles Rouse, had been committed to Saint Elizabeths Hospital, Washington, D.C. in 1962 after being found not guilty by reason of insanity of carrying a dangerous weapon, a misdemeanor with a one-year maximum sentence. After three years of confinement, he petitioned for release by a writ of habeas corpus alleging that he had not received psychiatric treatment during his confinement. The court refused to hear the claim because of a lack of jurisdiction. When the circuit court of appeals reviewed the case, Justice Bazelon's opinion echoed the editorial written six years earlier which first declared the right to treatment: "The purpose of involuntary hospitalization is treatment, not punishment . . . Absent treatment, the hospital is transformed into a penitentiary where one could be held indefinitely for no convicted offense."

The decision strongly implied that a constitutional right to treatment exists under the due process, equal protection, and cruel and unusual punishment clauses. The court stated: "Absence of treatment might draw into question the constitutionality of this mandatory commitment section . . . It has also been suggested that failure to supply treatment may violate the equal protection clause. Indefinite confinement without treatment of one who has been found not criminally responsible may be so inhumane as to be 'cruel and unusual punishment.'"

The Rouse decision established the issue of adequate treatment as relevant in habeas corpus hearings. In addition, the court dictated that the right to treatment exists regardless of the institution's lack of facilities or staff.

Rouse had been institutionalized after being found not guilty by reason of insanity. The next case raising the right to treatment was initiated by John Nason, an indicted murderer who had never been to trial. After spending five years in Bridgewater State Hospital, Massachusetts, because of incompetency to stand trial, Nason petitioned for habeas corpus on the grounds that the hospital was so understaffed that adequate psychiatric treatment was impossible. Nason claimed that treatment in Bridgewater was so inferior to that of other state institutions that his confinement denied him equal protection of the law.

The court also concurred that Nason's "confinement may have deprived him of liberty without due process of law." The court warned that if adequate treatment was not furnished within a reasonable time the legality of further confinement would be dubious. This decision began to strengthen the right to treatment for involuntarily committed mental patients on the constitutional grounds of due process and equal protection of the law.

Instead of seeking release for an involuntarily committed individual from a nontreatment situation, cases beginning with *Wyatt v. Stickney* argued for the implementation of adequate treatment for all residents of mental institutions and institutions for the retarded (44).

The courts are now demanding that treatment must be adequate in the light of our present knowledge. Lee Gurel points out how difficult it will be for the courts to develop such standards of treatment. He states that if mental health professionals are to help the courts move beyond a "numbers game" concept of hospital treatment—i.e., how many of what kinds of personnel define a level of adequate treatment—it becomes crucial that we follow up our attempts to refine our methodologies, concepts and measurements of the therapeutic and antitherapeutic effects of hospitalization itself. Adequate treatment requires an appropriate treatment climate. Until mental health professionals can provide a quantitative definition of that climate and an evaluation of its impact on treatment results, they are not likely to influence the evaluations of mental hospitals constantly taking place within the political arena (45).

DANGEROUSNESS AND EQUAL PROTECTION

The Baxstrom case is often cited to illustrate the extent to which psychiatrists over predict dangerousness. Although Johnnie K. Baxstrom in a sense "died with his rights on" a few weeks after his release, few cases have had such great impact on the disposition of mentally ill offenders. *Baxstrom v. Herold* was argued before the U.S. Supreme Court on December 9, 1965. On February 23, 1966, Chief Justice Earl Warren speaking for the Court said that equal protection of the laws required that when a male prisoner in the New York Department of Correction Hospital for mentally ill male prisoners neared the end of his criminal sentence he should be given a jury review of the determination as to his sanity in conformity with proceedings granted all others civilly committed under New York Mental Hygiene Law; he was also entitled to a hearing under the procedure granted all others to determine whether he was so dangerously mentally ill that he must remain in the Department of Correction Hospital (46).

In 1966 in New York the Baxstrom decision resulted in the abrupt and massive transfer of 969 men and women from Matteawan and Dannemora to the relatively open and less secure mental institutions of the New York Department of Mental Hygiene. It is worthy of note that prior to the Baxstrom mandate, such transfers had been sought for many of these men and women—in some cases on multiple occasions—but had been turned down. Several follow-up studies of the New York Baxstrom cases yielded extraordinary findings. It was found that although the transfers were viewed with much anxiety, in view of the alleged dangerousness of the Baxstrom patients, the patients proved to be relatively docile. Indeed, many were "model" patients from an institutional point of view—they were good workers—and many were subsequently discharged to the community. It was concluded that excessive clinical conservatism had prevailed in the prior management of these patients in strict security.

For many people, incarceration for many long years in strict security had been demonstrated by these studies to have been excessive and unnecessary. The risk to society of the massive transfer of such citizens to open facilities and to the community has proved to be minimal. It is our understanding that Pennsylvania is having a similar experience in implementing its Dixon decision (similar to Baxstrom) at Fairview Hospital. It is not clear whether or how many other states have applied the lessons of Baxstrom. At Bridgewater there has been a significant reversal of the clinical penal conservatism of the past. Thus, from a census high of 758 in 1963, the census on December 31, 1970, had dropped to 234. This occurred despite striking increases in the number of annual admissions (from 129 in 1960 to 478 in 1970). Clearly fewer men are being subjected to prolonged commitment and are being released much sooner than in the past. This is as it should be, both in Massachusetts and New York, and very likely as it should be elsewhere in the country (47).

Important recent judicial decisions and proposed legislative changes involving the confinement and treatment of so-called defective delinquents are of great concern in the area of constitutional law and should be included in any discussion of the violent offender, but an adequate review of the developments of the past few years would require many pages. Although we do not have the space to include this material, Alexander D. Brooks has covered this area quite satisfactorily in his book, Law, Psychiatry and the Mental Health System, which has just become available to the public. This book has excellent sections on the changes of the "sexual psychopath" laws and the frequent challenges in the courts of the Maryland Defective Delinquent Law and the programs this law has established at the Patuxent Institution (48).

A major revision of the Massachusetts Mental Health Code which became effective in November 1973 abolished the defective delinquent statutes and requires periodic reviews for all patients in mental hospitals. Among the other important changes was a provision that mentally ill persons have the right to refuse electroconvulsive treatment or lobotomy. A prominent group of legislators are presenting to the 1975 Legislature a bill to abolish the defective delinquent statutes in Maryland (49).

At present our courts are beginning to consider the rights of involuntarily committed patients who refuse treatment or demonstrate themselves to be untreatable. Does the rationale of Rouse v. Cameron that the hospital must continue its efforts to cure and improve the patient impose this duty on the hospital for patients who continue to refuse treatment?

The recent case of McCray v. Maryland represents one of the rare attempts by a court to deal with the problems surrounding the refusal of treatment. There, several patients confined to Patuxent Institution as defective delinquents filed habeas corpus petitions alleging that the institution's disciplinary procedures violated their constitutional rights. Responding to the practice of deliberately withholding rehabilitative efforts to "recalcitrant prisoners," the court declared that patients could not be confined indefinitely for purposes of treatment and then be deprived of all therapy unless the authorities first endeavored to discover the basis for refusal. Implicit in the obligation placed on the administrators to provide treatment was the necessity of distinguishing between the patient who is "so emotionally unstable that he refuses help" and the patient who is consciously hostile to treatment attempts. The court did not, however, indicate what the administrator was to do once he had decided in which category a patient belonged.

Release might be inapproprite for the untreatable patient, but the courts that have had to deal with that issue have chosen to sidestep it. For example, in *People ex. rel. Blunt v. Narcotics Addiction Control Board,* a narcotics addict whose sentence to a New York prison was predicated on his receiving treatment for addiction sought release on the ground that he was receiving no treatment.

In light of the undisputed evidence that Blunt in fact received treatment no different from nonaddict prisoners, the New York court's decision seems unduly restrained. The right-to-treatment theory could be seen to dictate that persons committed under statutes similar to the New York Drug Addiction Law or the Maryland Defective Delinquent Act who refuse treatment or demonstrate themselves to be untreatable should be returned to the custody of prison officials in order to serve the remainder of the statutory sentence of the crimes for which they had previously been convicted. Such statutes substitute treatment for conventional punishment of those persons convicted and sentenced for specified crimes whose mental condition is deemed to necessitate treatment. Though convicted initially by criminal standards, those persons are committed under civil procedures to confinement longer than that of the original statutory sentence. The release compelled by the logic of the Rouse test discussed earlier could at least be accommodated by "releasing" the dangerous patient unamenable to treatment to his former prison sentence.

Unfortunately, the availability of an effective enforcement mechanism solves only a few of the countless problems delaying widespread realization of the right to treatment. Judges will still have to formulate and apply admittedly awkward standards. In addition, many patients are unaware of their rights—due in part to their mental condition and in part to the fact that hospital officials do not apprise them of their rights. Even when aware, many are unable to obtain counsel. The judiciary still has to face the crucial issues involving nondangerous and dangerous persons who either refuse treatment or are untreatable (50).

One of the most potent judicial remedies that can enforce a right to treatment is the power to award monetary damages from the state for confinement in a nontreatment institution. In *Whitree v. State,* the plaintiff was committed to a state hospital after being found incompetent to stand trial. Whitree spent fourteen years in a New York state hospital without receiving adequate psychiatric care. The court found that his hospital record lacked both medical examinations and a treatment plan. It stated that "if that man had received proper and adequate psychiatric treatment such diagnosis (of insanity) would have been developed much sooner: and Whitree would have been released from Matteawan State Hospital much sooner." Supporting Whitree's claim of false imprisonment for the majority of his confinement, the court awarded him $300,000 in damages from the state (51).

Another attempt to be compensated for damages alleging inadequate care and deprivation of liberty without due process was argued in *Donaldson v. O'Conner*, a civil action against the superintendent of the hospital where Donaldson was involuntarily confined. Donaldson was awarded $38,500 money damage because he was confined for fifteen years without adequate treatment.

The specific details of this case and many of the cases we have only briefly described can be found in *Legal Rights of the Mentally Handicapped*, a good reference for recent legal explorations in the whole field of involuntary confinement of the mentally ill, including the violent criminal offender (52).

REFERENCES

1. Bazelon, L: The Perils of Wizardry. *Am. J. Psychiatry* 131:12, December 1974.
2. McGarry L: Demonstration and Research in Competency for Trial and Mental Illness: Review and Preview. *Boston University Law Review*, XLIX (1969), 46:50-53.
3. Halleck SL: A Troubled View of Current Trends in Forensic Psychiatry. *J. Psychiatry & Law* Vol. 2 No. 2 Summer 1974.
4. Zuzman J, Carnahan WA: Psychiatry and the Law: Changing the System Through Changing the Training. *Am. J. Psychiatry* 131: 8, August 1974.
5. Patch RK: The Mentally Disabled and His Lawyer. *J. Psychiatry & Law* Vol. 2 No. 1 Spring 1974.
6. Pollack S: Forensic Psychiatry—A Specialty. Bulletin of Am Acad Psychiatry & Law Vol. 2 No. 1 March 1974.
7. Morris, N: Psychiatry and the Dangerous Criminal. *Southern Cal. Law Review* Vol. 41: 514, 1968.
8. Supra, n. 4.
9. Supra, n. 1.
10. Halleck, S L: The power of the psychiatric excuse. *Psychiatry Digest* March, 1972.
11. Supra, n. 7.
12. Kaufman, E: Prison: Punishment, treatment or deterrent? *J Psychiatry & Law* Vol. 1, no. 3 Fall 1973.
13. Supra, n. 7.
14. Supra, n. 10.
15. Pugh, DG: *Wash. Univ. Law R.* 67, 93, 1973.
16. Arens, R: *Insanity Defense*. New York, Philosophical Library, 1974, p 302.
17. Supra, n. 1.
18. Arieti, S, (ed.): *American Handbook of Psychiatry*. Vol. 2, New York, Basic Books, Inc. 1965, pp 1192-93.
19. Supra, n. 16 at 289.
20. Supra, n. 1.
21. Brooks, A D: *Law, Psychiatry and the Mental Health System*. Boston, Little, Brown & Co., 1974, pp 305-9.

22. State of Maryland, Department of Public Safety and Correctional Services, Maryland's Defective Delinquent Statute, A Progress Report, Patuxent Institute, January 9, 1973.
23. Model Panel Code 7.03(3) (Prop. Final Draft No. 1 1961).
24. Advisory Council of Judges of the National Council on Crime and Delinquency, Model Sentencing Act 5 (a), 5(b) (1963).
25. Cavallin, H: Dangerous sexual offenders. *Medical Aspects of Human Sexuality.* June 1972.
26. Kozol, H W: Myths About the Sex Offender. *Medical Aspects of Human Sexuality.* June 1971.
27. Kittrie, N: *The Right to Be Different.* Baltimore & London, The Johns Hopkins Press, 1971, pp 175-82, 197-98.
28. Supra, n. 7.
29. Report of the American Psychiatric Association Task Force on Clinical Aspects of the Violent Individual. Draft No. 2, 1973.
30. Mass. Gen. Laws: ch 123, 1 (1971).
31. Miller, J: Dissenting in Hough v. United States. 271 F.2d 458, 465 (D.C. Cir. 1959).
32. Szasz, T: Civil liberties and mental illness. 131 J Nervous & *Mental Disease* 58,61 (1960).
33. Guze, S, Cloninger, C: Female criminals: Their personal, familial, and social backgrounds. *Arch Gen Psychiat* Vol. 23, December 1970.
34. Robins, L N: Deviant Children Grown Up: A Sociological and Psychiatric Study of Sociopathic Personality. Baltimore, The Williams & Wilkins Co., 1966.
35. Supra, n. 33.
36. Supra, n. 29.
37. MacAndrew C, Edgerton R B: Drunken Comportment. Chicago, Aldine, 1969, p 197.
38. Farnsworth, D L: The Second Report of the National Commission on Marihuana and Drug Abuse: Background and Recommendations. *Psychiat Annals* Vol. 3, No. 4, April, 1973.
39. Supra, n. 29.
40. Davidson, HA: Forensic Psychiatry. New York, The Ronald Press Co. p 17.
41. Supra, n. 21 at 251-54.
42. Parker v. State of Maryland: 414, 7 Md. App. at 167 (1968).
43. Wilkerson, E: Trying the Drugged Defendant. A Personal Communication.
44. Fremouw, WJ: A New Right to Treatment. J Psychiat Law. Vol. 2, No. 1, Spring 1974.
45. Gurel, L: Dimensions of the Therapeutic Milieu: A study of Mental Hospital Atmosphere. *Am J Psychiat 131:*4, April 1974.
46. Baxstrom v. Herold: 383 US 107, 1967.
47. McGarry, LA: Massachusetts operation Baxstrom: A follow up. *Mass. J Ment Health* Vol. 4, No. 3, Spring 1974.
48. Supra, n. 21
49. New Mass. Mental Health Code: Mass. Acts. Ch. 893, 1973.
50. Editors' notes and comments: *Maryland Law Review* Vol. XXXII, No. 1, 1972.
51. Supra, n. 44.
52. Ennis BJ, Friedman PR: *Legal Rights of the Mentally Handicapped.* New York, Practising Law Institute, 1973.

Therapy in Prisons

GARY J. MAIER

THE RANGE OF THE PROBLEM

In many ways the penal system is designed to negate the values of mental health. This chapter will only be able to relate the pain of two conflicting ideologies. One ideology stems from a Judeo-Christian revealed ethic where wrong actions are punished. The other stems from a youthful scientific tradition, less passionate, which aims at a search for "objective truth" (1). For this reason, any presentation related to therapy or treatment in the penal system will find itself immersed in many of the social issues of our day. Fundamental concepts, such as justice and injustice, punishment and treatment, personal and public civil rights, might be raised. The principles of law and the principles of mental health will be found intermingled.

At the same time, the field of penology in a world context has so many irregularities that it is nearly impossible to speak with common reference points. The prisons of the world themselves operate on the basis of different ideologies and different intents. While time-honored concepts like punishment, retribution and deterrence are general aims of the punitive system, more modern views stress rehabilitation and restitution (2).

David Ward (3) demonstrates the wide range of differences when he compares the inmate issues which led to the 1971 Attica Prison riot with those raised by the inmates of Osteraker Prison during their hunger strike in 1971. While visiting Sweden, Ward met the inmate council at Osteraker Prison and discussed with them the proposals which arose out of the 1971 riot at Attica. The Swedish prisoners were not prepared for the primitive level of some of the Attica prisoners' complaints. It had been years since the Swedish prisoners had been concerned with such problems as adequate food, water and shelter, true religious freedom and adequate medical treatment. Neither do Swedish prisoners seem to spend time filing appeals and writs in efforts to question their convictions. Part of the explanation for this difference from their American colleagues is that short sentences make the effort less worthwhile, but another part of the explanation seems to lie in the greater belief by Swedish inmates in the justice of the criminal process of their country. Compared to American prisoners, few complaints are heard about harassment, deception and discrimination by the police, prosecutors and judges. The efficiency and speed with which most cases are processed—that is, weeks compared to months, the availability of legal counsel, and ready access to the national ombudsmen—give inmates a sense that they have some recourse when action is taken against them.

Torsten Erikson, a former Swedish prison director, has described the policy regarding visits as follows:

> In Sweden we generally allow unsupervised visits in open institutions. An inmate may take a visitor to his private room, whether it's his father, mother, daughter, brother, sister, wife, fiancee or someone else close to him. Since the inmate has a key to his room nobody pays any attention if he locks himself in with his visitor. Moreover unsupervised visits in special rooms may be permitted in closed institutions also. I do not know whether sexual intercourse occurs during such visits although I can always hazard a guess. In my opinion, sexuality is strictly a personal matter. We do not ask questions. We make no special provisions. We merely decide whether the individual inmate can be trusted to receive a visitor without supervision (4).

The Swedes not only have this difference in attitude and policy but they also have a nearly one-to-one staff-inmate ratio, that is, in 1971 they had 4,700 staff to 5,000 inmates. This compares to the U.S. staff-inmate ratio of one to five, that is 71,000 staff to 363,000 inmates. The comparisons could go on (5, 6).

The confusion in the American penal system appears in two arenas. First in court, there is an increasing tendency for the judicial system to attempt to define treatment. In a distinguished article, (7) Judge David Bazelon has suggested that the court has a role in defining the right to treatment. His daring position has been challenged by the American Psychiatric Association, who took an official position in stating that "the definition of treatment and the appraisal of its adequacy are matters for medical determination" (8). At the same time the editors of the *Harvard Law Review* are equally concerned with the "difficulty of formulating standards of adequacy . . ." (9). Throughout the body of the paper, Judge Bazelon argues eloquently about the need for treatment plans in penitentiaries and the need for a built-in review system granted authority under the Criminal Code. In his opinion, the Review Boards should ideally, be peopled by an independent, multiprofessional group, one including such as a lawyer, a psychiatrist, a criminologist, etc. In contrast, Thomas Szasz (10) writes that the individual should be held entirely responsible for his behavior. He argues that the treatment of the offender must be dominated by the law rather than by psychiatric principle.

Halleck (11) states that a psychiatrist working in the American correctional system, the second arena, finds himself working in a basically bad system. Even when the system is not plagued with blatant corruption, it is a system that creates conditions which cause its victims to suffer great psychological pain. Sometimes the system seems diabolically conceived to create mental illness. It does not allow offenders to find intimacy; it does not allow them to express aggression; it does not allow them to be independent; and it does not allow them to be responsible. As a matter of fact, it comes down hard on people when they begin to search for these values. So one of the problems any professional has when he begins to work in a correctional area is that he is trying to create mental health in a system that is rigidly intolerant of mental health. This is a formidable and often impossible task. Further compounding it, psychiatrists can end up strengthening the oppressiveness of the system rather than changing it. The conclusion is drawn that the system itself is in need of treatment. The basic principles which underlie punishment of wrongdoers and the method of delivery ought to be the first concern of mental health workers in the correctional system. That is, it isn't this bad man that needs treatment, it's this bad system that needs to be corrected (12, 13, 14).

CLASSIFICATION OF THE INMATE: NAME-CALLING

Roth and Ervin (15) state that Karl Menninger recommended the following psychiatric services as indispensable to criminology in 1927: 1) a psychiatrist available to every court; 2) a psychiatric report made available before the sentencing of any felon; 3) a psychiatric service in every correctional institution; and 4) a psychiatric report on every felon before his release. Save for the California correctional system which makes some attempt to provide psychiatric evaluation for every offender, these recommendations have not been met.

Classification or diagnosis falls essentially into two areas: an assessment at the court stage; and then an assessment at the incarceration stage. Jablon, Sadoff and Heller (16) describe the forensic diagnostic hospital at Homesburg Prison, a unit similar to that at Oak Ridge, Maximum Security Division of the Mental Health Centre, Penetanguishene, Ontario, Canada. Typically, the patient is admitted for a sixty-day examination either for determination of competency before trial, or for evaluation and a recommended disposition after trial in preparation for sentencing. Great care is taken with those individuals examined in the pretrial stage not to discuss exculpatory material that may be used in a plea of insanity. The members of the unit wish to maintain neutrality with the court and do not become involved in adversary procedures dealing with criminal responsibility. In this latter respect the Homesburg Diagnostic unit is different from that at Penetanguishene.

In fact, the literature (17) time and again states the need for this kind of diagnostic unit. This would prevent those individuals with clear psychiatric illness from being immersed into the penitentiary system without treatment. Roth and Ervin found that compared to normal populations, alcoholism, drug abuse, epilepsy and schizophrenia were overrepresented within the federal penitentiary system (15). They found that 4 percent of the population experienced their first psychosis while incarcerated, and the 18 percent had at least one psychiatric encounter. There are a host of papers which attempt to define the epidemiology of the psychiatric illness within the prison system (18–21). This includes the diagnosis of the XYY syndrome, the relationship of criminality and violence in epileptic prisoners, suicide attempts and self-mutilation.

Once incarcerated, the prisoner is usually sent to a reception area where he is classified. Classification for treatment has as its intent the modification of the characteristics of the offender and/or the aspects of his environment which are responsible for his involvement in deviant activity. The problem is the treaters simply don't seem to know how to bring about changes in individuals via a treatment process. This is an important point when considering that the intervention strategies, which follow from offender typologies are not, by and large, made of new and unusual treatment methods, but rather consist of many of the old alternatives differentially applied to the various categories of offender. In an attempt to resolve this problem, Warren (22) took sixteen typological systems and cross-tabulated them. She found six offender subtypes: asocial, conformist, antisocial-manipulator, neurotic, subcultural-identifier and situational offender. These types lead to effective management and treatment, as they facilitated decision-making.

More pessimistically, people like R.D. Laing believe that someone whose mind is imprisoned in the diagnostic metaphor cannot see it as a metaphor. He succinctly outlines the diagnostic dilemma in stating that "the unintelligibility of the experience of the behavior of the diagnosed person is created by the person diagnosing him as well as by the person diagnosed" (23). Laing wishes to point out that the diagnostic or labeling process denies a social intelligibility to behavior and sanctions a massive ignorance of the social context in which the person was interacting. It also renders any genuine reciprocity between the process of labeling (the practice of psychiatry) and of being labeled (the role of the patient) as impossible to conceive as it is to observe. The diagnosis then only relieves strain on the system by allowing focus on the deviant, who is in large part a product of the inconsistencies existent in the system.

Kim and Clanon (24), in a short graphic paper, describe the integration of psychiatric services in the California correctional system. There are two reception-guidance centers, one in southern California for men at Chino and the other in northern California at Vacaville. All men committed to prison are first sent to a reception-guidance center where they are subjected, during a 60- to 90-day period, to vocational, educational, sociological, psychological and psychiatric studies on the basis of which they are assigned to one of thirteen California state prisons. Following the reception-guidance centers studies, three kinds of groups among the inmates are placed on "psychiatric referral status" to receive different levels of psychiatric care. Group one referral are those who require a psychiatric evaluation a year before their parole hearing, and who would need no special psychiatric attention. Group two referral are those who are not acutely psychotic but show significant emotional problems and/or personality disorders which seem to be related to deviant behavior, and who are thought to be in need of and capable of profiting from psychotherapy. There is an intensive psychotherapy program at Vacaville for this group. Group three referral are those with serious psychiatric disturbances requiring psychiatric treatment and management. The California Medical Facility has a 400-bed capacity for these patients. The treatment program for this group consists of occupational, recreational, drug and milieu therapy.

Clearly the last word in typologies has not been written.

PROGRAMS

The Milieu

The prison community run by the "con code" is well described in the American Correctional Association publication, *Riots and Disturbances* (5). A correctional institution is an unnatural environment which almost invariably contributes to the emotional stress of those incarcerated. There is limited personal freedom, monotony and boredom, regimentation, a sense of injustice and frustration, hopelessness, sexual deprivation, anxiety about family and friends, and many similar sources of emotional stress. Life in correctional institutions has been destructive to the human spirit often beyond the intention of the punishment and has defeated the possibility of rehabilitation in too large a proportion of people. Long corridors, repeated doorways, highly polished floors and hard finishes are hypnotic, and result in depersonalization of surroundings. It is not difficult to imagine that in certain inmates the combined depersonalization of human and physical environment can result in emotional stresses which seek release, and that sometimes this release can take the form of violence.

In this system, where the keeper and kept are separated by prejudice and fear, and where few keep many, an informal power structure arises which further confuses and threatens the inmate population. The solidarity of the inmate population becomes an important bond. Those inmates given informal power and those that "fink out" or "rat" on peers represent the two extremes which challenge con solidarity. To violate these trusts is punishable by death in the con code. Sandhu (6) points out how the population separated from nearly everything known to them, with many invisible barriers to dialogue, is victimized by rumor. In his book he gives a rather complete narration of the problems facing modern corrections particularly as it relates to authority, violence and sexuality. The American prison seems to have its sterotype prejudices, and with the exception of a few bright lights (see Butner's work, *Marion State Prison*, Illinois), the usual prison milieu is closer to that of Attica than to that of the therapeutic communities established by Butner.

Wheeler (25) did not find a clear parallel to the inmate code or prison solidarity observed in American prisons. In his study of

Scandinavian prisons he found that prisoners entered from a society which contained a lower incidence of anti-authority attitude than in the United States. There was less racial conflict. Because of the more liberal sexual attitude there was less homosexuality and, therefore, less need to have a prestige symbol such as a cute kid. Further description of differences would be unnecessary.

All over the world there have been attempts to change the prison milieu into a therapeutic milieu. These ideas were first expounded by Maxwell Jones as a result of work he began near the end of the Second World War. He coined the term "therapeutic community." Pioneers in this field have been Jones at the Henderson Hospital in England, Sturup at Herstedvester in Denmark, Barker at Penetanguishene Maximum Security Mental Hospital in Canada, Butner at the Marion State Illinois Prison, Cormier at the Dannemora Hospital in New York State, the group of workers at the Patuxent Maximum Security Institution, Maryland, Sandhu at the Hospital for Psychopaths in India. This list is not complete, but does give a picture of the attempt at a social systems level to treat the sick prison.

Kiger (26) defines the therapeutic community as a social matrix that affords the opportunity for people to use their initiative and ability in dealing with their problems through therapeutic processes. He lists the five basic principles first stated by Maxwell Jones—bilateral communication, confrontation, decision-making by consensus, multiple leadership and operation of living-learning groups. The basic foundation for the development of the therapeutic community is an active, functioning, democratic patient government, in conjunction with various group processes, all of which include and involve patients. The community meeting is one of the best settings in which to instill therapeutic principles and to facilitate their development. It should be the heart of any therapeutic community, as it involves everyone. The majority should rule. When this type of program is instituted, it combats many of the problems of the prison milieu. Each member of the community takes more responsibility in terms of individual problems, the problems of others and overall community involvement. There is better communication, which enables everyone, regardless of his position, to react in a more consistent fashion to a particular patient or problem. Being a part of discussion and decision-making engenders confidence in members who become involved in subsequent treatment processes. Teaching and research are greatly enriched, especially when each community meeting is followed by an intensive post-mortem. Patients become therapists instead of passive recipients of therapy. There is a minimum of authoritarian pressure and a maximum of peer pressure, which is especially conducive to the utilization of the assets and potentials of the psychopath. Staff-patient relationships are enhanced and patients become less dependent on individual staff members and more dependent on the program, on one another, and eventually on themselves.

Thus it is that we find Barker and Mason (27) writing the following as their principles for a therapeutic community: illness is miscommunication; dialogue is therapy; the patient is therapist. While these principles are typical of the guidelines for group process, Wilson and Snodgrass identified an aspect important to some therapeutic communities, namely, the tier levels system. They describe its function at Patuxent as "the major aspect of the therapeutic environment. This system grants greater freedom, privilege, and responsibilities to inmates of the highest level. The result is that the upper level is most characteristic of a therapeutic community, whereas conditions in the lower level are not unlike those found in a maximum security prison . . . (28). Promotion in the system is at least partially based on rehabilitative progress.

One of the greatest problems and continuing challenges to a therapeutic community is the staff attitudes. Sandhu (6) presents the dilemma explicitly. Because the staff have to deal with the inmates or patients at the closest proximity, they are often the most psychologically vulnerable. Their relationship becomes one of practicality. As they are the immediate target of all hostility, even if the hostility is intended for the administration, they must find ways of coping with this. Necessary strategies here might include acceptance of bribes, or offering themselves as sources of smuggled contraband, such as money, drugs and tobacco. Nevertheless, while this is a stark reality, the typical prison guard has a commitment to the reformation ideal. Sandhu supports these claims with a broad range of statistical analysis of guard attitudes.

The Group

If the therapeutic community is an attempt to organize a sick social system so that it can clarify itself and, because of an ongoing dialogue, homogenize prejudice, then the group, whether in the therapeutic community or merely as an isolated aspect of the prison life, has a central part in the dialogue of the community. Group therapy has more than a dialogue function. It sets up the space where men can come to share all parts of themselves, that is, their thoughts, their feelings and their behavior. The importance of group psychotherapy for the confined patient — therapy led by a staff member — is unquestioned in the literature. This is because the group acts as a safe dialogue medium where the two poles of con/screw can safely be dialogued out. It is a forum where trust can begin to build. Carney (29) describes some recurring therapeutic issues at Patuxent, the kind of issues which are the backbone of the group therapy process in a prison. These issues can be described as follows:

1. the belief that the director hates the patients;
2. the complaint that there are no rules;
3. concern with "craziness";
4. proving something to someone else.

One may expect that therapy will eventually deal with feelings about the self, home and family, and with individual problems of adjustment, and that these other issues are tangential to the central problem. However, it is possible that these other issues are not as tangential as they might appear at first. They might give important clues to the personality dynamics of criminal patients, and they might be the issues that lead to meaningful psychotherapy. It is Carney's view that criminal patients are largely unmotivated for therapy but successful therapy can result by dealing with the issues that they are willing to deal with.

In fact, once trust has been built and the therapy process has had some duration, the dialogue moves to exposure of life histories and criminal experiences, including details of sexual perversions, physical and sexual violence, homosexuality and accounts of family deprivation. R.G. Rappaport (30) describes how the inmate patient has a need to talk about his guilty feelings and conflicts, but requires a setting in which the likelihood of repercussions is minimal. His fear is not only that the other men in the group will be disdainful or uninterested, but that the prison administration, if informed of his true feelings, will inflict punishment and obstruct parole. The group process is often caught between trust in the group and trust in the administration. Rappaport observes that, paradoxically, there is little expression of rage in group therapy. While prisons are supposed to contain violent men, this release tends not to be expressed in a therapy group unless there is an extreme level of trust. Defenses usually remain high, particularly in relation to the hope and expectation of parole. Men try to appear more controlled than they actually are. In a note about therapists' style, Rappaport states that from his experience it is necessary for the therapist to abandon the traditional analytic stance and to be as human as possible. He discusses the difficulties of this position and sees that the therapist, too, stands in the middle of being an accepted group member on the one hand, and on the other a representative of the administration. In a follow-up study of one therapy group, he found only one member had returned to prison. The men had shown a heightened degree of self-awareness, improved ability to communicate ideas and feelings and increased insight into the origins of their behavior. Several men had renewed family relationships because of insights acquired within the group.

Elsewhere (31-33) other aspects of psychotherapy are discussed. In general it is clear that psychotherapy is important to the morale of the inmate and ward. This may be especially important for particular categories of patients, such as sex offenders, where there is already a marked prejudice against the patient. The problems of territoriality and homosexuality may also be seen in the group process.

Group counseling is a new form of treatment. Its aim is less dynamic and more educational. The general aim, however, is similar to that of group psychotherapy. The sessions contribute to staff-inmate participation, cooperation and communication. This leads to a better social climate in the institution. Group counseling is useful for the following reasons: 1) there is an economy of staff time and effort; 2) offenders who have picked up antisocial habits in association with the group can best be treated and resocialized in a group — a good number of offenders are most susceptible to peer influence, and for them, using the peer medium has a better effect; 3) group counseling invites greater participation from the staff, involves them in the process of effecting behavioral change, and gives them a sense of achievement — thus in this process, both the delinquent and the counselor change; 4) while the inmates share common problems with other members and develop a certain insight into their problems, they also get the viewpoint of the counselor — the staff becomes aware of the inmate's problems, and this in turn bridges the gap between the custodial and clinical staff; 5) a delinquent is weak in his capacity for maintaining adequate interpersonal relationships, and needs training and experience to improve this capacity — group counseling releases the offenders' latent emotional forces which helps them reestablish healthy human relationships.

Counseling is more problem-oriented than group psychotherapy. With the counselor, the group attempts to think of different ways of coping with problems either in the institution or on the outside. It has a commonsense philosophy (34, 37).

The Individual

Individual psychotherapy has its place in the spectrum of treatment programs for the offender. However, the exact public health value of the analyst has yet to be determined. In a system where the staff-patient ratio is hardly ever optimal, especially in North America, one wonders about the efficiency of such a treatment. There are several theoretical models for individual psychotherapy. Glasser's reality therapy model(38) has gained general acceptance in North America. Glasser is eminently readable and uses a commonsense approach such that the three R's of Reality, Responsibility, and Right and Wrong have become a popular way of approaching the rule breaker.

There seems to be some consensus that the individual therapy style most appropriate in the therapy relationship with the offender is one closer to C. Rogers than Freud. M. Schmideberg(30) describes the attitude of the therapist as propounded by A.P.T.O., the Association for the Psychiatric Treatment of Offenders, otherwise known as offender therapy. In their view the offender is seen to have a personality style which requires multi-channel feedback. He is predisposed to mistrust. He lives in an environment which denies him immediate feedback. Because of the nature of institutional living, it is fundamentally important that the therapist relate to the inmate as a whole person. The therapist must change from a passive observer to a more outgoing and supportive person in the role of medical doctor. Identification is a prime factor in treatment, and as there have been major deficits in the early identification processes with these "acting out" patients, there is a need to teach the patients by example. As part of offender therapy, the offender is taught how to fantasize, and secondly, how to recognize his feelings and describe them verbally.

John R. Lion and George Bach-Y-Rita(40) describe in some detail the problems of working with violent outpatients, and present guidelines helpful to those who deal with the incarcerated violent offender. Both authors support Schmideberg's therapy style. In dealing with the violent patient, they make several points which are important for the therapist to keep in mind. Violent patients are frightened of their own hostile urges and desperately seek help in preventing loss of control. The character-disordered patient is the most likely to become violent; because his aggression is poorly channeled and improperly sublimated, he has diffuse complaints, and for this reason may become dangerous. In the context of psychotherapy, acquisition of a weapon has a special significance. This is particularly true if the patient brings the weapon when visiting the physician. Then the therapist must share his anxiety with the patient. At the other end of the spectrum the violent patient often fears emotional intimacy with the therapist. To lessen feelings of helplessness and insecurity he may bring the weapon along. In a general way the patients are educated to seek controls for their hostile urges.

The violent patient may evoke negative feelings in physicians who are evaluating them. Lion and Pasternak (41) and others(42, 43) describe a common countertransference reaction to violent patients, feelings of fear and anger which interfere with effective management. They stress the importance of the physician being aware of this fear and how this fear may distort, by projection, his view of the patient as dangerous.

As the philosophy changes so that the individual offender is seen as having participated in a social system that has at least partially contributed to his crime, we find not only improved integration of treatment facilities within corrections but also an attempt to integrate the correctional system and the family system. Chaiklin(44) has presented such a paper. He describes a community reintegration project in a prison prerelease program that works with incarcerated men and their families to prepare both for reunion. Continuing problems are referred to the appropriate community agency. Coordinated treatment and rehabilitation planning in contrast to the traditional mode of treating prisoners as if they existed in a vacuum, isolated from community influences, has proven effective in reducing recidivism.

Learning Theory in the Prison

Schwitzgebel (45) has presented a general survey of learning-theory approaches to the treatment of criminal behavior. It is generally conceded that learning-theory approaches show an effectiveness in changing behavior that is comparable to the traditional psychoanalytical treatment of those disorders. Eysenck, Ullman and Krasner, Bandura, Skinner and others have championed a full literature discussing the theoretical basis and scientific application of learning theory. These programs can be divided essentially into two main theoretical streams: those based on a classical conditioning paradigm and those based on an operant paradigm.

Two important considerations are often overlooked in classical conditioning treatment programs. First, an attempt should be made to develop behavioral alternatives to the prohibitive behavior. Second, an attempt should be made to expose the patient gradually to actual life situations in which the behavior to be eliminated has previously occurred. This exposure should be gradual enough so that the old behavior will not occur and newly developed behavioral alternatives can be used by the patient. With this in mind we find that alcoholism, drug disorders, sex offenses (46) and the use of punishment with the psychopath and delinquent fall within the classical paradigm. Vallance (47) and Voegtlin (48) have reported two poles of follow-up in regard to alcoholics. Vallance found that approximately 5 percent or fewer alcoholics treated by standard psychotherapeutic methods in the psychiatric unit of a general hospital could be considered abstinent over a two-year follow-up period. Voegtlin found 51 percent of 4,096 patients treated by conditioning procedures were found abstinent for a two- to five-year period following treatment. Typically most studies tend to show a range abstinence between 10 percent and 35 percent over a period of one year or longer. Rachman and Teesdale (49) have summed up the effectiveness, in general, of chemical aversive therapy by stating that it seems to be effective in the treatment of certain types of alcoholics. However, they have been unable to locate adequately convincing evidence to prove this possibility beyond any doubt.

Sexual offenses usually fall into an aversive paradigm. Homosexuality, fetishes (50), sadism (51) and transvestism (52) have all been reported in the literature.

A common and somewhat justifiable criticism of certain conditioning methods is that they are unpleasant or inhumane. Aside from some of the extremely painful or hazardous procedures that might legally be prohibited, most of the patients traditionally treated by these methods have voluntarily chosen to participate because of the long-term negative consequences of their illegal or undesirable behavior. The harshness of the techniques over a short period of time should be weighed against the sometimes accumulatively more harmful effects of the untreated behavior. This situation is not as difficult when an adult voluntarily consents to treatment as when the treatment is involuntary. Naturally, the motivated patient is more subject to change. Criminals are often poorly motivated to accept treatment — (I'm right, and the system's wrong) — and this has been a problem with such treatment procedures.

type of classical conditioning. Caldwell (53) has presented an interesting follow-up of whipped patients. In Delaware 1,302 offenders were whipped between the years of 1900 and 1942. In a special study of 320 whipped offenders 61.9 percent were later reconvicted of an offense. Of those whipped twice, 65.1 percent were again convicted of a subsequent offense. Only 37.5 percent of those offenders placed on probation were later convicted for similar crimes. Scura and Eisenman (54), using Checkley's clinical profile of the psychopath, have presented a paper to test the hypothesis that the psychopath would show punishment learning deficit and he would be able to make less effective use of social negative reinforcers than those with fewer psychopathic characteristics. In a cohort of 60 prisoners they found there was no significant effect for social or nonsocial reinforcement, although the trends were in the predicted direction. Altogether the results tended to cast some doubt on the usual belief that a psychopath cannot learn from past experience.

Operant conditioning is also popular as a method of behavioral change. When this is applied at the level of a ward, the token economy program is one of the most popular. Lawson, Greene, Richardson, McClure and Padina (55) have described such a program at the Dannemora State Hospital in New York. Forty-one low-functioning male patients selected were indifferent, apathetic, dependent and institutionalized. The results indicate that behaviorally inactive patients will engage in reinforced activities in order to gain access to a variety of reinforcers. Token economy programs can be an effective treatment method in a maximum-security correctional center. A one-year follow-up study indicated that none of the twelve patients transferred from Ward 5 had returned to the ward and that the two patients discharged from the hospital to the New York prison system had not been readmitted to the hospital.

McKee and Watkins (56) have both described the attempt at the Draper Correctional Center in Alabama to effect a change in the organization of the institute so that the primary aim of the prison would be to treat or change behavior and not to punish prisoners. Over the past six or seven years the Draper Correctional Center has gone from a cheerless institution with little to offer in the ways of education, recreation and mental stimulation to one pioneering in the forefront of behavioral change for the state. McKee describes eloquently the problems of applying behavior modification. He accurately presents the importance of working with the staff, the organization of staff potential, and at the same time he makes it clear that the institution is to serve the inmate. In considering the treatment triad — intervention, generalization and the measurement of behavioral change — McKee feels generalization is the name of the game; it is the principle that makes intervention go. The challenge to modify criminal behavior is well laid out for the pie-in-the-sky behavior modifier in the final sentence. The road to good clean living is not easy for any of us. "But if any of you behavior modifiers are looking for some free-wheeling opportunities to try out your talents on a vast human laboratory come and get locked up with me" (57).

Industrial, Vocational and Educational Programs

Elliott (58) and Terl (59) describe industrial work programs in Atascadero, California, and Jessup, Maryland, respectively. Both programs seem to be highly developed and sophisticated with a clear philosophy, patient work assignment, and reporting system. At

Atascadero each patient is assigned to a job in the first group, three weeks after admission to the hospital or as soon as he is emotionally and physically able to leave his ward unescorted and to work under supervision up to twenty-four hours a week. He is required to stay on that assignment throughout his stay in the hospital regardless of his educational level, personal interest or previous vocational skills. That rule virtually eliminates the manipulation of work assignments and prevents patients from jumping from one job to another to avoid confronting their problems. It also maintains stability in the essential jobs and ensures a continuing relationship between patients and their work supervisors. The latter is necessary to provide a reasonable picture of the patient's emotional and social progress over a long period of time.

As soon as the patient is working satisfactorily at his basic assignment, he is encouraged to take an assignment in the second category. The ward team must approve the second assignment. They decide on the basis of the patient's emotional stability, personal interest, previous skills or future vocational plans. The system thus encourages patients to assume responsibility for an appropriate share of the necessary work and also allows them to receive training or do work in which they are interested. It is a laudable system.

Terl, at Jessup, describes a more psychodynamically based work-for-pay program, yet there is great similarity to the philosophy of the Atascadero plan. With the instrumentation of an effective work program, the con code has been broken. The general level of trust has improved, so that Terl reports that workshop patients have their own razors. Of fifty-seven patients who were in the workshop program, ten have been discharged, and three returned for further treatment. The figure is 25 percent below the overall hospital return rate. Those who did return seemed to have had longer periods of remission.

Release Programs

Work release, half-way houses and the parole system are all programs which will come into greater importance as the rehabilitation ethic replaces the punishment ethic. Brown and Spevacek (60) describe a work release program to the community from an institutional setting. In their summary they point out that to the extent that a critical assessment of one's place in the world is one goal of the work release program, community placement appears clearly more effective than institution placement. Once placed in the community, it can then become the role of the work release staff to follow up the client's own initial evaluation by guiding both his further examination of the community and his adjustment to that community. It would seem apparent that it would be most useful to locate each work release program as close as possible to the actual community to which the client will be returning, thereby permitting the fullest possible evaluation by the client of his real community, and of his capacity for making pro-social adjustment to it.

In line with this philosophy, the half-way house stands in the community where the inmate is to be rehabilitated. Sullivan, Seigel and Clear (61) explain the major factors influencing changes in rates of recidivism of half-way house residents. It is clear that in all of the research examined, some factors of considerable weight have been avoided or overlooked, particularly those related to half-way house climate and managerial behavior of staff. Without information about the effects of staff behavior, and management practices, conclusions should not be drawn about the effectiveness of the half-way house. The keeper-kept dichotomy is always the essential relationship to be examined. From the review it would appear that we should be less than optimistic about the functioning of the half-way house.

Tanz, Deluca and Suarez (62) described the pre-release program for federal prisoners in the Los Angeles area. In general they showed it has been proven effective in reducing recidivism. They point out the need for close examination of each of the individual pre-release programs, stating that specific feedback is needed. They also highlight the structure of the bureaucracy of a prison which encourages isolation of the staff from inmates and, thereby, makes it more difficult to appraise the inmate at the time of his release date. They blame the shortage of manpower, lack of funds and the prison code as the major obstacles to a successful rehabilitation or a successful parole.

Evaluation: The Effectiveness of Correctional Programs

Robison and Smith (63) have written a comprehensive paper examining carefully the literature reporting on the effectiveness of correctional programs. This paper will be partly summarized in the following paragraphs. They write that research in the correction system has been concerned with answering five basic questions about the behavior of convicted persons: 1) Will they act differently if we locked them up rather than place them on probation? 2) Will they recidivate less if we keep them locked up longer? 3) Does educating and treating in prisons reduce recidivism? 4) Does supervising them more closely in smaller parole case loads reduce recidivism? 5) What difference does it make whether we discharge prisoners outright or supervise them on parole?

Answering the first question, the authors carefully examine two published studies: the California Youth Authorities Community Treatment Project and the Northern California Service League Project. The authors are led to conclude that there is no support to any claim that institutional confinement is more effective than community supervision. At the same time, they found little support for the thesis that probation is superior to institutionalization for reducing the recidivism rate.

Concerning the relationship between time served and probability of recidivism, the authors suggest that it is difficult to escape the conclusion that the act of incarcerating a person will impair whatever potential he has for a crime-free future adjustment, and that the longer he is kept in prison the more he will deteriorate and the more likely it is he will recidivate. In any event, it seems almost certain that releasing inmates from prison earlier than is now customary in California would not increase recidivism.

In regard to the relationship between treatment, education and recidivism, the authors did not find many hard data studies. Much of the published research on group counseling in a prison setting deals with simple descriptions of the program, theoretical justifications or shoddy evaluations without an adequate control group, and random assignment of cases. However, a study by Cassibaum, Ward and Wilner (*Prison Treatment and Its Outcome*, to be published by John Wiley) was found to be sufficiently vigorous in randomizing assignment and control group size. Results are quoted from that study. There were no differences in parole outcome by treatment status measured at six, twelve, twenty-four and thirty-six months after release, no treatment or control group differences on the number of misdemeanors or felony arrests recorded in the parole records, no difference in the total number of weeks spent in jail, no difference in the most serious disposition received within three years after release. The same study also showed that the group counseling and community living treatment schemes had no effect in reducing either inmate adherence to the prison code or prison discipline problem frequency. The authors conclude that there are still no treatment techniques which have unequivocally demonstrated themselves capable of reducing recidivism. This is further supported by a recent Canadian study by Carlson at the Guelph Correctional Centre in Ontario (64). R. Martison presents the same unpleasant picture (65).

To answer the fourth question, which considered case-load size and recidivism, reports from three intensive supervision parole programs are taken. The California Department of Corrections conducted a four-phase experiment over twelve years with the special intensive parole unit. In the first three phases, variation in case-load size saw no evidence of superiority for the reduced case load. The fourth phase matched parolee and case worker on personality characteristics, but failed to produce significant results. In a second California program, the work unit gave some indication on superficial examination of favorable outcome for reduced case-load supervision. But when controls for parolee risk level were introduced, the difference in favorable outcome between the work unit and the conventional unit was erased, and conventional supervision was found to have a significantly lower rate of technical prison return. A thoroughly randomized experiment by the Federal Probation System San Francisco Project yielded similar results. Thus the small case load has not been demonstrated to be more effective in reducing recidivism.

Relatively little attention has been given to comparing those considered to have benefited from prison and now discharged, with men on parole. Of 4,854 male felons discharged at sentence expiration from the California Department of Corrections, 47 percent were first releases. It seems reasonable to assume that many of these men were kept the full time because of problems in their prison adjustment or concern about releasing them. One would expect men discharged from prison to be poorer risks than those placed on parole. Examination of the figures available indicated that discharged men have fewer returns to prison than men released to parole supervision. The authors warned that it may be the facts of technical violation that make parolees significantly poor risks.

If this comprehensive search of the literature and examination of the California system leaves us in doubt as to the efficacy of our programs and our intelligence in knowing what we're doing in regard to the convicted criminal, let Walter C. Bailey[67] help us out with an article in which he examined one hundred evaluation reports of correctional outcome covering a twenty-year period of the literature in 1960. He discovered that on the basis of this sample with all of its limitations, evidence supporting the efficacy of correctional treatment is slight, inconsistent and of questionable reliability, although on the positive side there is impressive evidence of an increasing concern with correctional outcome research and progressive improvement in the caliber of the scientific investigations conducted.

Conclusion

Corrections do not correct, reformatories do not reform. No matter what kind of program we institute, recidivism remains high. We are having an awareness at the present time that we need to improve the caliber not only of programs but of research tools used to investigate them. There is a growing consciousness of these needs. At the same time programing in institutions does change the quality of life. There is less impersonality and depersonalization, and morale seems to be higher with an active program. What these factors have to do with recidivism has yet to be determined.

While there is serious discussion at each level presented here, and a treatment plan to accompany it, there will be little progress toward successful reintegration of the rule breaker into his community until there is respect for him. The culture which realizes and accepts human limit will offer a "penal program" where the keeper and kept are helpful to each other and encounter each other as persons[67].

REFERENCES

1. Belle OS: Correctional reform — myth or reality? *Corr Psychiat J Social Ther* 16:69-73, 1970.
2. Working Paper Number 3. The Principles of Sentencing and Despositions. Law Reform Commission, Canada. March 1974, Information Canada.
3. Ward D: Inmate rights and prison reform in Sweden and Denmark. *J Crim Law, Criminol, Pol Sci* 63:240-255, 1972.
4. Ibid p 246.
5. *Riots and Disturbances in Correctional Institutions: Causes, Preventative Measures, and Methods of Controlling.* American Correctional Association. Woodridge Station, Post Office Box 10176, Washington, 1970.
6. Sandhu S: *Modern Corrections, The Offenders, Therapies and Community Reintegration.* Springfield, Illinois, CC Thomas, 1974.
7. Bazelon DL: The right to treatment: The court's role. *Hosp Comm Psychiat* 20:129-135, 1969.
8. Ibid p 129.
9. Ibid p 129.
10. Szasz TS: Justice in the therapeutic state. *Comp Psychiat* 11:433-444, 1970.
11. Halleck S: Psychiatry and correctional justice. *Bull Menninger Clin* 35:402-407, 1971.
12. Miller JG: Professional dilemmas in correction. *Sem Psychiat* 3:357-362, 1971.
13. White B: Penology — the new science? *Corr Psychiat J Social Ther* 17:14-17, 1971.
14. Belle OS: Confession and punishment in authoritarian relationships. *Corr Psychiat J Soc Ther* 16:69-73, 1970.
15. Roth LH, Ervin FR: Psychiatric care of federal prisoners. *Amer J Psychiat* 128:56-62, 1971.
16. Jablon NC, Sadoff RL, Heller MS: A unique forensic diagnostic hospital. *Amer J Psychiat* 126:139-143, 1970.
17. Chalke FCR: *General Progress for the Development of Psychiatric Services in the Federal Correctional Services in Canada.* Solicitor General of Canada, W. Allmond, 1972.

18. Clarke GR, Telfer MA, Baker D, Rosen M: Sex chromosones, crime, and psychosis. *Amer J Psychiat* 126:1659-1663, 1970.

19. Gunn J, Bonn J: Criminality and violence in epileptic prisoners. *Brit J Psychiat* 118:337-343, 1971.

20. Beigel A, Russell HE: Suicide attempts in jails: Prognostic considerations. *Hosp Comm Psychiat* 23:361-363, 1972.

21. Cooper HHA: Self-mutilation by Peruvian prisoners. *Int'l J Offender Ther* 15:180-188, 1971.

22. Warren MQ: Classification of offenders as an aid to efficient management and effective treatment. *J Crim Law, Criminol Pol Sci* 62:239-258, 1971.

23. Laing RD: The obvious, in Cooper, (ed): *To Free a Generation.* New York, MacMillan, 1968.

24. Kim LIC, Clanon TL: Psychiatric services integrated into the California correction system. *Int'l J Offender Ther* 15:169-179, 1972.

25. Wheller S: Socialization in correctional institutions, in L Radzinowicz, and ME Wolfgang (eds), *Crime and Justice* (vol 3), *The Criminal in Confinement.* New York, Basic, 1971.

26. Kiger RS: The therapeutic community in a maximum security hospital — treatment in vocations. *Corr Psychiat J Social Ther* 17:34-47, 1971.

27. Barker ET, Mason MH: Buber behind bars. *Canad Psychiat Ass J* 13:61-72, 1968.

28. Wilson JM, Snodgrass JD: Prison code in a therapeutic community. *J Crim Law, Criminol, Pol Sci* 60:472-478, 1969.

29. Carney FL: Some recurring therapeutic issues in group psychotherapy with criminal patients. *Amer J Psychother* 26:34-41, 1972.

30. Rappaport RG: Group Therapy in Prison. *'Int'l J Group Psychother* 21:489-496, 1971.

31. Moore RT, Zimmermann RR, Estelle J: Program of psychotherapy for inmates at the Montana State Prison. *Psychol Reports* 30:756-758, 1972.

32. Marcus AM, Conway C: A Canadian group approach study of dangerous sexual offenders. *Int'l J Offender Ther* 15:59-66, 1971.

33. Roth LH: Territoriality, and homosexuality in a male prison population. *Amer J Orthopsychiat* 41:510-513, 1971.

34. Brown BS, Dupont RL, Kozel J. Spevacek JD: Staff and client views of the role of the correctional client: Conflicts and its implications for treatment. *Social Psychiatry* 6:83-88, 1971.

35. Keefe TW, Smith TH: A group counselling and group counsellor training program in an Airforce correction setting. *Corr Psychiat J Social Ther* 16:97-102, 1970.

36. Pew ML, Speer DC, Williams J: Group counselling for offenders. *Social Work* 18:74-79, 1973.

37. Joselson M: Prison education: A major reason for its impotence. *Corr Psychiat J Social Ther* 17:48-56, 1971.

38. Glasser W: *Reality Therapy: A New Approach to Psychiatry,* New York, Harper and Row, 1965.

39. Schmideberg M: Offender therapy as a tool of research: An Anglo-American study. *Int'l J Offender Ther Compar Criminol* 16:61-65, 1972.

40. Lion JR, Bach-Y-Rita G: Group psychotherapy with violent outpatients *Int'l J Group Psychother* 20:185-191, 1970.

41. Lion JR, Pasternak SA: Countertransference reactions to violent patients. *Amer J Psychiat* 130:207-208, 1973.

42. Bach-Y-Rita G, Lion JR, Climent CE, Ervin FR: Episodic dyscontrol: A study of 130 violent patients. *Amer J Psychiat* 127:1473-1478, 1971.

43. Kalogerakis MG: The assaultive psychiatric patient. *Psychiat Quart* 45:372-381, 1971.
44. Chaiklin H: Integrating correctional and family systems. *Amer J Orthopsychiat* 42:784-791, 1972.
45. Schwitzgebel RK: Learning theory approaches to the treatment of criminal behavior. *Sem Psychiat* 3:328-344, 1971.
46. Feldman MP: Aversion therapy for sexual deviations: A critical review. *Psychol Bull* 65:65, 1966.
47. Vallance M: Alcoholism: A two year follow-up study. *Brit J Psychiat* 131:348, 1965.
48. Lemere G, Voegtlin W: An evaluation of aversion treatment of alcoholism. *Quart J Stud Alc* 11:199, 1950.
49. Rachman S. Teesdale J: *Aversion Therapy and Behavior Disorders: An Analysis.* Coral Gables, Florida University of Miami Press, 1969.
50. Marks IM, Guilder MG: Transvestism and fetishism: Clinical and psychological changes during faradic aversion. *Brit J Psychiat* 113:711, 1967.
51. Mees HL: Satistic Fantasies modified by aversive conditioning and substitution: *Case Stud Behav Res Her* 4:317, 1966.
52. Lavinn I, Thorpe JG, Barker JC, Blakmore CB, Conway CG: behaviour therapy in a case of transvestism. *J Nerv Ment Dis* 133:346, 1961.
53. Caldwell RG: *Red Hanna Delaware's Whipping Post.* Philadelphia, University of Pennsylvania Press, 1947.
54. Scura WC, Eisenman R: Punishment learning in psychopaths with social and non social reinforcers. *Corr Psychiat J Social Ther* 17:58-64, 1971.
55. Lawson RB, Greene T, Richardson JS, McQure G, Padina: Token economy program in a maximum security correctional hospital. *J Nerv Ment Dis* 152:199-205, 1971.
56. Watkins JC: Organization of institutional resources for behaviour change: A model. Paper Delivered at the 97th Annual Congress of Corrections, Miami Beach, Florida, August 22, 1967.
57. McKee JM: Draper experiments of behaviour modification. Presented at the Behaviour Modification Institute, Tuscaloosa, Alabama, May 13, 1969.
58. Elliott AE: Industrial therapy in a maximum security hospital. *Hosp Comm Psychiat* 20:215-217, 1969.
59. Terl BG: A dynamic work program for maximum security patients. *Hosp Comm Psychiat* 19:381-383, 1968.
60. Brown BS, Spevaeck JD: Work release in community and institutional settings. *Corr Psychiat J Social Work* 17:35-42, 1971.
61. Sullivan DC, Seigel LJ, Clear BT: The half-way house, ten years later: Reappraisal of correction innovation. *Canad J Criminol Corr* 16:188-197, 1974.
62. Tanz HA, Deluca KT, Suarez JM: Pre-release planning for federal prisoners in a Los Angeles area. *Corr Psychiat J Social Ther* 18:4-9, 1972.
63. Robison J, Smith G: The effectiveness of correctional programs. *Crime Delinq.*: 67-81, 1971.
64. Carlson KA: Some characteristics of recidivists in an Ontario institution for adult male first-incarcerates. *Canad J Criminol Corr* 15(4), 1973.
65. Martinson R: What works? — questions and answers about prison reform. *Public Interest,* 1974.
66. Bailey WC: Correctional outcome: An evaluation of one hundred reports. *J Crim Law, Criminol, Pol Sci* 57:153-160, 1966.
67. Dawson R, Emond B: A personal communication. Thank You.

Psychological Approaches
to Violence

DENIS J. MADDEN

Almost from the beginning of time, man has left behind a history of violence. Today, it seems, however, that that history of violence is more prominent and prevalent than ever before, especially in America.

In 1968 more Americans were the victims of murder and aggravated assault in the United States than were killed and wounded in seven and a half years of the Vietnam war and almost half a million persons were the victims of homicide, rape and assault, according to the National Commission on the Causes and Prevention of Violence (1).

It would seem that, as Santayana warned, we are condemned to repeat history, this time our history of violence. The National Commission on the Causes and Prevention of Violence states that:

> Our nation was conceived and born in violence — in the violence of the Sons of Liberty and the patriots of the American port cities of the 1760's and 1770's . . . Violence has formed a seamless web within some of the history: The birth of the nation (revolutionary violence), the freeing of the slaves and the preservation of the union (Civil War violence), the occupation of the land (Indian Wars), the stabilization of frontier society (vigilante violence), the elevation of the farmer and the laborer (agrarian and labor violence) and the preservation of law and order (police violence) . . . The patriot, the humanitarian, the nationalist, the pioneer, the landholder, the farmer and the laborer (and the capitalist) have used violence as the means to a higher end . . . (1).

Arthur Schlesinger, Jr., the Pulitzer Prize-winning historian, has commented on our history by saying that "we began, after all, as a people who killed red men and enslaved black men. No nation, however righteous its professions, could act as we did without burying deep in itself — in its customs, its institutions and its psyche — a propensity toward violence."

These comments by philosophers and historians do not give any real explanation of why man acts in a violent manner. The question to be considered here is whether or not psychology can offer anything by way of explanation. From the time of Freud to the present a number of plausible theories have been advanced to explain man's violent acts. Despite the fact that many a worthy theorist has come forth, no one theory seems complete in itself. In addition to this, many of the theories seem to be so divergent that behavioral scientists find themselves differing from one another on this vital topic. It seems that no one theory is complete in itself because man's violent acts do not stem from one cause alone but are rather symptomatic of multivariate deficits in the personality.

The purpose of this chapter will be not to offer an exhaustive coverage of what psychology has learned about human aggression but, rather, by reviewing a specific literature, to offer some information on determinants of the personality that are seen to influence man's violent behavior.

A brief overview of the psychological approaches to this subject is given first. The major studies of violence have taken an ethological, psychoanalytic and environmental approach.

Ethologists have been studying the similarities and differences between species. In a recent work, Tiger and Fox (2) attempted to demonstrate an unbroken continuity existing between the behavior of monkeys, apes and man. Montagu (3), in reviewing their work, stated that although experts might disagree on some of the interpretations of such a study, there can be little doubt that just as man bears the marks of his origins from such creatures in his physical structure, so too he carries within him evidences of his behavioral relationship to the lower primates. It is unfortunate, as Megargee (1) points out, that many of the more popular ethological reports (2,3,4,5) have emphasized the similarities and continuities between man and animals without sufficiently warning against the dangers of uncritically applying ethological data to human problems.

For a more detailed treatment of non-human aggression the reader is referred to Anderson's chapter. Ethologists in their view that aggressive drives are innate have suggested ways in which this drive can be redirected and sublimated. This approach has been opposed by those who have taken an environmental approach. The environmentalists feel that an innate theory fails to give proper attention to environmental factors such as poverty, slums, etc., that instigate aggressive behavior. They also feel that the channeling of this drive into mild aggressive activity actually creates aggressive habits that can later result in violence.

In the fall of 1971 Kelsey (6) wrote a paper entitled "Aggression, Violence and Emotion: The Psychology of the Punitive Element in Man," in which he states that if one is to understand human behavior, and violence as a part of this behavior, one must first understand human nature. This is something, as simple as it might seem, that must be kept in mind as one considers the various theories of aggression that have been put forth. How each theorist views the nature of man will certainly have an effect on his explanation of violence. Freud, as a physician, was long engaged in physiological research before turning his attention to the psychological nature of man. This fact, coupled with the Darwinian spirit of his times, led him first to arrive at a theory of human behavior that stressed man's animal nature. At first, Freud referred to aggression as a component of the sexual impulse. In 1917 he hypothesized that aggression was aroused when pleasure-seeking or avoidance of pain was blocked. Aggression was seen then as a result of frustration. Only later, as a result of the study of depression, did he refer to aggression as an independent and primary drive with a destructive component which he called the death instinct (7,8,9).

Jung, like Freud, spoke of instincts, but he went beyond Freud. Jung (10,11) viewed man as having instinctual and archetypal elements at work destructively within him, but having a creative force opposing them. Jung sees conflict as inherent to man because the psyche is made up of polar opposites, conscious and unconscious poles. The interaction of these poles creates a constant flow of energy. This energy cannot be dissipated or destroyed, and if repressed at one place it will find expression somewhere else. Conflict, therefore, cannot be avoided, nor the tension that accompanies it. Man, once he realizes his own instinctive potential for destruction, can initiate a choice and stand up against it. But this is only a beginning and not always successful. There is also a destructiveness that can surge through man which he cannot control directly. Man can only resist his own and those demonic impulses toward violence as man's ego is directed and empowered by the creative aspects of his being. And it is only as man becomes conscious of their existence that he is able to control those forces that are coming from the unconscious.

Storr attempted to incorporate the materials provided by Lorenz (4) within a modified psychoanalytic framework. He suggests that a combination of purely biological and psychological factors is responsible for this trait and its problems in man. He felt that the body contains a physicochemical system which subserves the emotions and actions which we call aggressive, and that this system is easily brought into action both by the stimulus of threat and also by frustration.

For the past thirty years much research in aggression has centered around the frustration-aggression theory. This theory was first proposed by a group of psychologists at the Institute of Human Relations at Yale University in 1939 (12). Very simply, it says that frustration produces a state of readiness to aggress, and that aggression is always preceded by some frustration. While this may have oversimplified the problems of studying aggression, it did permit the formulations to be tested empirically. The Yale group did not state whether this relationship was innate or learned. They merely stated that it was a necessary relationship no matter what its origin. Most experimental psychologists now believe that aggression has antecedents other than frustration. People may aggress to obtain a goal or they may aggress after being exposed to some other environmental stimuli.

In this brief overview of some of the approaches to the study of violence, two things become apparent. First, we have yet to tap the root source of violence, and there is need for further research in this area. Secondly, although methodology may differ greatly in the approaches that have been undertaken, there seems to be much that can be taken from each of the separate approaches that will give greater understanding to the problem. It seems that the developmental nature of man must be taken into consideration. In addition to this, one would have to consider the situational variables that have some effect on the personality and in some cases lead men to commit violent acts. Wallach (12) has noted that research involving the study of personalities requires that the experimenter take into account "the complex internal differentiation of predispositions" which the subject brings to a situation. Thus, before one may legitimately make statements regarding personality-environmental interactions, there must be some knowledge of the possible effects of the combination of moderating variables.

For the advancement of knowledge in the area of violence, it seems most important to isolate as many variables as possible and determine how each of these variables, coupled with particular personality types, leads to violent acts. Theorists have stated that man has basic needs which, if unmet, may cause the person to commit a violent act. One of these needs that has been singled out as being particularly potent in leading to violent acts when unmet is the dependency need (Erikson,

1963; Bandura and Walters, 1959; Maslow, 1970; Wolberg & Kiddahl, 1970; Hamilton, 1971; Kalogeriakis, 1972). Years ago, Adler (1929) recognized a fundamental tendency in man which he called a "will to power." May (1972) feels that there is today more than ever before a feeling of powerlessness, a feeling that we cannot influence others, that we are not in control of the situation. This feeling of powerlessness provides the existential situation that leads to many acts of violence. It is for this reason that we now turn our attention to some of the research that has dealt with the variables of dependency, power and powerlessness.

Dependency

Although Freud does not treat the subject of dependency explicitly, it is implied in much of what he wrote. In his writings he puts forth the thesis that the life-preservation function of dependence on the object is universal in man. Freud states that the recurrence of need forges the cathexis of the object and dependence upon it and secures the formation of persisting object relations (13). Helplessness leading to anxiety and, in turn, to dependence on the object — and then on the object's love — is a principal adaptive sequence of earliest childhood. The child learns early to seek shelter from mounting anxiety by turning to the object. In *An Outline of Psychoanalysis* Freud wrote:

> ... in the space of a few years the little primitive creature must turn into a civilized human being ... This ... can almost never be achieved without the additional help of upbringing, or parental influence, which, as a precursor of the superego, restricts the ego's activity by prohibitions and punishments, and encourages or compels the setting-up of repressions. We must therefore not forget the including of the influence of civilization among the determinants of neurosis ... Since the demands of civilization are represented by family upbringing, we must bear in mind the part played by this biological characteristic of the human species — the prolonged period of its childhood dependence — in the etiology of the neuroses (14.)

Earlier, Freud wrote that "the child is brought up to a knowledge of his social duties by a system of loving rewards and punishments; he is taught that his security in life depends on his parents loving him" (15).

Freud's thought led Himsie and Campbell (16) to define dependency in the following terms: it is "the unconscious wish for maternal protection, to be encompassed by the mother, to regain the peace, protection, and security of her sheltering arms. This stems from the original intense and forgotten gratifications of the infantile nursing period, when the infant's prehensile mouth anchored it to the mother's nipple and breast. To the child, to be fed means to be loved, i.e., to be protected, ergo, to be secure." This dependency need, or need for security is viewed by Maslow (17) as one of the basic or lower order needs.

Developmental Theorists and Dependency Needs

Maslow viewed man as being motivated by a number of basic needs "which are species wide, apparently unchanging, and genetic or instinctual in origin" (17). According to Maslow's schema, as the lower needs are satisfied other higher needs emerge, and these dominate the organism, and when these in turn are satisfied, again new and higher needs emerge, and so on. It is only after the basic dependency needs are satisfied that we can speak of the needs of intimacy and love. If one is not able to love and to maintain intimate relations with others, not having his dependency needs met, the person remains suspicious and hostile. Maslow generalized this same notion of unmet dependency needs possibly leading to hostile action to cultures and communities, as have others (18,19).

Some cultural determinants of intrapsychic structure and psychopathology were examined in the context of modern American society by Hamilton (19). Two basic hypotheses were treated. In the first, it was seen that as the American culture has developed, the superego system has become progressively less meaningfully internalized, and that this change has then exerted a definite effect upon the formation of psychopathological syndromes and the consolidation of a meaningful ego identity. The second theory suggests that in lending widespread support to a doctrine of pseudo-equality, with the emphasis upon pregenital modes of gratification and reward, the frustrations which understandably accompany such conditioning will give rise to primitive oral and anal types of rage. This leads to violent forms of acting-out behavior, the common denominator being that of unresolved dependency strivings.

Chyou Niem (20) attempted to discover if there were cultural differences between a group of Chinese and American children in kind and amount of aggressive behavior and in parental discipline of aggression. Subjects were 17 Taiwanese and 17 American four-year-old children. Results were based on daily records kept by the mothers for thirty days, describing aggressive incidents of the children and disciplinary methods used. Chinese subjects were found to show significantly less physical aggression and more tantrums and more verbal aggression than American subjects. Chinese parents were significantly more love-oriented and less non-love-oriented in their techniques of discipline.

Erikson (21) also speaks of the possible negative results if one's dependency needs are not satisfied. He presents an epigenetic chart of the eight stages of development in man. The first four of these stages are basic trust vs. basic mistrust; autonomy vs. shame and doubt; initiative vs. guilt; and industry vs. inferiority. It is during these stages of development that one is most dependent on another. As is the case with all of these modalities, their basic conflicts can lead in the end to either hostile or benign expectations and attitudes. If these basic needs, which, taken together, can be understood as dependency, are not met, man becomes "a great potential danger to his own ego — and to that of his fellow men" (21).

AGGRESSION AND DEPENDENCY

Early Childhood Development

The less the affected satisfaction of dependence, or warmth, the infant and child receives (in other words, the more the reserve, neglect or rejection), the less developed is his subsequent personality likely to be and the less quickly he matures. He is likely to be apathetic, unresponsive, vegetative and incapable of independent action. He is also likely to have less strength of character and a sense of self, leading even to the development of a psychopathic personality that feels no responsibility to others (22). Clinically, this personality type offers the least amount of hope for remission, and his aggressive activities, accompanied by no remorse or pricks of conscience, make him a most dangerous person. His actions are an attempt to make contact, in some way to receive some warmth and recognition from another. This has led some theorists to go so far as to say that the individual whose dependency needs have not been met by his parents, who has had no affective parent-child relationship, is the primary perpetrator of violence today (24). Love and respect helps children to mature adequately and become loving, responsible and productive spouses, parents and citizens. Those reared in such a way that they hate their parents will also hate other persons for life. If persons such as this repress, this pathological hostility causes neuroses; if acted out, "it results in crime, tyranny, revolution, and aggressive war" (25).

It has been suggested by some theorists, however, that children may refrain from aggressive behavior even when abused by parents. Dollard and Miller (12) believe that the strength of inhibition of any act of aggression increases with the amount of punishment anticipated as consequence of that act. This hypothesis is supported by other investigators (26) who feel that even if the youngsters are frustrated by the situations surrounding them, they may have developed response tendencies incompatible with aggressive behavior. Their frustrating parents may have taught them, implicitly or explicitly, to inhibit their hostility. They suggest that the child will refrain from engaging in aggressive behavior, even though the mother and father he loves are often cold to him, if he has learned that he cannot gain the affection he desires unless he conforms to his parents' demands. In this case, the child experiences relatively frequent thwarting of his dependency wishes but has learned that satisfaction of these wishes is contingent upon acceding to his parents' dictates. He then hides whatever aggressive inclinations he might have.

Recent studies suggest, however, that even though the child who is reared in such a deprived situation may not directly agress at that time, it is likely that he will at a later date (27).

Most of the specialists in the mental health disciplines seem to agree that aggressive personalities are the product of many severe emotional thwartings. Radke's (28) summary of the research literature up to the end of World War II suggests that a variety of socialization conditions which probably can be regarded as frustrating to the child, such as parental rejection and parental disharmony, seem to be related to aggressiveness in the child. Psychoanalytic conceptions and the frustration-aggression hypothesis of Dollard and his colleagues maintain that frequent thwartings yield a heightened instigation of aggression, and parents tend to be fairly consistent in their actions toward their children. The youngsters who are treated with hostility by their mothers when they are infants are usually still treated in this manner as they approach adolescence (29). Nevertheless, as Bandura (30) points out, we cannot satisfactorily explain the development of every hostile person by saying that he has been frustrated as a child. Frequent deprivations throughout childhood may lead to withdrawal reactions or apathy as well as to some form of aggression. Thus, although no attempt is being made to imply that all aggressive persons have suffered severe emotional deprivations in their early childhood, a sufficient number have suffered such thwartings. For these persons, at least, we might hypothesize that this has had some effect on their emotional development.

It has been found that affectionally cold mothers tend to describe their children as highly aggressive (30). The college-student offspring of this type of mother generally shows a relatively high frequency of aggressive responses on psychological tests (31). When child-abusing mothers have been studied, an inability to empathize with their children, severely frustrated dependency needs, and a probable history of emotional deprivations were noted (32).

The role of the father is also important with regard to the dependency strivings of the child and aggression. In situations where the father is absent from the home or is absent because of divorce, boys were found to be more aggressive and less able to delay gratification; also, the later the father's absence occurred, the more aggression was manifested.

In addition to not having their dependency needs met, children of homes where there is something lacking in the relationship with their parents do not learn to tolerate frustrations. A recent study compared psychological test and interview data for a group of twenty-six hyperaggressive adolescent boys, who had been in trouble with authorities for antisocial aggression, with a matched group of youngsters who were "neither markedly aggressive nor markedly withdrawn" (26). The aggressive boys apparently had received enough love and attention from their mothers during infancy to develop further desires for aid and comfort (i.e., they had acquired fairly strong dependency needs). As they grew older, however, the boys experienced coldness and neglect from their fathers, and to some extent from their mothers as well. It was hypothesized that because of their rejection and their mothers' inconsistent reactions to their earlier dependency behavior, they developed not only strong aggressive inclinations but also relatively intense dependency anxiety.

Several other investigations have found that when comparing groups of aggressive adolescents with "normal" groups, there seemed to be little indication of emotional warmth and a lack of fulfillment of dependency needs among the aggressive group (22,27,35,36).

This lack of fulfillment of dependency needs theoretically leads to another characteristic frequently observed in aggressively antisocial youngsters, i.e., such boys generally are reluctant to enter into close relationships with other people (39). The highly aggressive group of adolescents expressed little affection for either their parents or schoolmates (26). Possibly as a result of their strong dependency anxiety and hostility toward their parents, highly aggressive preadolescents have been found to construct relatively few stories containing themes of dependency upon parents when given TAT-like pictures (36).

It becomes apparent that a crucial factor in the development of aggressive-destructive patterns of reaction is, as Freud pointed out, the long period of dependency of the human child with protracted inequality of power, which makes envy, hate and destructive impulses virtually unavoidable. These could be mitigated if the powerful "significant" others, the parents, were able to exert their influence in the service of the child's growth and autonomy.

The literature supports the theoretical position that unmet dependency need in itself creates a predisposition to aggression. Aggressive cues must be present if such behavior is actually to occur. Prior learning to behave aggressively, through which the individual learns to perceive aggression-evoking cues, may also be necessary in order to produce the habitually hostile person. Bandura (30) has obtained some evidence indicating that a history of frequent frustration in childhood is not sufficient to explain childhood aggression, and indeed, may not even be necessary in the formation of such behavior patterns. One such aggressive cue which may lead a person to act in an aggressive manner is a feeling of powerlessness.

Adler, like Freud, recognizes the existence of the unconscious with forces which direct man's psychic life and which can upset it. But the fundamental tendency is not, in Adler's view, the libido or sexuality. It lies in the effort made by the person to assert himself; a drive towards the affirmation of his personality, a tendency towards self-preservation, or, as he called it, "a will to power."

In Adler's Individual Psychology the immanent finality of the preservation of the self is fundamental. On the other hand, every child soon learns of his dependence on others. And with this, we can begin to have a better notion of the relationship between the two variables of dependency and power and, in turn, their relationship with aggression and violence. For much longer than any animal, the child is dependent upon his parents and incapable of pursuing his own life in the complex society developed by man. Even when his spiritual faculties and conscious ego begin to develop, he experiences all kinds of desires which are quite unrealizable (41). As the child begins to be aware of his dependence on others he becomes aware as well of his powerless position. Adler would hold that in reaction to this, there develops in the child an unconscious drive toward superiority.

> The child finds himself in the predicament of either having to assert his individuality, or being psychically drowned in the mass of superior beings. This is the foundation, the universal source, of the drive to assert one's personality, to assert oneself; under the influence of the feelings of inferiority, the fundamental need — that of self-preservation — is changed and converted into an impulse of self-assertion, a will to power (41).

The concept of power is basic to understanding May's (42) theory of man and his theory of violence. Power, which he defines as "the ability to cause or prevent change," is seen as one of the basic needs of man. May goes so far as to state that it "is essential for all living things." He presents the argument that there are five levels of power "present as potentialities in every human life." These are:

1. The power to be;
2. the power of self-affirmation — not only to be but to be significant;
3. the power of self-assertion — "I demand that you notice me";
4. aggression — taking some of the power of another for oneself;
5. violence — largely physical because the other phases, which can involve reasoning and persuasion, have been ipso facto blocked off.

According to May's theory, man must be able to choose and live a proportion of what he has to do freely. If he then realizes that there are other things that he is required to do, he will not delude himself and will be able to preserve his own autonomy and humanity. May states that love and power have been traditionally cited as being opposed to each other. This, he believes, is based on superficial reasoning and leads to errors and endless troubles. "The endeavor to love with the renunciation of power is a product of the tendency toward pseudoinnocence." He goes on to state that "the docile overcontrolled individual," the one who appears kind all the time, can be the one who releases his aggression in one big blowup. This accords with his thesis that violence occurs when a person cannot live out his needs for power in normal ways. Other investigators also held that the calm, placid person who usually only arouses friendly feelings can produce marked aggression under certain circumstances (12,43,44,45,46).

In Love and Will and Power and Innocence, May provides an existential approach that presents a theory that appears to integrate the theories and research findings that have been advanced thus far. Although his theory is not yet strongly supported by research dealing directly with powerlessness, related research points positively in that direction, and he himself presents arguments that call for further research.

In Love and Will May states that in our times of transition the individual is forced to turn inward; he becomes obsessed with the new form of the problem of identity, namely, if I know who I am, I still have no significance, I am unable to influence others. The next step is apathy. And the step following that is violence. For no human can long endure the perpetually numbing experience of his own powerlessness (47).

Hopelessness has been cited as being the common factor to both violent and suicidal persons (48). Studies have shown that individuals who eventually committed suicide showed an attitude of hopelessness that became a delusion that could not be shaken by reason or psychological intervention. In England between 1950 and 1962 one-third of those convicted of murder committed suicide. In the United States a study of 600 convicted murderers showed a high suicide rate of 9 percent. Policemen who committed suicide when they had their records examined showed that one-third had histories of aggressive behavior.

Research on suicides among young blacks in New York City found a combination of self-hatred and homicidal rage directed toward a racist society that made the blacks feel helpless and powerless (49). Among blacks who engaged in hostile activities was found an angry diffuse reaction to the frustrations of unrealized expectations and a loss of hope (50).

May feels that there is today perhaps more than ever before a feeling of powerlessness, facelessness and an inability to influence others. Sullivan said some years ago that "one must consider especially the states characterized by the feeling of ability or power. This is ordinarily much more important in the human being than are the impulses resulting from a feeling of hunger or thirst . . . We seem to be born, however, with something of this power motive in us" (51). May holds that deeds of violence in our society are performed largely by those trying to establish their self-esteem, to defend their self-image, and to demonstrate that they, too, are significant.

H.G. Wells in *Time Machine Philosophy* says that we can make people nonviolent by making them powerless (52). This state, however, prepares them for a future violence, for powerlessness leads to apathy and finally to violence. Deeds of violence in our society are performed largely by those trying to establish their self-esteem, to defend their self-image, and to demonstrate that they, too, are significant. Violence has often been thought to be a reaction to impotence. Feelings of impotence and the need for attention lead to violence, and this violence can lead to hostile acts against oneself or others.

Hans Toch in *Violent Men* states that the black kids and the white cops — their pride, their fear, their isolation, their need to prove themselves, and, above all, their demand for respect — are strangely alike; victims both, prisoners of an escalating conflict they did not make and cannot control (53). Time after time it is clear that the policeman is fighting an impotency-potency battle within himself that he expands and projects on the concept of "law and order." For some, violence is a response to the myth of our society that all are equal, and for others, on a more individual plane, it is a way of asserting one's self-esteem (54).

Woods (55) feels that the violence associated with homosexual panic is an attempt to restore masculine self-esteem via aggressive demonstrations of power and strength while at the same time denying the passivity and dependency symbolically linked to femininity. For such persons, violence is a restorative act.

Ransford (56) in studying a group of blacks after the Watts riot found that racial isolation, i.e., low degrees of intimate white contact, is strongly associated with a willingness to use forms of violence, under two conditions: when these individuals feel a sense of powerlessness in society; and when they are highly dissatisfied with their treatment as blacks. In another study Ransford (57) found that dark blacks as opposed to light blacks expressed stronger anti-white system sentiments. Again, those who felt powerless to exert control through institutional channels were more prone to resort to violence.

With regard to militancy in general, Crawford and Naditch (58) studied high and low discrepancy in an individual's distance from his ideal life-style. Results tended to support the view that a large difference between "want" and "get" leads to political militancy. Willingness to use violence was lowest with those subjects who felt a low life-style discrepancy and who felt that the control of their life-style was in their own hands. Persons who felt a high discrepancy and who also felt that their life-style was "fated" or out of their own control were more willing to engage in violent actions.

In a study which included the simultaneous analysis of a father and son, it was found that the father tended to beat his son and resort to other violent actions whenever he felt threatened or powerless in the relationship (59). Gold (60) in his study found that adolescents tended to engage in delinquent behavior when they felt powerless, in the sense of not being able to influence others. This resorting to violence is not limited to adolescents when the feeling of powerlessness is present. Jensen (61) reports that medical students who felt powerless during the Cambodian invasion to exert any political influence when tested by means of a checklist showed more anxiety, depression and hostility than college students tested at "normal" times. Two weeks later, after there had been opportunity for constructive political activity, retesting showed significant decreases in anxiety and hostility, although the depression scores remained high.

It was also found that editors who had community power status tended not to report conflict in local government (62). In general, it was found that such editors who felt powerful in being able to influence community activity tended to protect community institutions rather than attack them. In the business field, executives who were successful had high scores on a test of power and low aggression scores when compared with a group of executives who were not successful (63).

Although the literature does not seem to present us with as many studies as might be desired on the effects of powerlessness and violence, it does seem to indicate that this is indeed a variable that, as May hypothesizes, does lead persons to act in a violent manner.

PRACTICAL IMPLICATIONS

In the preventive sense, these studies stress the importance of child-rearing practices that lead to the healthy development of independent persons. In this, the role of the parents is of primary importance. Children must experience warm accepting relationships with their parents or parent surrogates if their dependency needs are to be met. In addition to having their dependency needs met, children, and especially adolescents, must also experience success and thus have a feeling of power.

Within the community the variables of dependency and power are of great importance in the relations of the authorities with the members of the community. If those in positions of authority are not themselves well adjusted with regard to dependency and power, their actions can be damaging as they fulfill their "lawful duties." Thus, those with authority roles in the community are aware of their own needs and the needs of the people they come in contact with. The policeman whose own feeling of power is threatened will overreact and be much more punitive than will a policeman who does not feel so threatened. Those who work in areas where there is much poverty, many broken homes, and high crime rates must be made to realize that their duties require an understanding of the needs of the people who live in such areas. Thus, special training programs are needed that will allow this understanding to take place.

Those in the helping professions must also have an understanding of their own needs for power. If this is not done, then there is a good possibility that the client, patient or student may become the victim of an unconscious drive for power operating in the supposedly helping person.

REFERENCES

1. Eisenhower M (Chairman), et al: *To establish justice, to insure domestic tranquility: Final report of the National Commission on the Causes and Prevention of Violence.* Washington, D.C., United States Government Printing Office, 1969.

2. Tiger L, Fox R: *The Imperial Animal.* New York, Holt, 1971.
3. Montagu A: Human Behavior: An innate violence from ape ancestors. *Chicago Sun Times Book Week,* September 26, 1971, 1.
4. Lorenz K: *On Aggression.* New York, Bantam Books, 1967.
5. Morris D: *The Naked Ape.* New York, McGraw-Hill, 1967.
6. Kelsey M: Aggression, violence and emotion: The punitive element in man. Unpublished manuscript, Notre Dame University, 1971.
7. Freud S: Three contributions to the theory of sex, in A Brill (ed): *The Basic Writings of Sigmund Freud.* New York, Random House, 1938 (first published 1905).
8. Freud S: *Beyond the Pleasure Principle.* New York, Bantam Books, 1959 (first published by Liveright, 1928).
9. Freud S: *Civilization and Its Discontents.* London, Liveright, 1930.
10. Jung C: In *Collected Works.* Vol 9, Part II. Princeton University Press, 1959 (first German edition 1951).
11. Jung C: *Memories, Dreams, and Reflections.* New York, Vintage Books, 1961.
12. Storr A: *Human Aggression.* New York, Bantam Books, 1970.
13. Freud S: *Group Psychology and the Analysis of the Ego.* London, Hogarth Press, 1955 (first published in 1921).
14. Freud S: *An Outline of Psychoanalysis.* London, Hogarth Press, 1964 (first published in 1940).
15. Freud S: *New Introductory Lectures on Psycho-analysis.* London, Hogarth Press, 1964 (first published in 1933).
16. Himsie L, Campbell R: *Psychiatric Dictionary.* New York, Oxford University Press, 1960.
17. Maslow A: *Toward a Psychology of Being.* New York, Van Nostrand, 1962.
18. Wolberg L, Kildahl J: *The Dynamics of Personality.* New York, Grune and Stratton, 1970.
19. Hamilton J: Some cultural determinants of intrapsychic structure and psychopathology. *Psychoanalytic Review* 1971, 58, 2, 279-294.
20. Chyou Niem T, Collard R: Parental discipline of aggression behaviors in four year old Chinese and American children. *Proceedings of the Annual Convention of the American Psychological Association,* 1972, 7, 95-96.
21. Erikson E: *Childhood and Society.* New York, W.W. Norton & Company, 1963.
22. Child I: Socialization, in G Lindzey (ed): *Handbook of Social Psychology.* Reading, Mass., Addison-Wesley, 1954.
23. Kleem H: Contact needs of the aggressive child. *Praxis der Kinderpsychologie und Kinderpsychiatrie,* 1969, 18, 6, 215-233.
24. Saul L: Personal and social psychopathology and the primary prevention of violence. *American Journal of Psychiatry,* 1972, 128, 12, 1578-1581.
25. Saul L: *The Hostile Mind.* New York, Random House, 1956.
26. Bandura A, Walters R: *Adolescent Aggression.* New York, Ronald Press, 1959.
27. Kalogeriakis M: Homicide in adolescents: Fantasy and deed, in J Fawcett (ed): *Dynamics of Aggression.* Chicago, American Medical Association, 1972.
28. Radke M: The relation of parental authority to children's behavior and attitudes. *University of Minnesota Institute of Child Welfare* Monogram Series, 1946, No. 22.
29. Schaefer E, Bayley N: Consistency of maternal behavior from infancy to pre-adolescence. *Journal of Abnormal Social Psychology,* 1960, 61, 1-6.
30. Bandura A: Relationship of family patterns to child behavior disorders. Progress report to NIMH on grant M-1734. Stanford University Press, 1960.
31. Bornston L, Coleman J: The relationship between certain parents' attitudes toward child rearing and the direction of aggression of their young adult offspring. *Journal of Clinical Psychology,* 1956, 12, 41-44.

32. Meinick B, Hurley J: Distinctive personality attributes of child-abusing mothers. *Journal of Consulting and Clinical Psychology,* 1969, 33, 6, 746-749.
33. Santrock J, Wohlford P: Effects of father absence: Influence of the reason for and the onset of the absence. *Proceedings of the Annual Convention of the American Psychological Association,* 1970.
34. Offer D: Coping with aggression among normal adolescent boys, in J Fawcet (ed): *Dynamics of Aggression.* Chicago, American Medical Association, 1972.
35. Glueck S, Glueck E: *Unraveling Juvenile Delinquency.* New York, Commonwealth Fund, 1950.
36. Kagan J: Socialization of aggression and the perception of parents in fantasy. *Child Development,* 1958, 29, 311-320.
37. McCord W, McCord J, Howard A: Familial correlates of aggression in non-delinquent male children. *Journal of Abnormal Social Psychology,* 1961, 62, 79-93.
38. Rolde E, Goethals G: Adolescent aggression and dependence, in J Fawcett (ed): *Dynamics of aggression.* Chicago, American Medical Association, 1972.
39. Redl F, Wineman D: *The Aggressive Child.* New York, Free Press, 1957.
40. Adler A: *Problems of Neurosis.* London, Kegan Paul, 1929.
41. Nuttin J: *Psychoanalysis and Personality.* New York, Mentor Books, 1962.
42. May R: *Power and Innocence.* New York, W.W. Norton and Company, 1972.
43. Megargee E: The role of inhibition in the assessment and understanding of violence, in J E Singer (ed): *The Control of Aggression and Violence; Cognitive and Physiological Factors.* Academic Press, 1971, p. 125-147.
44. White W, McAdoo W, Megargee E: Personality Factors Associated with Over and Under-Controlled Offenders, *FCI Research Reports,* 1971, 3, 5, 1-6. Federal Correctional Institution, Tallahassee, Florida.
45. Blackburn R: Emotionality, extraversion and aggression in paranoid and non-paranoid schizophrenic offenders. *British Journal of Psychiatry,* 1968, 114, 1301-1302.
46. Haven H: Descriptive and developmental characteristics of chronically over-controlled hostile prisoners. Unpublished Doctoral Dissertation, Florida State University, 1972.
47. May R: *Love and Will.* New York, WW Norton and Company, 1970.
48. Stotland E: *The Psychology of Hope.* San Francisco, Jossey-Bass, 1969.
49. Hendin H: *Black Suicide.* New York, Basic Books, 1969.
50. Grier W, Cobbs P: *Black Rage.* New York, Bantam Books, 1968.
51. Sullivan H: *The Interpersonal Theory of Psychiatry.* New York, W. W. Norton and Company, 1953.
52. Wells H: *The Time Machine.* New York, H Holt and Company, 1946.
53. Toch H: *Violent Men: An Inquiry into the Psychology of Violence.* Chicago. Aldine Publishing Company, 1969.
54. Berkowitz L: *Roots of Aggression.* New York, Atherton Press, 1969.
55. Woods S: Violence: Psychotherapy of pseudo-homosexual panic. *Archives of General Psychiatry,* 1972, 27, 2, 255-258.
56. Ransford H: Isolation, powerlessness, and violence: A study of attitudes and participation in the Watts Riot. *American Journal of Sociology,* 1968, 73, 5, 581-591.
57. Ransford H: Skin color, life chances, and anti-white attitudes. *Social Problems,* 1970, 18, 2, 164-179.
58. Crawford R, Naditch M: Relative deprivation, powerlessness, and militancy: The psychology of social protest. *Psychiatry,* 1970.

59. Kolansky H, Moore W: Some comments on the simultaneous analysis of a father and his adolescent son. *Psychoanalytic Study of the Child*, 1966, 21, 237-268.
60. Gold M: Juvenile delinquency as a symptom of alienation. *Journal of Social Issues*, 1969, 25, 2, 121-135.
61. Jensen G: Emotional response of students to a political crisis. *American Journal of Psychiatry*, 1971, 128, 3, 356-358.
62. Olien C, Donohue G, Tichenor P: The community editors power and the reporting of conflict. *Journalism Quarterly*, 1968, 45, 2, 243-252.
63. Cummin P: TAT correlates of executive performance. *Journal of Applied Psychology*, 1967, 51, 1, 78-81.

Suicide and
Self-destructive Behavior

GEORGE GALLAHORN

This chapter on self-destructive behavior is drawn from a review of behavioral sciences literature from January 1973 to September 1974. Some research involves both completed suicides and suicide attempts — other articles are devoted to only one of the subjects. First, there will be a description of the research on completed suicides and then on suicide attempts. Finally, miscellaneous papers which touch on a variety of issues related to suicide will be summarized.

COMPLETED SUICIDE

Epidemiology

The epidemiology of those individuals who complete suicide has been studied extensively in the past. The rate of successful suicides has remained unchanged in all the epidemiological data gathered so far. In the following series of papers the authors attempt to look at new epidemiological variables or refine old concepts in a new way.

Weissman (42) in a general review of the epidemiology of suicide attempts noted that those individuals who complete suicide often have a prior history of suicide attempts. Patients who were hospitalized and later killed themselves usually did so within the first two years following hospitalization for an attempt.

Humphrey et al. (18) focused on disruptive events in the lives and past history of individuals who complete suicide. The authors agreed with Gibbs' position that the disruption of social relations is the one crucial etiological factor in suicide. The authors' study showed there were familial and social losses, followed by loss of student roles, followed by marital problems, loss of occupational roles and finally the loss of health. These losses culminated in a completed suicide.

A persistent debate centers on the contagion effect of sensational newspaper stories about completed suicides. The thesis is based on Durkheim's suggestion that imitation is a significant factor in suicide. A paper by Blumenthal and Bergner (6) studied the suicide rate in New York City during a partial newspaper strike. There was no change in the suicide rate and thus no apparent relationship between the *partial* cessation of newspaper articles on suicide and the suicide rate for the year as a whole. There were several problems with the study: (1) the strike was a partial one and the other daily papers were available, although not subscribed to at a rate equal to that of the papers on strike; (2) there were 12 television stations in the central city and 19 others in fringe areas, so there was no complete news black-out. Also, the impact of different media (television versus newspapers) in conveying suicide stories is not explored in this paper.

Phillips (29) in his article on the influence of suggestion on suicide used a different approach to study this issue. He evaluated the suicide rate of nations on a month-by-month basis following front page (*New York Times, Daily News,* and *London Mirror*) stories of the suicides of famous people. The author was able to demonstrate a rise in the suicide rate in the months following the death of a famous person, such as Marilyn Monroe. There was no corresponding dip in the months following the increase. There are three possible hypotheses: "(a) the excess suicides after a suicide story would have killed themselves anyway, but several months or several years later; (b) the excess suicides would not have killed themselves if the suicide stories had not occurred; (c) a third hypothesis, combining the two previous ones, is also possible: newspaper suicide stories precipitate some suicides, and create others."

Phillips also speculated that joining a social movement would reduce an individual's anomie, and he noted that there was a drop in the suicide rate in a region where a social movement came to town. Additional data to support this concept were not available in the current paper.

Sanborn et al. (33) studied the relationship between occupation and suicide. They found that fourteen of twenty-two individuals who completed suicide had experienced some form of job change in the year prior to the suicide. Of these only one individual was promoted. Fifty percent of the males were unemployed at the time of suicide. Over half of those employed were disappointed with their jobs. The authors felt that the loss of a sense of pride and identity which was obtained by one's occupational status could be quite damaging to one's self-image. This poor self-image could lead to suicide.

An attempt was made by Zung and Green (47) to relate suicide to seasonal variations. They found that completed suicides are not significantly related to weekdays versus the weekend, months of the year, seasons of the year, special days of the week (holidays) or the week following a holiday. There was a statistically significant (P = < .05) incidence of suicide by days of the week, with the highest number on Mondays and the lowest on Saturdays. The authors do not speculate on this interesting finding. Perhaps it can be related to the beginning of the work week and dissatisfaction with one's job, as noted in Sanborn et al.'s paper (33) or an increasing sense of emptiness and despair because of unemployment.

Flanagan and Murphy (16) studied the possible association of body donation and suicide. They found that while the donation of one's body may have been prompted by thoughts of suicide, the risk is remote and a screening procedure of body donors for probable suicides is unlikely to be useful.

H.M. Babigian (3) compared black and white homocide and suicide rates in Monroe County over a four-year period. There had been an increase in self-destructive deaths of blacks via "victim precipitated" murder or through accidents. Thus the low black suicide rate may be artificially low, and the changing role of the black male in society could result in increased stress and increased suicide-like deaths.

A cross-cultural study was done by Ripley (31) on suicide in Edinburgh and Seattle. The incidence of completed suicide in both cities has remained stable since 1958. Edinburgh had a lower rate than Seattle (15.8 versus 20.8 per 100,000 population). Some factors throught to be related to this lower incidence in Edinburgh are "lower incidence of alcoholism, more integrated and less mobile society, a smaller percentage of foreign born and racial minorities, and a cultural condition of more controlled and less violent behavior."

Edinburgh has an increase in the number of deaths caused by drugs and a decrease in the number of deaths by gas over the period of time for the study. No significant changes in methods of completed suicide were noted for Seattle. In this city, guns, followed by drugs, were the most frequently used methods of completed suicide. Often the method was related to specific issues for the individual patient, such as a man with a gun collection. The rate of female suicide in Edinburgh was almost equal to the male rate. The author suggested that women have a significantly changing role in Edinburgh, as compared with Seattle, but this hypothesis is not well supported.

Conrad and Kahn (12) studied suicide among Papago Indians. There were ten completed suicides in four years, which gives a rate of 18 per 100,000. Alcohol was involved in eight of the ten. Eight of the ten lived in the urban areas adjacent to the reservation or on the reservation just outside a major city. Only two of those who killed themselves lived in isolated areas. Eight of the ten were men between the ages of twenty and twenty-nine. Six of those who killed themselves were unemployed. Five had completed some education beyond high school. The higher suicide rate among this tribe, as compared with others, was felt to be related to the poorly defined role of the Papago man due to problems of acculturation and poor role definition. Roles previously filled by the male in this tribe had been taken over by the government and government agents, such as physicians in the Public Health Service.

Rose and Rosow (32) reviewed death certificates in California for a three-year period to determine the suicide rate of physicians. Physicians were twice as likely to commit suicide as the general population. There were no significant differences between various medical specialists. The methods of death were 55 percent by drug ingestion, as compared with 12 percent by firearms. This propensity for death by ingestion is interesting and not explained by access to drugs, since the rate of death due to drug ingestion is lower for dentists (35 percent) and pharmacists (40 percent). Reasons for this propensity for death by drug ingestion are not explored further in the article.

Intrapsychic and Family Dynamics

Shneidman's paper (35) on suicide notes attempted to evaluate suicide notes as a "special window . . . into the thinking and feeling of the deed itself." Until now, studies of suicide notes have been disappointing. The author reviewed a number of notes and attempted to classify them from an epistelomogical viewpoint. While this can be done, it adds little to a dynamic understanding of suicide. Shneidman noted that "we tend to confuse the drama of the suicidal situation" with the expectation that notes will be dramatic and revealing. Instead, they were "always secular and usually constricted," and little light was shed on intrapsychic conflicts and suicide.

Weissman (42) noted that there was a diagnostic group of patients who often have completed suicides. These were patients with hysterical depression and hostility. The author warned that the hysterical personality should not lead observers to underestimate the suicide potential of the patient.

Dorpat (13) challenged the assumption that "accidental" barbiturate overdoses are caused by drug automatism. The author noted that there was no good evidence to support the drug automatism hypothesis. He felt the persistence of this hypothesis as an explanation for fatal overdoses was an attempt by relatives, friends and the physicians involved to deny the suicidal intent of the victim.

Stone (39) evaluated six disturbed suicidal adolescents and their families. Of these, three actually killed themselves eventually. The ones who completed suicide came from more "unworkable" families that had significant psychopathology. The adolescents who committed suicide were seen as acting out the parents' wishes, or suicide was seen as the only way out for them from an impossible situation. Of those who survived at the time of the paper, two out of three were felt to be in significant danger of killing themselves. One solution proposed by the author was the enforced separation from the family of the adolescent in an attempt to free the patient from their enmeshment in destructive family dynamics.

Treatment and Prevention

Androlia (2), in a brief communication on the possible iatrogenesis of suicide, warned that therapists who saw suicidal patients as merely making gestures are likely to convey this message to the patient. The patient may feel he is viewed by the therapist as someone who should stop playing around and get this business of suicide over with.

Fabian et al. (15) studied suicide attempts and completed suicides on an inpatient ward. There were only three patients with lethal attempts and thus the data are highly speculative. If other patients making serious, potentially lethal attempts were included, several issues became apparent. The most serious attempts were made during the early afternoon when there were a number of activities, groups and staff on the ward. Also, most patients making a serious attempt were diagnosed as being depressed. The authors did not speculate as to why most serious attempts were made in the early afternoon. Perhaps the patients' anomie was more acute at this time with so much activity going on around them while they remained isolated, depressed and alone.

Wold and Litman (45) studied suicide after contact with a suicide prevention center. They noted that patients who frequently contact a suicide prevention center are responded to in the manner of an emergency, and often chronic feelings of severe depression and helplessness were not appreciated. This helplessness and exhaustion makes it difficult for the suicidal person to make use of remaining relationships. A program was being initiated by the authors to reach out to these individuals by phone contact or have home visits to combat the feelings of helplessness and exhaustion experienced by them.

This theme of hopelessness noted by Wold and Litman (45) was found in another group of patients. Kiev (20) found in a follow-up study of patients who attempted suicide and later completed a suicide attempt that the patient was unable to mobilize himself or herself to change his interpersonal relations. There was a chronic sense of rejection in the patient's life and his interpersonal relations. The patient's diagnosis or the lethality of the previous attempt was not related to this pervasive sense of hoplessness and helplessness.

Yamamoto et al. (46) evaluated the effect on the suicide rate of certain "community psychiatry" treatments, such as crisis intervention and a major emphasis on keeping patients in the community. There was no significant change in the rate of completed suicides. The importance of follow-up care was shown by data which demonstrated the highest incidence of suicide occurring within six months of the last clinic contact.

SUICIDE ATTEMPTS

Epidemiology

Weissman's extensive review (42) of articles on suicide attempts called attention to the increase in attempts, particularly by young (under twenty-five) single or divorced females. This group of attempters has a history of drug abuse, social disorganization, hostility and impulsive behavior. These characteristics make them difficult to engage in suicide prevention programs.

Some of the characteristics of Weissman's group of patients were found by Buglass and Horton (8) in a review of individuals who repeated a suicide attempt within one year of a previous admission for suicide in Edinburgh. This group of patients was compared with a control group, and a number of items were found which contrasted between suicide repeaters and the control group. The repeaters had problems with alcohol and drug abuse, a history of sociopathy and criminal behavior, previous suicide attempts and inpatient treatment, and social class 5 and unemployment. These characteristics were noted to be similar for both sexes.

Pederson et al. (27) delineated some differences between white and nonwhite suicide attempters. Nonwhites had a higher rate of attempts (160 versus 53 per 100,000). The ratio of women to men was twice as high for nonwhites (6 to 1 versus 3 to 1). The nonwhite group had more single or separated/divorced individuals and came from a lower socioeconomic level. Whites who had a history of previous suicide attempts were sixty-four times as likely as nonwhites to kill themselves. "For nonwhites . . . suicide attempts appear to be negatively related to further self-destructive behavior." However, despite this data it is important to consider material on homicide and suicide of white versus nonwhites. These authors did not note such data.

Parkin (25) in his study of three cultural groups in Fairbanks, Alaska, found several factors that were related to non-native suicidal behavior. These included the "myth of Alaska," in which the state was seen as a last frontier and a last chance for some individuals. Many patients developed marital problems because of travel and isolation related to employment in Alaska. Finally, being housebound for many months of winter was a significant factor in the depression among women.

Natives who recently migrated to the city were at higher risk because of problems with the culturation in the city. This was felt to be related to city problems of prejudice, loss of cultural norms, and increase in excess alcohol consumption. Because of cultural prohibitions against direct expression of hostility, Eskimos often became depressed and suicidal, while Athabascans (native indians) were more aggressive, and their suicidal behavior had a more angry manipulative quality.

Intrapsychic and Family Dynamics

Freud and Abraham's concepts of depression as hostility turned inward were modified by Weissman et al.'s study (44) of hostility and depression associated with suicide. The suicide attempter was characterized as an individual who has poor defenses and engages in acting out his hostility. The controls in this study were depressed individuals who presented an interesting contrast of compliance and passivity in the interview.

Lester and Perdue (21) compared Rorschach protocols of suicide attempters and murders. The results suggested that a certain sign (Martin's) on a test which had previously been associated with suicidal behavior was more related to general aggressive acting out. This finding is consistent with that noted in the previous study by Weissman et al.

Minkoff et al. (23) studied hopelessness and suicidal intent. The population was of low socioeconomic status who were admitted to a general hospital. It was found that hopelessness was a stronger indicator of suicidal intent than depression. This is important in planning therapeutic intervention. The authors stressed the importance in correcting distorted negative expectations of the future as a way of combating the hopelessness of the suicidal patient. This therapeutic plan is likely to encounter difficulty with patients who have a negative set (for masochistic reasons among others), and are extremely difficult to reach in attempting to correct the set. The authors also noted that if the hopelessness is objective, an intervention may be initiated to alter the difficult reality situation.

Treatment and Prevention

A study was done by Paykel et al. (26) on the treatment of suicide attempters who came to a general hospital emergency room. The study found that only a small percentage of patients required medical hospitalization. About 50 percent of the patients were hospitalized in psychiatric settings, and 40 percent were referred for outpatient therapy. The remainder either signed out of the emergency room against medical advice or a few were not referred for any follow-up treatment.

A number of factors were considered in the decision to hospitalize patients. These included previous suicide attempts, slow onset of suicidal preoccupations, self-directed hostility, and a number of other factors previously described by Weissman and Worden (43) in a paper not discussed here. Other issues such as socioeconomic status, race and countertransference feelings of the therapist were not significantly related to the decision for hospitalization.

A second issue evaluated by the study was the decision regarding site of psychiatric hospitalization. Significant factors entering into this decision included financial consideration and social status. In addition, countertransference feelings of a negative nature often resulted in patients being admitted to the state hospital rather than to other psychiatric facilities.

The final area for investigation related to outpatient follow-up. Of the patients who were referred for outpatient treatment, only 50 percent came for an initial interview. Attempts to discover a reason for this were unsuccessful, partially because of a rather small sample. However, some general impressions were that non-attenders were often young and black, and therefore perhaps alienated from the more middle-class psychiatrist.

Drye et al. (14) developed a method in dealing with suicide patients on an outpatient basis. They asked the patient to make the following statement: "No matter what happens, I will not kill myself, accidentally on purpose at any time." The author would ask the patient to make this statement preferably for a six-month contract but would allow for shorter time periods. The authors recommended hospitalization for any patient who would not make the statement exactly as quoted. They noted that approximately six hundred patients had made the "no suicide decision" in the past five years with a fatality rate of 0. The authors do admit to several problems associated with this particular tactic in dealing with suicidal patients. They are award that there are special difficulties encountered in using this maneuver with long-term therapy patients as well as patients whose character structure includes persistent suicidal feelings. Finally, they also state that this is not a reliable method of dealing with patients who are alcohol or drug abusers.

Another new method described in dealing with suicidal patients is the use of operant techniques. Bostock and Williams (7) described the use of this method with one individual patient. For this patient the method was quite successful in an inpatient setting. The authors recommended that operant techniques be used more frequently because many patients are unable to verbalize certain feelings or symptoms and therefore they remain chronically suicidal.

An interesting technique in treating the suicidal patient was described by Resnik et al. (30) in which there was video tape confrontation with the patients who attempted suicide after they regained consciousness. This video tape showed, among other things, all measures used to treat the patient from the time of his entry into the hospital. The authors noted that special attempts were made to interview family members as well as many close-ups of the patient's facial expression on admission. The authors felt that the use of video tape enabled the therapist to break through the denial and despair that patients frequently expressed. They noted that issues related to the suicide attempt often persisted in therapy for a significantly longer period of time following video tape confrontation than from a control group of patients. Because this was a pilot project, additional studies of a more extensive nature are planned.

Orten (24), in a paper on transactional approaches to suicide prevention, emphasized the importance of the therapist's engaging the patient's "adult" rather than the patient's "child." The author feels that it is the patient's "child" who is suicidal and one must speak to the "adult" in order to prevent a suicide attempt. He recommends that this be done by the therapist not becoming immediately enmeshed in trying to resolve the acute suicide crisis without discovering some other pertinent facts about the patient as a human being. It is interesting to note the similarities between Orten's recommendations and some of the papers (20,34) calling attention to problems in dealing with patients who are chronically suicidal.

Burstein et al. (9) attempted to study the ability of psychology and psychiatry trainees to assess suicidal risks of patients. They used as their authority one experienced clinician and his decision about the patient. The study seemed to indicate that psychology trainees were able to learn faster and better how to assess suicidal risk in agreement with the one particular clinician used in the study. The authors also felt that the use of a semi-structured interview by the psychology trainees was of importance in helping them assess a patient's suicidal risk.

Maltsberger and Buie (22) discussed the extremely interesting issue of countertransference hate in the treatment of suicidal patients. They reviewed the literature relating to countertransference — particularly countertransference in relation to suicidal patients. The authors noted that this type of reaction is a major obstacle in the treatment of suicidal patients. They emphasized that the therapist must become aware of all of the manifestations of his anger and hatred toward the suicidal patient. If the therapist can obtain this awareness, the likelihood of a successful treatment is considerably increased.

Schwartz et al. (34), in an article on the suicidal character and treatment problems, noted that current treatment programs are set up with an emphasis on the acutely suicidal patient. They feel that the maternal caring response, which is often preferred by various suicide prevention centers, reinforces the suicidal character's personality structure. They note that it is only with great difficulty that the long-term treatment of these individuals is undertaken.

Kiev (20) studied prognostic factors in attempted suicide and notes that there were three factors related to prognosis: interpersonal conflict, symptoms of stress and the social setting of the attempt. The author found that if there is a persistent interpersonal conflict the suicide risk remains high. However, it was also found that patients who have a lack of interpersonal conflicts may either be well on the verge of recovery or be so socially isolated that they are not encountering such conflicts. In the latter case the prognosis is quite grim. Patients who complain of symptomatology were felt to have a favorable prognosis. Finally, the authors noted that the setting of the attempt (i.e., how likely the person was to be discovered) should not be considered a factor in ruling out serious suicidal intent. In this study all of those individuals who ultimately killed themselves initially made an attempt in which there was a high likelihood that they would be discovered.

In a somewhat different approach to conceptualizing suicide and treatment of the suicidal individual, Tabachnik (40) noted that for some people, feelings of suicide constitute a creative crisis. This concept applied only for a small group of individuals, but the author felt that these patients needed special treatment. He felt that crisis therapy was inappropriate for these patients, and that the "suicide-like states" through which this group passes were important in their creative development and were precipitated by turning away from a disappointing unfulfilling world.

Horton (17) also pointed to a somewhat unusual concept in the treatment of suicidal patients. He noted that for three severely disturbed schizophrenic patients the ability to achieve mystical states when they were stressed was a significant preventive aid against the patient acting on suicidal feelings. The author felt that these mystical states were related to remnants of primary narcissism, and that they were potentially useful to the patient until the patient was able to work through this particular stage. The author likened the mystical state to Winnicott's concept of transitional object, and felt that as the patient improved, the dependence on these states was slowly given up.

Suicide attempts on inpatient psychiatric facilities were studied by several authors. Fabian et al. (15) noted that the most serious suicide attempts are made in the early afternoon by depressed patients. There was a much greater frequency of suicide attempts in the evenings, and these were often made by schizophrenic patients or adolescents with adjustment reactions. It would be helpful if additional studies were done to determine how generalizable the findings are, as well as reasons why the attempts occurred when they did.

A very practical paper by Benesohn and Resnik (5) on suicide-proofing a psychiatric unit was written because of the increasing number of court decisions holding hospitals liable for suicides of patients on the grounds. Many of the recommendations in the article are standard procedure at most hospitals, such as counting silverware, staff specials when indicated, etc. However, there were several interesting recommendations. One is that patients should spend a minimum amount of time in their bedrooms and suicidal patients should not be put in single rooms. In addition, because the bathroom is a place for a high number of lethal suicide attempts, curtain and shower rods should be made of a "break away" type. The authors also noted that with open hospital wards the area immediately surrounding the open ward should be suicide-proofed with screens, etc., as well as the hospital ward itself. They also recommended that the patients residing on a ward be consulted regarding various potentially dangerous aspects of ward routine and milieu to the suicidal patient.

MISCELLANEOUS ISSUES

Forensic Psychiatry

There were several articles emphasizing the importance of legal responsibility for the suicidal patient. It was noted that suicide is increasingly becoming a basis for malpractice actions. The authors (both Slawson et al. (38) and Perr (28)) decry the increasingly conservative measures that are necessary to deal with suicidal patients because of these court decisions.

Self-Mutilation

There were several articles dealing with self-mutilation. Bach-y-Rita (4), in an article on habitual violence and self mutilation, notes that certain prisoners exhibited hyperactivity, hyperexcitability, poor impulse control, depression, withdrawal and aggressive behavior indiscriminately directed at self or others. He felt that these patients were often mislabeled as "manipulative" and not treated appropriately. Indeed, from the author's description it appeared as if many of these patients were borderline schizophrenic and not only lacked what the author states as "inhibitory or superego mechanisms" but also were deficient in certain aspects of ego functioning.

Female self-mutilation was discussed by Siomopoulos (37). The author felt that repeated self-cutting was an impulse neurosis and was related to conflicts around masturbation. He found that the cutting began usually when the patient stopped masturbating in preadolescence or adolescence. The author felt that the cuttings "appear to symbolize little female genitals . . . which become available for uninhibited touching, handling, and all sorts of manipulations."

Simpson (36) described a single case of a female patient who engaged in direct genital self-mutilation. The syndrome is extremely rare in females, the author's patient being one of four cases described in the literature. This behavior would appear to occur in extremely disturbed individuals with many other associated symptoms such as anorexia, bulimia and frequent drug ingestions.

Therapist's Suicide

In a general article on suicide and psychiatric education, Kelly (19) recommended that more attention be paid to the emotional problems developed by psychiatric residents during their training. The author felt that preventive psychotherapy could be recommended for many individuals during this period of time which hopefully would lead to a decreased vulnerability of psychiatrists at a later stage in life to depression and suicidal behavior.

Ables (1) described a child's response to the loss of a therapist through suicide. It was noted that the child went through a typical mourning process with no unusual reactions. The authors recommended that efforts should be made to facilitate the mourning process rather than inhibit it in similar situations.

One year after the suicide of a psychiatrist, Chiles (11) followed up five of the seven patients who were in therapy with the psychiatrist at the time of her suicide. These patients described several similar concerns. First, that they were in some way responsible for the death of the therapist. Second, that the therapist was not omnipotent as they had fantasied. Third, they were concerned about continuing their own therapy. The author recommended that some intervention with patients of therapists who kill themselves be regularly undertaken by the psychiatric community.

Relatives of Those Who Are Suicides

There are two recent books which address themselves to the problem of the survivors of someone who has killed himself. Wallace (41) in his book *After Suicide* includes verbatium tape-recorded interviews of twelve women whose husbands had killed themselves. The book begins with the marriage of each of these couples and deals with the widows' reactions to the deaths of their spouses. While limited in content to the widows' own words, the book is quite eloquent in this respect. Nine of the twelve widows did anticipate their husband's death, but for three, it was unexpected. Two of the widows noted that they had anticipated their husbands' death becuase of the persistent physical illness, and in seven there was a downward life spiral which was unremitting. This book provides not only a glimpse of what the marriages were like between the women and their husbands but also presents a follow-up on current difficulties in adjusting to widowhood.

A somewhat more scholarly book by Albert Cain (10) on *Survivors of Suicide* is a compendium of articles written over the years on families who survive the suicide victim and the difficulties they encounter. The various articles in the book cannot be reviewed here, but it is important to note, as the author does in his introduction, that there are some common clustered reactions which include: "(1) Reality distortion, (2) tortured object relations, (3) guilt, (4) disturbed self-concept, (5) impotent rage, (6) identification with the suicide, (7) depression and self-destructiveness, (8) search for meaning, (9) incomplete mourning."

SUMMARY

Out of the many articles summarized in this chapter, several issues become apparent: (1) there is an increasing recognition that some patients are suicidal as a way of life and that these people need special treatment methods to engage them in a meaningful therapeutic encounter; (2) some new techniques such as video tape confrontation hold promise in the treatment of the suicidal patient; (3) also helpful is the therapist's awareness of his own feelings toward the suicidal patient; (4) epidemiological data continue to point to anomie from among a variety of causes as a crucial precipitant for suicide.

REFERENCES

1. Ables BS: The loss of a therapist through suicide. *J Child Psychiatry* 13:143-152, 1974.
2. Andriola J: A note of the possible iatrogenesis of suicide. *Psychiatry* 36:213-218, 1973.
3. Babigian HM: Multiple aspects of suicide. *J Forensic Sciences*, 19:267-275, 1974.
4. Bach-y-Rita G: Habitual violence and self-mutilation. *Am J Psychiat* 131:1018-1020, 1974.
5. Benesohn HS, Resnik HL: "Suicide proofing" a psychiatric unit. *Am J Psychother* 27:204-212, 1973.
6. Blumenthal S, Bergner L: Suicide and newspapers: A replicated study. *Amer J Psychiat* 130:468-471, 1973.
7. Bostock T, Williams CL: Attempted suicide as an operant behavior. *Arch Gen Psych* 31:482-486, 1974.
8. Buglass D, Horton J: The repetition of parasuicide: A comparison of three cohorts. *Brit J Psychiat* 125:168-174, 1974.
9. Burstein AG et al: Assessment of suicidal risk by psychology and psychiatry trainees. *Arch Gen Psych* 29:792-793, 1973.
10. Cain AC: *Survivors of Suicide*, Springfield, Charles C Thomas, 1972.
11. Chiles JA: Patient reactions to the suicide of a therapist. *Am J Psychother* 28:115-121, 1974.

12. Conrad RD, Kahn MW: An epidemiological study of suicide and attempted suicide among the Papago Indians. *Am J Psychiatry 131:* 69-72, 1974.

13. Dorpat TL: Drug automatism, barbiturate poisoning and suicide behavior. *Arch Gen Psych 31:*216-220, 1974.

14. Drye RC, Goulding RC, Goulding ME: No suicide decisions: Patient monitoring of suicidal risk. *Am J Psychiatry 130:*171-174, 1973.

15. Fabian JJ, Maloney MP, Ward MP: Self-destructive and suicidal behavior in a neuropsychiatric inpatient facility. *Am J Psychiatry 130:*1383-1385, 1973.

16. Flanagan TA, Murphy GE: Body donation and suicide. *Arch Gen Psych 28:*732-734, 1973.

17. Horton PC: The mystical experience as a suicide preventive. *Am J Psychiatry 130:*294-296, 1973.

18. Humphrey JA: The process of suicide: The sequence of disruptive events in the lives of suicide victims. *Dis Nerv Syst 35:*275-277, 1974.

19. Kelly WA: Suicide and psychiatric education. *Amer J Psychiatry 130:*463-468, 1973.

20. Kiev A: Prognostic factors in attempted suicide. *Am J Psychiatry 131:*987-990, 1974.

21. Lester D, Perdue WC: The detection of attempted suicides and murders using the Rorschach. *J Psychiat Res 10:*101-103, 1974.

22. Maltsberger JT, Buie DH: Countertransference hate in the treatment of suicidal patients. *Arch Gen Psych 30:*625-633, 1974.

23. Minkoff K, Bergman L, Beck AT et al: Hopelessness, depression, and attempted suicide. *Amer J Psychiatry 130:*455-459, 1973.

24. Orten JD: A transactional approach to suicide prevention. *J Clin Soc Wk 2:*57-63, 1974.

25. Parkin M: Suicide and culture in Fairbanks. *Psychiatry 37:*60-67, 1974.

26. Paykel ES, Fallowell C, Dressler DM et al: Treatment of suicide attempters. *Arch Gen Psych 31:*487-491, 1974.

27. Pederson AM, Awad GA, Kindler AR: Epidemiological differences between white and nonwhite suicide attempters. *Am J Psychiatry 130:*1071-1076, 1973.

28. Perr IN: Suicide and civil litigation. *J Forensic Sciences 19:*261-266, 1974.

29. Phillips DP: The influence of suggestion on suicide: Substantive and theoretical implications of the Werther Effect. *Am Sociological Rev 39:*340-353, 1974.

30. Resnik HL, Davidson WT, Schuyler D et al: Videotape confrontation after attempted suicide. *Amer J Psychiatry 130:*460-463, 1973.

31. Ripley HS: Suicidal behavior in Edinburgh and Seattle. *Am J Psychiatry 130:*995-1001, 1973.

32. Rose KD, Rosow I: Physicians who kill themselves. *Arch Gen Psych 29:*800-805, 1973.

33. Sandborn DE: Occupation and suicide: A study of two counties in New Hampshire. *Dis Nerv Syst 35:*7-12, 1974.

34. Schwartz DA et al: Treatment of the suicidal character. *Am J Psychother 28:*194-207, 1974.

35. Shneidman ES: Suicide notes reconsidered. *Psychiatry 36:*379-394, 1973.

36. Simpson MA: Female genital self-mutilation. *Arch Gen Psych 29:*808-810, 1973.

37. Siomopoulos V: Repeated self-cutting: An impulse neurosis. *Am J Psychother 28:*85-94, 1974.

38. Slawson PF, Flinn DE, Schuartz DA et al: Legal responsibility for suicide. *Psychiatric Quart 48:*50-64, 1974.

39. Stone M: The parental factor in adolescent suicide. *Int J Child Psychother 2:*163-201, 1973.

40. Tabachnick N: Creative suicidal crises. *Arch Gen Psych* 29:258-263, 1973.
41. Wallace S: *After Suicide*, NY, John Wiley and Sons, 1973.
42. Weissman MM: The epidemiology of suicide attempts. *Arch Gen Psych* 30:737-746, 1974.
43. Weissman MM, Worden JW: Risk-rescue rating in suicide assessment. *Arch Gen Psych* 26:553-560, 1972.
44. Weissman MM et al: Hostility and depression associated with suicide attempts. *Amer J Psychiatry* 130:450-455, 1973.
45. Wold CI, Litman RE: Suicide after contact with a suicide prevention center. *Arch Gen Psych* 28:735-739, 1973.
46. Yamamoto J, Roath M, Litman R: Suicides in the "new" community hospital. *Arch Gen Psych* 28:101-102, 1973.
47. Zung WW, Green RL: Seasonal variation of suicide depression. *Arch Gen Psych* 30:89-91, 1974.

Nonhuman Aggressive Behavior: Trends and Issues

D. CHRIS ANDERSON
J. VICTOR LUPO

This paper is concerned with recent trends and issues in the area of nonhuman aggressive behavior. A comprehensive survey of the research on nonhuman aggression is not possible for several reasons, one being that the number of relevant papers simply is too large to be summarized in the allotted page space. Second, it is doubtful that any single organizational framework could readily integrate the diversity of variables, paradigms, subject populations and different outcomes that characterize the present state of the literature. Nowhere better are these problems of synthesis and organization highlighted than in the opening statements of many that have recently summarized portions of the literature. For relatively recent surveys and analyses of various facets of nonhuman aggression research, the reader is referred to Scott (108,109), Lorenz (82), Carthy and Ebling (27), Eleftheriou and Scott (46), Garattini and Sigg (54), DeReuck and Knight (41), Southwick (116), Cole and Jensen (39) and Knutson (74).

As an alternative to a comprehensive survey, the present paper takes up selected topic areas that have received much recent experimental and theoretical attention. Even this has proven to be a problem. Both the number of areas and the amount and diversity of recent literature within each has made it unfeasible to cover thoroughly all that has been reported. Thus, we have found it expedient to be somewhat arbitrary in the selection of areas to summarize, as well as with the choice of articles that seem especially important within each. We wish to apologize in advance to those whose research may only be partly referenced or, in some cases, regrettably, omitted altogether.

WHAT IS "AGGRESSION"?

It is not unusual in the recent plethora of volumes and texts on the topic of aggression to encounter an initial statement that lists, in a rather awesome manner, recent statistics dealing with the rise in crime in the streets, the atrocities of war, the problems of brutalized children and related indices of social illness. Following this, the reader is often treated to a series of topics that deal variously with children that may (or may not) strike a Bobo Doll, college students that attempt to electrically shock a colleague, restrained monkeys that vigorously bite a proximal rubber hose following electric tail shock, stickleback fish that attack a red oval object, rats that kill mice when housed with the latter over a 24-hour period, and so forth. In addition, some investigators of some of these phenomena may defend their findings as more properly indicative of aggression than alternative approaches (e.g., 37, pp. 42–45). Such can be taken as suggestive of the apparent diversity of situations to which the term "aggression" has been applied.

In addition, some authors have championed the position that there are several kinds of aggression. For example, Moyer (91, pp. 12–14), in revising earlier listings (89,90), appears to envision two basic kinds of aggression: hostile feelings and hostile habits (i.e., instrumental aggression). He further subdivided hostile-feeling aggression into several kinds, namely, predatory, inter-male, fear-induced, maternal, sex-related and irritable. Ulrich, Dulaney, Arnett and Mueller (125, p. 83) and Hutchinson (61, p. 178) seem in agreement with Moyer's classification of aggression into hostile feelings (i.e., aggressive attack coupled with "emotional arousal," e.g., anger) and instrumental aggression (aggression without arousal), but make no further subdivisions. Knutson, however, apparently at least partially concurs with Moyer, and has published data to suggest that different ontogenetic variables can affect different kinds of aggression, and thus can be used to identify one form from the other (74, Ch. 3; 76).

To further complicate the possibility of achieving a univocal usage of the term, many disagree as to the particular ingredients that should be included as part of a definition of aggression. For example, the following have been viewed by some as conditions that are necessary if a given behavior is to be labeled as aggressive: there must be (1) *intention* by the aggressor to do harm or injury (69; 49); (2) *execution* of a particular act or response sequence; (3) *harm* or injury to the target; and (4) *a socially significant target.* While there is disagreement as to how necessary each of these ingredients are, the presence or absence of each has often provided controversy in attempts to label particular behaviors as aggressive. The most inclusive definition has been one that requires the presence of all four elements, namely, *intention, action, harm* and a *social target.* Some, mostly of a biological persuasion, have apparently substituted for the ingredient of "intention" the question of whether or not a given behavior serves a functional or evolutionally adaptive role for a given species in surmounting physical conflict (cf. 44, Ch. 15; 82; 109, p. 683; 115). Otherwise, the latter definitional approach seems somewhat like the more inclusive ones that have often been adopted by many contemporary social psychologists who have engaged more exclusively in an analysis of human aggression.

Less inclusive definitions have included three or fewer of these ingredients. For example, some have considered it sufficient to label an action as aggressive if harm was intended to a social target but no actual injury resulted. An assassin that fired a rifle at a victim and missed, or the unsuccessful attack behavior of a shark on a human victim that was being retrieved into a ship, are examples of this kind of definition.

Other authors have focused more simply on the outcome of an action in order to determine whether it qualified as being aggressive, and have been unconcerned as to the possibility of intention or whether the target was a social one. Studies in which an organism bites a rubber hose to tail shock exemplify this definitional approach. Yet others have been concerned primarily with the specific topographical features of a response and the injury that is "triggered" in the presence of certain features of the target object. Little concern is voiced for the intention of the subject in such a definitional framework.

In spite of these many differences in usage of the term, there nonetheless are also some apparent commonalities. First, all investigators seem to agree that some action or response sequence, whether verbal or nonverbal, must occur as part of the condition(s) that define aggression. From this, it can be seen that the ingredient of "intention-to-harm" per se is not a sufficient (even though many view it as a necessary) defining condition. Second, there appears to be no definition of aggression that is couched solely in terms of the overt movements of an organism, independent of whether intention or harm to a social or nonsocial target resulted from that behavior.

But what can be concluded from this discussion regarding any general or uniform meaning of the term "aggression"? This question is especially cogent for anyone who would undertake a partial survey of the literature. Clearly, before conducting an evaluation of any phenomenon, it is well to begin with an unambiguous statement as to what the phenomenon is and is not. Such a statement has the value of establishing the boundary conditions as to what material should be included and what should be excluded as part of the survey. But how can any solid boundary conditions be located for the term "aggression," since it has been used to label highly diverse situations, which many view as being composed of manifold subdivisions, and on which there is little agreement regarding the ingredients that are necessary for its definition?

The answer to this question depends upon whether it is possible to reconcile these differences in current usage. While a final reconciliation may not be immediately forthcoming, it now seems possible to point in that direction. Note first that most applications of the term have involved certain predilections or predispositions on the part of the user as to what aggression actually is and is not. Typically most investigators have viewed the operations of their experiments only as being indicative of what aggression "really is." It is as if the term were applied to some entity or thing, and that the operations of the experiments that have been performed are but ways of partially revealing this more basic form. As such, the term largely seems to have served a connotative rather than a denotative function for most. Rather than being used simply as a label for a particular set of experimental conditions and measurements, the term instead has frequently been employed as a more encompassing concept. The operational ingredients of any given procedure have been viewed merely as a part or a reflection thereof.

Obviously, if this usage of the term was firmly grounded in empirical demonstration, such would be an entirely proper scientific procedure. If one set of experimental conditions and behavioral measures, labeled as aggression, was empirically shown in the some manner to be related to another quite different set of experimental operations, then some scientific justification would be provided for the application of the same label in both cases. For example, if it were possible empirically to show a relationship between the aggressively labeled performance of college sophomores who electrically shock a colleague when thwarted and the shock-induced hose biting of a monkey, then it would be scientifically proper to apply the label "aggression" to both paradigms. Knutson (74) seems in agreement with this analysis.

Unfortunately, many scientists have not used the term in this manner. Instead of relying upon empirically derived relationships, they have applied the term to a wide diversity of situations on more exclusively, often unclearly articulated, rational bases. Usually, these bases for labeling a particular behavior as aggressive have been anchored in the judgments and the values of the particular experimenter. Aggression is often viewed implicitly as something that can be grasped intuitively. As such, it is often considered analogous to other concepts and features in the world that have, as a primary distinguishing feature, the tendency to *stand out* and literally court a label. Examples of these include "dog," "table," and perhaps various colors and tastes. Each represent sources of differential sensory experience that repeatedly impinge upon all of us. The consistency and the obtrusiveness of these experiences into the daily lives of each of us makes it possible to come to a consensual agreement in labeling such events. Much of the language of common sense consists of names for these objects of direct experience. They need no definition aside from that of listing the observable (experienced) attributes which characterize that object. When asked to explain, for example, what one means by "dog," one generally proceeds by listing the observable attributes of dogs. Thus, a dog means the attributes of being four-legged, covered with hair, having a tail, and a collection of various behavioral qualities. In essence, the term "dog" is a shorthand statement for a combination of other words that denote the attributes of certain kinds of objects or things.

But what set of qualities does one list when asked to report the meaning of the term "aggression"? As indicated, one might list the qualities of harmful intention, the execution of a particular action, whether the act actually was injurious, and the social nature of the target of that action. However, these qualities are not of the same kind as those that would be listed for the concept "dog." Whereas the attribute of four-leggedness can easily be specified through pointing, the presence or absence of a harmful intention cannot be so readily designated. Indeed, to list a harmful intention as a defining attribute of aggression is the equivalent of assuming that the *attribute* of intention and the *object* of aggression can both be easily recognized intuitively, even though neither is firmly nor consistently (reliably) anchored in experience.

But, a little thought will indicate that aggression is not something that *stands out* in the same sense that the concept "child" or "thunder" stands out. Instead, aggression seems to be a feature of the world that must be *carved out*, as it were. It is not some "thing," the properties of which provide universally distinct and consensually recognizable sensory experience. It has no general meaning above and beyond the specific conditions of measurements by which it may be defined. In a sense, the concept of aggression is much like the concepts of, for example, "anxiety" or "motivation." Aggression is a behavioral feature of the world that can be discerned only under certain specified conditions.

In order to more fully illustrate this point, consider any typical aggression experiment. The label of aggression is invariably prescribed, at least implicitly, in terms of two ingredients. One of these is a behavioral measurement of some sort. The other consists of the conditions that are arranged by the investigator so that the measurements can be taken. That is, *a definition of aggression for a particular experiment can always be known in terms of (1) the conditions of a measurement, and (2) the measurement itself.* Illustratively, given an environment of a specified description that contains a female wolf in estrus, an experimenter equipped with certain recording devices may label as aggressive the occurrence of a cluster of behaviors for two proximally located male wolves. These measures might include piloerection on the neck and shoulders, fang baring, and certain vocalizations. In other situation, an experimental psychologist may define as an occurrence of aggressive behavior his observation of a dead mouse in a confined space in which the only other organism is a fully alive rat. To ask whether either measure is really aggression would make little sense in terms of the present discussion. Both have been similarly labeled. To conclude, however, that they were reflections of a more fundamental entity would not be scientifically proper unless it was demonstrated that (1) the variables that influenced one measure had a similar effect on the other, and (2) that these measures correlated in a similar manner with other different dependent variables that also were labeled as "aggressive behaviors."

Berkowitz (18) has provided a good example of this approach in certain of his laboratory studies of human aggressive behavior. He was able to show that exposing college sophomores to the movie *The Champion*, followed by a "thwarting" verbal interchange, produced similar increments in two separate behaviors that independently had been labeled "aggressive." College sophomores both produced higher scores on a paper-and-pencil test (one measure of aggressiveness) and delivered more electric shock to a colleague (the second measure) following the movie and the "thwarting" episode. However, had these two measures not been shown to be influenced by the same manipulation, little justification other than the predisposition of the experimenter would have been supplied for the assumption that each might be a reflection of some more global index termed "aggression."

Unfortunately, many investigators have not seemed to adopt this view when discussing their experimental findings. It has not been unusual for authors to make sweeping integrative statements regarding the implications of their findings for a general understanding of the term "aggression" (e.g., 45, Ch. 5, 7). There seems a clear gap, under this circumstance, between the use of the concept of aggressiveness as a definition-type label that has exclusive reference to a particular set of experimental conditions and the use of the term as an underlying trait-type concept that has a more global "thing-like" connotation. Since few attempts have been made to relate empirically the many different ways in which the label of aggression has been applied, the present source of confusion seems to reside in the fact that the term nevertheless is frequently treated as if such relationships have actually been established.

To summarize, the present argument is that it is improper (premature) to speak of the term "aggression" as a thing or an entity. Instead, the term at best should serve as a label for a particular behavior of an organism in a given circumstance. Used in this manner, it would not be correct to state that an organism evinced "aggression"; instead, it would be more proper to say that under a set of specified conditions, an organism "behaved aggressively." By speaking in this way, it would then always be possible to discern what was meant by aggressiveness for a particular study simply by referring to the conditions of measurement that were reported and the outcome of those measuring operations. This approach has the major advantage of taking one "off the hook" as to any alignment with any particular position as to what aggression "really is." By defining aggressiveness in terms of measuring condition(s) and the measurement itself, it is possible to conduct a thoroughgoing examination of what is meant by the label without any such theoretical allegiance. This would be achieved by an experimental analysis of the boundary circumstances under which the specified behavior(s) does and does not occor.

Once having explored, for a given set of conditions and measurements, those variables that affect the occurrence of that behavior, it is then possible to evaluate the effect of the same variables on other measures that have been labeled as aggressive. Illustratively, assume that the amount of mouse-killing by rats (i.e., labeled as aggressive behavior for the set of conditions specified for such studies) was found to fluctuate as a function of the duration of prior peer-group isolation rearing. The question then could be posed as to whether other measures of behavior labeled as aggressive were similarly influenced by the variable of isolation rearing. Although unfeasible because of practical consideratons, it "in theory" would be possible to then question whether, for example, a college sophomore would be more or less likely to depress a button to shock a colleague following thwarting (i.e., a different label of aggressiveness) if reared in isolation (perhaps approximated by comparing students raised as single children, i.e., in relative peer-group isolation, with those raised as part of a large family of brothers and sisters). Experiments of this type would provide the scientifically necessary empirical foundation for those that would conclude that certain independent variables that influence one measure of aggressiveness exerted a similar effect upon other different measures that have been similarly labeled. When two measures are affected in the same way by the same independent variable, one can tentatively conclude that a similar "process" is involved. If comparable manipulations produced similar consequences for an even larger number of behaviors that had been labeled as aggressive, it could then be concluded that these different indices may reflect a more "fundamental" behavioral phenomenon termed "aggression."

This discussion provides the background for our organization of the following survey. Were this survey to have been organized in terms of the kinds of variables that have been studied, it could be taken as acquiescence to the notion of "aggression-as-an-entity." Often, the kind of variable that has been studied has been confounded with a particular way (i.e., experimental paradigm) that aggressiveness has been defined. To classify the outcomes of such research in terms of the effects of different variables could thus be taken as tacit approval that the different measurement procedures that have been used are but reflections of the same phenomenon. The present survey was organized instead in terms of the general experimental procedures (i.e., paradigms) that have been used to study nonhuman aggressive behavior. Even here, graded differences in methods have blurred the distinctions between various paradigms. Nonetheless, the present survey of nonhuman aggressive behavior was organized in terms of the (1) measurement conditions involved, and (2) the measurements that have been taken as a way to distinguish the various paradigms from one another.

Much of the current conceptualization regarding aggressive behavior derives from the current writings of biologically oriented behaviorists and/or ethologists. Generally, these investigators have employed natural and seminatural conditions in order to gather observations about the aggressive behavior of organisms. The first section takes up some of the notions, methods and findings of this research strategy. Following this, various laboratory approaches are discussed. These include procedures that have entailed the explicit introduction of antecedent and/or consequent stimulus manipulations as part of the conditions that provide for the measurement of aggressive behaviors (i.e., pain-elicited, contingent-reward, and schedule-induced paradigms), and those procedures that have been used mostly to examine genetic and ontogenetic variables (i.e., mouse-mouse, rat-mouse, and related interspecies aggression paradigms).

REPRESENTATIVE PARADIGMS USED TO STUDY NONHUMAN AGGRESSIVE BEHAVIOR

1. *Aggressive behavior in the natural (and seminatural) setting.* Contemporary ethological theory seems to have had a decided influence upon the data collected by its adherents. Thus, it has been difficult to separate data from theory in any exposition of the work in this field. The present survey unfortunately, is no exception in this regard. Perhaps Lorenz (82), Ardrey (6) and Eibl-Eibesfelt (44, 45) have had the greatest influence in both popularizing and promulgating the current ethological viewpoint regarding both nonhuman and human aggression. The basic starting point of the ethological position on aggression is that it refers to a class of more or less instinctively controlled behaviors that, for each species, can be identified by the form (i.e., topography) of the responses involved, the stimuli that "release" such reactions, and their effect upon the environment. Aggressive behavior typically is discussed primarily in connection with two types of activities: namely, (1) pre-attack, ritualized responses, and (2) the actual attack reactions that can occur between members of the same species. Interspecies predatory behavior is generally excluded in ethological discussions of aggression. Eibl-Eibesfeldt (44) thus has noted that ". . . these two forms must be clearly distinguished. Intra- and inter-specific behaviors often employ quite different behavior sequences: a cat attacking a mouse behaves quite differently than it does when attacking a rival. These two basically different behavior patterns can be activated through electric stimulation of quite different parts of the brain.'

On the grounds that intraspecies aggression is perhaps the most pervasive of all the kinds of behavior that occur throughout the animal kingdom (ethologists have observed aggression for all species, with the possible exception of those animals that are not equipped for attack, such as amphibians, although Scott (108), reported nonspecific attack behavior between frogs), ethologists see the presence of such behavior as being of central evolutionary significance. As instinctively based behavior, aggression serves the function of distributing conspecifics more widely apart over the geographic terrain. This is seen to accomplish more effective utilization of extant resources. Intraspecific aggression thus serves the vital function of "distance-maintaining."

This relationship between aggression and distance-maintaining behavior has been integrally linked to territoriality. Ethologists contend (44) that an animal that has acquired no territory often cannot breed. Territorial behavior, which is seen to consist largely of aggressive responses, thus is viewed as an important mechanism of population control. Further, by maintaining a territory, overpopulation cannot occur to the point where the essentials of life are exhausted. Pressures from neighboring members of a species can also lead to less favorable areas being developed and populated. Territoriality can thus be seen to aid in the preservation of a species, since such areas can supply reserves during the resettlement of more favored areas if the normal population has been decimated by epidemics or other catastrophies. This distribution function, served by territorial or distance-maintaining aggressive behavior, can also apply in the case of animals that live in closed groups. In such cases, it is the groups that exercise pressure on one another to ensure that each keeps its distance.

Ethiologists point to a general tendency of vertebrate males to fight with their own kind in the mating season, as a further advantage of aggressive behavior. The stronger and healthier vertebrate is thus selected for reproduction. This is seen as a particularly important factor in cases where the males are responsible for the defense of the young. As an example, the sea lions of the Galápagos Islands are reported to swim up and down the coastline chasing back the young from their own harem that go too far out into the sea. Because of the presence of sharks, this is conceived as protective aggression. The stronger of the lions is seen as best suited for this task.

A considerable number of examples of territorial aggression have been listed in support of its focal place in nature. Thus, ethologists point to free-living monkey groups in which territoriality is seen as a widespread characteristic (26). Here, members of different groups threaten and fight one another. Wilson (133) studied such fights in rhesus monkeys on Cayo Santiago. In these conflicts, the groups line up opposite one another as if part of an organized tournament. Several females from one group then rush forward in apparent attack, fight briefly, and return. Females that waited then rush forward to continue the fight. Intraspecific fighting between groups also has been observed for Norway rats (119). Aggression-maintenance behavior of territory has been reported for such diverse species as reef-dwelling fish (122), large birds such as herons (50), hamsters, antelope (130), mice and rats

(43), insects of various kinds, and a wide variety of other organism-types.

Because of the potential danger for a given species, ethologists contend that aggressive behavior cannot go uninhibited. Once territorial preservation is accomplished, the aggressive behavior that was involved must be terminated. Ethologists have introduced the notion of instinctually based, aggression-inhibiting mechanisms (cf. 82) to account for this feature. Actually, there are two ways in which the destructive influences of nonspecific aggression are checked. One is through pre-attack threat, which can often serve to curb actual physical contact. Examples of the kinds of data used in support of this view are the observations of Ellefson (47). He observed gibbons over a 21-month period, and found that the conflicts between two or more groups involved little direct physical contact. Instead, the adult mules engaged in much gesturing, vocalizing loudly and chasing that could span over an hour but never entail direct contact. Similarly, Washburn (131) has reported that the greatest majority of conflict between nonhuman primates is ritualized, and is designed to protect the young, elevate social position, or gain access to food, grooming or sex. Usually the conflict starts with a slight gesture. If that does not work, more gestures follow, including facial expressions, piloerection, movements of the ears, scalp and tail. Finally, the dominant animal may move threateningly toward the other. Washburn (131) noted that the vast majority of intraspecific primate aggression occurs in the form of "bluffing," all of which may be taken to suggest the presence of a pre-physical-contact, aggression-curtailing mechanism.

But how is destruction prevented when physical contact occurs? Lorenz (82) and Eibl-Eibesfeldt (44) have noted that occurrence of nonspecific stereotyped behavior patterns that are different from those that occur for contraspecific physical conflict. An example of this has been cited in the intraspecific aggression between horned animals. Walther (129) contends that such behavior is of a different nature than when a horned subject must defend against a predator. Whereas in the latter case the horns are lowered so as to wound through puncturing, intraspecific fighting typically involves head butting and other far less lethal posturings (129). Other forms of inhibition through contact involve escape behaviors, such as can occur rather quickly after several biting attacks by one hamster upon another, or via morphological adaptations that ensure that subjects may not seriously harm one another as in the case of the manner in which fiddler crabs "grasp" one another during conflict (1, 32).

The inhibition of aggression is seen to be "triggered" by certain key stimuli. One "releaser" for curbing further aggression is the so-called "submission" posture. Lorenz is widely cited for his account of defeated wolves "turning off" their assailants by exposing the jugular vein. Much as been made of the significance of this posture in terms of its ontogenetic and evolutionary importance (44). However, Lorenz's interpretation recently has come under major attack. For example, Barnett (16) has argued that so-called "submission" signals have highly variable effects on the responses of foes. Both Kuo (77) and Schenkel (107) have made convincing arguments to the effect that attempts to forestall further attack more likely take the form of displays of counteraggression or escape, and that Lorenz may have mistaken his observation of submissiveness for an actual preparatory-challenging posture by the attacked subject.

Both the methods, data and theory of contemporary ethology have received rather solid criticism. For example, the general concept of instinct-released, specific behavior patterns has been soundly assailed on both logical and empirical grounds (79, 87). With regards to the instinctual basis of aggression in both human and nonhuman species, both Montagu (88) and Bandura (14) have marshaled a sizable body of evidence to suggest that the data of Ardrey (6) were misleading and the interpretations of Lorenz (82) overly extravagant.

By way of discussing certain of the limitations of the theory and data presented from the ethological viewpoint, consider some of the following problems. First, no solid reason (cf. 27, 44) is given for labeling intraspecific fighting as aggression and intraspecific conflict as something else. If, for example, evolutionary grounds are given for such a distinction, convincing reasons why one form of attack should be more evolutionally significant than another simply have not been forthcoming. Indeed, at least as strong an argument can be made for the adaptive value of predatory attack as that suggested by the ethologist for intraspecific conflict. Consider, for example, the statement of Kenny (70) on the significance of predatory attack by the shark: ". . . like any predator, it may improve the prey animals by taking misfits out of the breeding stock." Such logic obviously can apply to the effects of any predator upon the genetic constituency of the population(s) upon which it preys.

Consider some of the problems that are posed by the ethologist's lack of separation between data and theory for his collection of measurements of aggressive behavior in the natural setting. As noted, aggressive behaviors need not involve actual contact with a foe. They can be response patterns that constitute ritualized, "threatlike" behaviors. Unfortunately, very little specification has been given as to the exact nature of a "threatlike" response pattern and how to identify it. This may well explain why it was possible for Lorenz and Schenkel to attribute essentially opposite meanings to apparently similar response patterns in connection with the submission-inhibitory vs. preparatory-attack behaviors of a "defeated" wolf.

Actual physical contact can also qualify as aggressive behavior. However, even here there is a certain lack of clarity. Contact can occur in a variety of contexts and ways, including those that sometimes may be affilial in nature. Obviously, then, only certain kinds of contact qualify as aggressive. These variously have been described as head butting, pushing and shoving, tail fanning, biting, and so forth. But since many of these descriptive phrases could also be used in connection with "playing" and other non-aggressive response categories, additional criteria for the identification of an aggressive behavior are needed. Such criteria have been slow in forthcoming. This difficulty of specification is compounded by the fact that ethologists typically have emphasized the nondestructive nature of intraspecific physical conflict. This precludes the identification of an aggressive response solely in terms of its harmful or injuring consequence. It seems clear that the ethologist has something more in mind when he labels a behavior as aggressive than, simply, the patterned response sequence of an organism. It is not clear, however, what these additional determining ingredients are.

Contemporary ethologists have viewed their data as theoretically suggestive of the presence of certain instinctlike organizing forces in the CNS. Lorenz (81), Tinbergen (121), Hess (57) and Eibl-Eibesfeldt (44) have all elaborated on the assumption that the occurrence of aggressive behaviors can be understood in terms of the interplay of key environmental events and the genetico-physiological makeup of the organism. Aggressive behavior that is characteristic of a given species is seen to have, as its core, a genetically preformed, centrally blueprinted physiological substrate. Releasing stimuli serve as primary "triggering" or activating sources for CNS-blueprinted aggressive behaviors, although an excess of aggressive energy can also purportedly cause spontaneous behavioral discharge (81). A "releaser" releases from the CNS what has been termed action-specific energy (ASE). This CNS structure thus provides the source of energy for an aggressive response pattern as well as supplying the response pattern per se. Ethologists have made much of what they observe to be highly invariant, stereotyped components of the aggressive behavior of a given species. It is this component of any aggressive response sequence, termed a fixed action pattern (FAP), that is seen to be the portion of behavior that is genetically blueprinted and CNS-directed.

The variability in aggressive-response displays between members of the same species is due to those modifiable components of behavior that are possible for almost all animals. The ethologist does not deny the possibility of an associative or acquired basis of behavior, but seems disposed to the bias that the more basic component of any aggressive response sequence is (1) innate or unlearned, (2) unmodifiable by experience, (3) independent of maintaining stimuli, (4) invariant in form and, upon occasion, (5) capable of occurrence in the absence of a triggering event (87). The latter stipulation underlies the ethologist's concept of an "aggression drive." As underscored by Eibl-Eibesfeldt (45), "A noteworthy feature of intraspecific aggression is its spontaneity. Aggressive behavior is by no means simply released by specific key stimuli; what we observe, rather, is that animals that have been unable to fight for a long time will grow steadily more ready to fight, clearly on the basis of drive mechanisms peculiar to them. These pugnaciously disposed animals will then actively seek out a releasing stimulus situation which will permit them to work out the fighting drive evidently building up within them." He stated further (44, p. 71): ". . . many animals are preprogrammed in such a way that they react to particular signals with aggressive behavior patterns. The basic patterns of motor sequences thus activated are inherited as fixed action patterns. Fighting behavior, furthermore, is not always purely reactive. The spontaneity and appetitive behavior for fighting which are demonstrable even in socially inexperienced animals lead one to suppose the existence of innate drive mechanisms."

Moltz (87) has shown that the concept of the FAP is untenable on logical, definitional and empirical grounds, and Lehrman (79) and Hinde (58) have convincingly discussed the absence of neurophysiological evidence to indicate that functional behavioral activities generate their own motivational energy which builds up in the absence of releasers. These criticisms are not to be taken, however, as an indictment of the potential that may be derived from the naturalistic study of aggressive behavior. There is much to be said for the wealth of anecdotal observation that has been gathered by biologically oriented students of behavior. Many have made convincing arguments as to the efficacy of the study of nonhuman aggression in the natural setting. However, many also seem to agree that laboratory-controlled research provides a setting that is more ideally suited to an investigation of systematically manipulated variables upon aggressive behavior. The problem is that of artificiality. Are the behaviors that have been studied in the natural setting also available for study under tightly controlled laboratory conditions? While several authors have attempted to address this issue (cf. 37), much of the jusitification thus far supplied as to whether naturally occurring and laboratory-inspired physical contact are the same has largely been of a rational rather than empirical nature. Notwithstanding the merits and the limitations of these arguments, a number of laboratory paradigms nonetheless have been developed to evaluate nonhuman aggressive behavior. One such paradigm is that of pain-elicited fighting behavior.

2. *Pain-elicited fighting.* In 1939 O'Kelly and Steckle (98) showed that when two rodents were caged with each other in close proximity, the presentation of a brief and painful electric shock was correlated with apparent vigorous fighting behavior. Over two decades later Ulrich and Azrin (124) repeated the basic features of this study with essentially the same outcome. The findings of Ulrich and Azrin (124) seem to have prompted literally dozens of follow-up experiments, many of which have duplicated most of the procedural features of this earlier work.

The conditions requisite to the measurement of aggressive behavior in this situation have usually included the presence of an observer-scorer who has been given prior training in cataloguing the behavior to be measured. The observer initially is instructed as to what kinds of behavior are to be scored, and then is given practice with the use of the scoring procedure. Usually, a fighting response has been defined in terms of the extent of physical contact made by a pair of adversary pigeons or rats. If the subjects are rodents, biting and vigorous flagelation of one another by the paws sometimes has been a major part of the fight-scoring criteria. In order to correlate and tally on a scoresheet the occurrence or nonoccurrence of such responses, the observer typically is cued by a light or some other stimulus that indicates that the electric shock has been delivered to the subjects.

Many of the pain-induced fighting procedures have included temporally subdivided "blank" or shock-free durations that correspond to the periods when shock ordinarly would have been presented. The observer will usually continue to record the occurrence of fight responses during "blank" periods in an attempt to discern whether the latter have become associated with apparatus noises. Another measure that sometimes has been collected is "posturing." Posturing is defined as an upright positioning of the two subjects facing each other. The occurrence of posturing between shock presentations or during "blank" trials has proved only of marginal utility in most of this kind of research.

The non-automated nature of this procedure has prompted many to evaluate the reliability of the measurement technique. Pre-experimental reliability coefficients have often been calculated on the basis of independent observations made by multiple observers of the same pairs of subjects. Often two or more observers separately tally the occurrence of fighting and/or other responses that occur for a series of shock and nonshock (blank) presentations. The percentage of occasions that produce interobserver agreement and nonagreement are then computed. Although the reported interobserver coefficients are high within laboratories (often in excess of 90 percent), different laboratories have reported wide discrepancies in the percentage of observed fighting behaviors when highly similar procedures and apparatuses were employed (cf. Ulrich, Hutchinson and Azrin, (126), for a partial discussion of this issue, and Follick and Knutson (52), for additional reasons for discrepant percentages).

Some have attempted to quantify laboratory fighting with automated procedures as a way to circumvent such large between-laboratory scoring discrepancies. Azrin, Hutchinson and Hake (11) restrained target animals in devices that resulted in switch closures when attacked. In addition, various inanimate devices have been used as targets for attack, including a rubber tube attached to a pneumatic switch in order to record the number of bites (62). This technique has mostly been used with small monkeys. This latter procedure has been criticized because of the use of a nonsocial target. In order to avert this objection, the "bite-hose" measurement technique has been employed in several studies that have involved variables with a known influence upon dyadic, pain-elicited fighting. The effects of most such variables have been the same on both dependent measures. Ulrich et al. (125) thus concluded that "Most squirrel monkeys will attack such a hose functionally in much the same way as they will attack each other, and in the way that a rat will attack a rat or a pigeon will attack a pigeon."

One measure of the utility of a paradigm is whether it can be employed to evaluate a wide variety of variables. If scientific success can be measured in this manner, then the pain-elicited fighting procedure has been a fruitful one. Illustratively, variations in a wide variety of aversive environmental conditions have been investigated in terms of correlated increases in the percentage of fighting behaviors. Thus, the delivery of a physical blow (7), foot or tail shock (13, 102, 103, 124), painful brain stimulation (105), intense air puffs (126), and an abrupt and intense auditory stimulus (64) have been shown to produce attack behavior. Each of the latter stimulus conditions qualify as aversive in that, if given an opportunity, subjects very likely would have escaped from them in other situations. Indeed, Azrin, Hutchinson and Hake (11) and Ulrich (123) found that if actually given the opportunity to escape or avoid certain of these events, subjects would do so rather than engage in fighting.

The latter stimuli can be distinguished from other events in that it is their onset that affects fighting behavior. Neither the continued tenure nor the offset of these events produces as much correlated attack behavior. There also are circumstances, however, in which stimulus offset can produce increments in fighting. Again, these situations can be described as aversive in character because each independently has been shown capable of producing escape behaviors. Thus, the removal of food, water or an attractive sexual object from a hungry, thirsty or sexually aroused organism has been correlated with increments in fighting behavior (10, 19). Further, Emely, Hutchinson and Brannan (48) found that morphine withdrawal resulted in increased fighting.

The environmental events thus far discussed and which produce correlated increases in fighting can be described as unconditioned stimuli. Prior experience with them is not necessary to produce the observed attack (and the strong autonomic responses that accompany them). However, initially neutral stimuli that have been paired with these unconditioned events can similarly produce correlated increases in fighting. Vernon and Ulrich (127) paired the onset of a light repeatedly with shock-elicited fighting. After extensive pairings, the light was occasionally presented without shock. The percentage of fighting responses during the tenure of the light stimulus was higher than those that occurred by chance alone. Termination of an initially neutral stimulus that previously had been paired with food can similarly result in a correlated increase in fighting behavior (63, 65).

How pervasive is pain-elicited fighting? A wide variety of species have been subjected to either the onset or to the offset of stimulus events that produce fighting behavior in laboratory rodents, pigeons and monkeys. Although variable in magnitude, fighting has been reported throughout much of the phyletic span of the animal kingdom; from arthropods and insects (crayfish, stinging wasps), through Reptillia and Aves (snakes, pigeons), to primates (from various species of New World monkeys to man). These data are summarized by Hutchinson (61, p. 168). As pervasive as these data seem, Bandura (14, p. 156) has noted that they do not invariantly support a nativistic aggression theory of "push-button" control by aversive stimuli. He indicated, for example, that aversive stimuli did not produce much fighting in at least two species primarily noted for aggressiveness in the natural setting, namely, Siamese fighting fish and fighting cocks. Further, shock also has sometimes failed to produce fighting in certain docile species (124).

It should be noted, however, that both Bandura's (14) arguments, as well as any others raised in connection with the development of a general theory of aversion-based aggression, can be considered cogent only if one adopts a "generalist" view of "aggression-as-thing." But such viewpoints would make little sense for a more operational analysis of "aggressiveness," as defined in terms of behavior measurements within a particular paradigm. Until it can be shown that those variables that affect pain-elicited aggressiveness similarly affect a variety of other behaviors that also have been labeled as aggressive, notions about any general aversion theory, or whether or not it really is general, seem premature.

The effects of a number of stimulus parameters on the relative frequency of fighting have been investigated. In most instances, these parameters have been investigated in connection with the effects of both stimulus onset and offset. In general, increases in intensity, duration and the repetition of such events have resulted in increases in the relative rate of fighting behavior, as measured either in terms of the "vigor" (force, intensity) of physical contact, the duration of the attack, and/or the absolute or relative frequency of fighting.

Although not always the case, many of the pain-elicited fighting phenomena have been evaluated within the framework of an operant methodology (cf. 112). The general experimental design has been an ABA approach in which (A) an initial *baseline* performance rate of the response to be studied is measured, followed by (B) an introduction of the condition(s) designed to promote *correlated increases* in the rate of the measured behavior, and then followed by (C) a *reversal procedure* in which the aggression-maintaining stimulus conditions are removed. Thus, the behavior obtained during the initial so-called "blank" trials of the pain-fighting paradigm conforms to a baseline-recording session (Period A). Presentation of the on- or offset of an antecedent stimulus and the concomitant recorded increase in the rate of fighting conforms to the experimental manipulation (Period B). Occasionally, periods in which the antecedent stimulus is removed are given (i.e., Period A). The observed rate of behavior correspondingly decreases, often in a precipitious fashion. Justification thereby is provided for the conclusion that some aspect(s) of the antecedent stimulus condition of period B is the critical determinant of fighting.

Modifications of this ABA procedure have been employed. Illustratively, a *multiple baseline procedure* has occasionally been used in which more than one response has been measured coincidentally with each stimulus. presentation. If the antecedent stimulus influences only one of the two response baselines, then an added conclusion can be drawn—namely, that the stimulus condition selectively influenced the particular *stimulus-response contingency* under study. When a multiple-response baseline was employed in the pain-elicited fighting paradigm and one of the responses was an attack and the other an escape-from-pain reaction, subjects differentially escaped rather than fought (80). Under conditions in which the escape response required "social confrontation," electric shock provoked some fighting. But successful escape quickly displaced the attack reaction and fighting reappeared only when escape became impossible (11, 134). Further, Knutson (73) has shown that in an environment that was not optimal for attack, even close social contact did not provoke fighting over escape behavior.

These data suggest that aversive stimuli do not invariantly (i.e., reflexively) provoke attack behavior. Indeed, it could be argued that the so-called fighting responses observed by Azrin, Ulrich, Hutchinson and colleagues actually may be some form of escape and/or avoidance-of-pain behavior, at least when antecedent-stimulus onset is involved. Related to the revelation that fighting is not the invariant, reflexive outcome of pain are the findings of Powell and Creer (103), Payne et al. (102), Maier, Anderson, and Lieberman (83), Knutson and Hynan (75), Powell, Francis, Francis, and Schneideman (104), and Anderson, Lupo, Cunningham and Madden (5), all of whom have shown that various kinds of prior experiences, both with aversive and nonaversive stimulation, can markedly attenuate the fighting behavior normally produced by shock onset.

3. *Instrumental aggressive behavior—non-hostile aggressiveness?* As noted by Ulrich et al. (125), experimental focus upon responses that are stimulus-induced constitutes a departure from the traditional operant research strategy. They view the fighting responses that are measured in the pain-fighting paradigms as being closely akin to what has been termed *respondents* by Skinner (113). More traditionally, operant procedures have been used to study the development and the maintenance of behaviors that occur in connection with correlated consequences or, more commonly, reinforcers. The question can thus be asked whether attacklike behavior, such as the kind described in previous paragraphs, can be established and maintained by an operant response-reinforcement contingency method. This could entail the use of a response-shaping procedure in which a reinforcer was made available for the occurrence of any pattern of behavior that resembled, at least superficially, the physical-attack response that is elicited by pain. Thus, food reward or pleasurable brain stimulation might be delivered to an appropriately motivated subject for a hose-biting response, or for physical contact by the paws and the mouth with another con- or contra specific, or for some similar behavior. A variation on this procedure might be to use the offset of a negative or aversive stimulus as the reinforcing event for the occurrence of one of these behaviors. This latter procedure would conform to Miller's (86) pioneering report of instrumental attack by two rats to escape shock.

Hutchinson (61) has summarized those situations in which the onset of a rewarding stimulus or the offset of an aversive one has been used successfully both to increase the frequency of and to maintain attack behavior. The reinforcing stimuli that have been used successfully, classified respectively in terms of reward-onset or aversive-offset effects, to train attack behavior include the delivery of food (8), pleasurable brain stimulation (118) and target contact per se (12) as reward-onset, and the removal from conspecific attack (111, 9), tail shock (11), or from contraspecific attack (61, p. 177) as aversion-offset conditions.

One major difference between rewarded and stimulus-induced attack responses is that the latter are invariantly accompanied by a host of ANS changes. Some of these ANS changes include the occurrence of vocal and facial responses that can be said to resemble "anger." In contrast, attack behaviors that have been established instrumentally are not accompanied by comparable emotional changes (4). This difference might be taken as support for Moyer's (91) distinction between hostile feelings (i.e., stimulus-induced attack?) and hostile habits (instrumentally mediated attack?).

Ulrich et al. (125) have pointed to the possible close association between stimulus-induced fighting and instrumentally established responses. This interrelationship may have been shown in a laboratory demonstration in which subjects that did not engage in pain-induced attack behavior were subsequently trained instrumentally to evince fighting responses. The experimental design entailed an initial demonstration that the monkeys would not engage in shock-induced biting on a proximally located hose (Period A). Subjects then were food-deprived and reinforced (i.e., response-shaped) to bite the hose for food (Period B). The biting response was placed on an intermittent reward schedule until stable responding occurred. Training was then stopped, the subjects were given *ad libitum* food, and then returned to the experimental chamber, where biting could occur in the absence of further food reward (extinction). Once the monkeys no longer bit the bar, they were repeatedly given brief tail shocks (Period A). Although they previously showed no attack behavior to shock, they now regularly bit the hose. This demonstration seems to indicate that aggressive behavior can be established by one set of conditions, and then can be amplified and maintained by another different set of circumstances.

4. *Schedule-induced aggressive behavior.* Azrin, Hutchinson and Hake (10) discovered that indices of aggressive behavior by pigeons increased immediately following extinction of an rewarded response. Thompson and Bloom (120) also showed this phenomenon for domestic rats. This extinction-produced fighting paradigm has been

seen by some as being analogous to the experimental conditions that characterize the study of pain-induced attack. The abrupt transition from the stimulus conditions of food reinforcement to those of nonreward (viz., extinction) can be taken as being equivalent to the onset of an aversive event. The notion of abrupt food removal as being unpleasant is not inconsistent with the many findings of Amsel regarding the behavioral effects of nonreward (2, 3, 4). A direct demonstration that extinction can be aversive was shown by Daly (33). She reported that animals will show persistent escape behavior from conditions that have been associated with an abrupt reward-nonreward transition. The extinction-produced fighting results of Azrin et al. (10) could thus be viewed as but the addition of yet another index of the aversive consesquences of frustrative nonreward. Moreover, such an analysis is consistent with the frustration-aggression hypothesis of Dollard, Doob, Miller, Mowrer and Sears (42).

Simply stated, the frustration-aggression hypothesis is that interference with goal-directed activity can be labeled as frustrating. In turn, the latter (i.e., "being frustrated") can serve as a source of motivation for behavior that can injure a person (or the thing) that appears to function as an obstacle. Berkowitz (17) has already noted that the data of Azrin et al. (10) indicated support for the frustration-aggression hypothesis. In addition, it has been suggested that certain schedules of reinforcement may also supply frustration-produced unpleasantness because of intermingled periods of reward and nonreward. The possible presence of aversiveness, induced by the frustration of embedded periods of nonreward within a rewarding context, may have aggressive-behavior-eliciting properties. Daly (34) has supplied solid evidence that rats will escape from the conditions that have been associated with an intermittent reward schedule.

Gentry (55) concomitantly examined the aggression-producing properties of an extinction procedure with that evoked by a reinforcement-scheduling procedure. The basic procedure involved initial exposure of two pigeons to each other prior to training one of the birds to peck a key on a fixed ratio (FR) schedule of reinforcement. Following training to peck the key on a FR 50 (i.e., reward was given following each "set" of 50 consecutive responses), the second bird (which served as a target subject) was reintroduced into the situation. FR scheduling continued, and the number of attack responses was recorded again. Following several sessions with this procedure, the pecking key was taped over, and the reinforcement mechanism was made inoperative. Attack responses were measured during this period of non-reinforcement. Finally, the entire procedure was repeated.

Table I.

The total frequency of attack responses for no-reinforcement and FR 50 conditions (from Gentry, W.C., *Journal of the Experimental Analysis of Behavior*, 1968, *11*, 813-817, p. 815).

Subject Pair	No. Reinf.	FR-50	No. Reinf.	FR-50
1	25	1888	85	299
2	555	6780	345	4521
3	0	85	0	95

Gentry's (55) procedure thus followed an ABAB design. Attack responses between two birds was measured in the absence of reward (Period A), during a period when a FR schedule of reinforcement was in effect (Period B), again during a nonreinforcement period (Period A), and then finally during a period when the same schedule was again in effect (Period B). Table I (taken from Gentry, 55, p. 815) summarizes the frequency of attack responses for each of three pigeons during the respective nonreinforcement (A periods) and intermittent reinforcement conditions (B periods). While some attack behaviors occurred during the nonreinforcement periods, this rate of fighting was no greater following exposure to the FR schedule than prior to it. However, the rate of attack increased precipitously during the tenure of the FR schedule. Gentry (55) reported that most attacks occurred immediately following the delivery of the reinforcer (this period has been termed the "post-reinforcement pause").

In a similar study, Hutchinson et al. (63) trained squirrel monkeys to press a lever for food on several FR schedules, during which time it was possible for each to bite a proximally located rubber hose. Biting consistently occurred during postreinforcement pauses and during the early portions of the response sequence following the last reward. In addition, there was a correlated increase in biting frequency when the requirements of the FR schedule were increased from an FR-2 (i.e., reinforcement following every second response) to an FR-45 requirement. Higher FR schedules also resulted in more biting during extinction than did lower requirements. Knutson (72) has reported a similar finding, as have Cole and Parker (30) using pigeons. However, Hymowitz (66), using rats, reported only marginal attack behavior on high-requirement FR schedules.

Cherek, Thompson and Heistad (28), in a somewhat more complicated procedure, attempted to demonstrate the differential aversiveness of longer intervals between reinforcements on an fixed-interval (FI) schedule of food reward (i.e., the first response after a fixed period of time is reinforced). In extending the interval between reinforced responses for pecking one of two keys, they showed that pigeons also would increase pecking on a second key in order to attack a target subject. Pecking rate and attack frequency were a positive function of the duration between food rewards when the interval value of the reinforcement schedule was varied from one minute to 5 minutes. Responding on the target was not maintained in the absence of an intermittent schedule of food presentation for pecking on the alternative key. In addition, pecking to obtain the target bird occurred almost exclusively during the postreinforcement pause of the FI schedule. The findings of Cherek et al. (20) were similar to those of Flory (51), who discovered that when food reward was presented *independently of behavior* at fixed intervals, attack responses invariantly occurred during the food-absent interval.

Rilling and Caplan (106) measured aggressive behavior in a study that combined interval-based food reward scheduling with periods of extinction. Pigeons were trained to peck on a variable-interval (VI) schedule of 30 seconds (i.e., the *average* period between rewarded responses was 30 seconds) when the key was green. It was further possible to train the pigeons not to peck the key when it was dark in such a manner that this differential responding to green and not to black was accomplished without, in most cases, a single error. Once differential responding was established, an attack object (a target bird) was made continuously available. During training, the rate of target attack in the presence of the dark key was higher for each pigeon than was the operant attack level before training. Thereafter, attack did not decrease during forty-five sessions of discrimination training. Rilling and Caplan (106) also found that reinforcement during presentation of the green stimulus was a determinant of the attack during extinction because removal of the reinforcer eventually eliminated attack during extinction.

5. *Other laboratory analyses of aggressive behavior: studies of mice and rats.* The studies summarized below differ from the preceding experiments in that (1) less focus is given to the specific antecedent and/or consequent controlling stimulus conditions of the fighting environment, and (2) between-subject rather than within-subject designs have been employed more frequently. In addition, the following experiments have frequently involved a graded-scoring procedure to measure aggressiveness, such as the one employed by Lagerspetz (78, pp. 40-41). Illustratively, the latter is a seven-point scale that presumably reflects gradations of aggressive performance, from relative docility to vigorous attack.

Scott (108, 109), consistent with other biologically oriented behaviorists, preferred the phrase "agonistic behaviors" as a substitute for the term "aggression" in his 1966 survey of the literature dealing with rats and mice. Furthermore, he attempted to relate the conspecific fighting behaviors of these species to a more global system (i.e., agonistic behaviors) of which fighting was only a component pattern. This more global system was described as being composed of response patterns that served the common function of "adaptation to situations involving physical conflict between members of the same species (109, p. 683)."

The variables of interest in the present section have most often been concerned with the genetic composition of the subject and with developmental history (ontogenetic variables) as they relate to fighting behavior. Ontogenetic variables have included the effects of early handling, peer group social interactions, prior exposure to various "stressors," and manipulations of the maternal object as each may determine subsequent aggressive behavior.

The mouse has been an ideal subject for an analysis of the genetic mechanisms of aggression because of its rapid proliferation. Highly inbred strains can be produced quickly. It has thus been possible to select mice that exhibit a particular phenotype (i.e., a measurable "trait"), and systematically inbreed them with one another in order to maximize the appearance and magnitude of the characteristics in question. Through sibling intermating over a sufficient number of generations (usually, twenty is regarded to be an acceptable number), it has been possible to approach a condition of genetic homogeneity with regard to a wide variety of behavioral and morphological characteristics. "Genetic homogeneity" refers to the notion that each mouse will be genetically like every other mouse except for sex chromosomes. In essence, such inbreeding procedures are tantamount to an explicit "magnification" of particular genotypes. When accomplished, members of succeeding strains will be sufficiently genetically alike so as to provide an experimenter with a preparation that remains virtually unchanged from one study to the next. The strains of mice that typically have been used in studies of aggressive behavior have been designated BALB/c, C57BL/6, DBA/2, C3H/J, A/He. These strains respectively have been found to be representative of a rather wide range of aggressive performances (cf. 117).

Mouse-mouse and rat-rat aggressive behavior of the kind discussed in this section typically is studied through placement of the subjects in some sort of fighting chamber. Aggression-training has often been given by initially "dangling" a docile male conspecific by the tail in front of a trainee. Approach by the trainee is followed by dragging and pulling away the "dangled" mouse. Through a series of exploratory episodes and concurrent "dragging-away" procedures, rather vigorous fighting has been reported, for example, for C57BL/10 mice (108). Until a recent study by Cairns and Milakovich (22), such training has been viewed as a necessary prerequisite for fighting. Measurement of fighting has usually involved observers who, armed with a recording technique either identical with or somewhat like that of Lagerspetz (78), tally the number and the magnitude of aggressive encounters within a specified period of time (often, 15 minutes or less).

Certain unique problems can arise in connection with this kind of fighting procedure. Almost all of the present kind of aggression studies involve either dyadic (twosome) or foursome subject groupings in the fighting chamber. These measurements thereby always involve a "social" situation. This can pose major methodological problems when conducting an evaluation of the relative aggressiveness of different strains. For example, a typically aggressive mouse may be more or less pugnacious, depending upon the extent and the kind of aggressive behavior displayed by its partner. A "testy" combatant may extract far less aggression from the same subject than a normally docile one. Moreover, continued experimentation with a particular partner in a particular situation may result in a progressive decay (or increase) in aggressive performance.

In order to surmount these problems, a modified "paired-comparisons" procedure has sometimes been employed (cf. 56, 108). Here, individual subjects from one strain are tested against individuals from every other strain that are being compared. When a large number of strains are evaluated, a modified Greco-Latin square design can sometimes be used in which representative matchings are chosen from the larger set of total possible paired-comparisons that could be made (cf. 117). In this manner it has been possible to rank a large number of inbred mice in terms of amount of aggressive behavior. Thus, in a comparison of 14 strains, Southwick and Clark (117) were able to compute an overall index of aggressive performance for each. The average scores ranged from 11.3 to 82.2. Their findings suggested that the BALB/c mouse was, for example, considerably more aggressive than the A/He strain (composite scores of 62.7 vs. 11.3).

There is a growing literature which indicates that *contextual factors* cannot be ignored in studies of ontogenetic variables on aggressive behavior. For example, a seemingly innocuous variation in level of illumination during testing can dramatically alter the amount of aggressive behavior displayed by different strains of mice (71). The latter investigators paired C57BL/6 (pigmented) males with BALB/c (albino) males under two levels of illumination. With high illumination the

C57BL males won 90 percent of the fights that resulted in submission by the other subject. In contrast, low-illumination resulted in less than half of the bouts being won by the C57BL males.

The sex of the animal has frequently been noted as an important determinant of aggressiveness. There is a marked difference, in fighting, between males and females. Females, whether wild or domestic, simply do not fight as much as males. Moreover, this trend is consistently present in a wide set of circumstances. Presumably, this difference is related to the male sex hormone (31). Interestingly, the presence of a female can offset male aggression, although not uniformly. A female can markedly reduce male-male aggressiveness in one strain of mice, but may have little effect on the aggressive behavior of males of another strain (53).

Age can also influence aggressive behavior. Generally, mice and rats show little fighting before one month, and then only with unfamiliar (strange) conspecifics (110). Fighting among familiar conspecifics (cage mates) usually does not appear until three months of age, and then apparently recurs unabatedly throughout adulthood. There seems to be no available evidence on fighting behavior in the later portion of the life span for mice or rats or, for that matter, any mammalian species-type.

There is a plethora of recent reports on the various roles of peer-group rearing and maternal influences on subsequent mouse-mouse aggression. Denenberg and his colleague have reported extensively on these variables (36; 37). For example, their data suggest that the absence of peer-group interaction between birth and weaning can produce a significant increase in adult aggressive behavior, regardless of the nature of the postweaning, peer-group interaction (cf. 37, p. 46). Moreover, the presence of conspecific (but not contraspecific) peers after weaning was reported to enhance aggression in adulthood, regardless of the social experience of mice prior to weaning. Apparently, rearing with contraspecifics (such as rats) as cage-mates may not have major effects upon mouse-mouse aggressive behavior, as compared with being reared in isolation. Indeed, Denenberg concluded that a key variable is the presence versus the absence of conspecific cage-mates following weaning in producing the increments or the decrements in adult aggression that he and his colleagues have reported. All of these findings employed C57BL/10J mice.

Both Cairns and Nagelski (23) and Scott and Frederickson (111) have reported data that seem at odds with the findings of Denenberg. For example, Scott and Frederickson (111) showed that mice, reared from birth in groups over a long period, are less aggressive either with new or with familiar conspecifics than when mice are reared in post-weaning isolation.

Maternal-rearing variables have also been found important for the presence and the magnitude of adult mouse-mouse aggressive behavior. Consider, for example, a study by Southwick (114). Southwick employed a cross-fostering technique that involved two strains of mice: an aggressive (CFW) and a more docile (A/J) strain. Three groups of mice were formed within each strain. Group 1 involved fostered animals that were placed with the females of the alternate strain within 24 hours of birth; Group 2 entailed in-fostered mice that were removed from their biological mother and placed with another female of the same strain, also within 24 hours of birth; and Group 3 consisted of control animals that were handled in the same way but returned to the biological mother. Aggressive behavior scores were collected using a modified paired-comparison test procedure and a composite scoring technique following weaning of the subjects.

Southwick reported that young A/J males, reared by a more aggressive CFW mother, showed enhanced aggression scores when compared with control animals. But, normally aggressive CFW males, reared with more docile A/J mothers, showed no depression of aggressive behavior. In addition, although rearing by an aggressive CFW mother increased A/J aggressive behavior, the latter remained below that of any of the CFW groups, regardless of rearing conditions. To summarize, being reared by a more aggressive mother increased aggression, while rearing by a less aggressive mother did not. Further, the gain in aggressiveness that resulted from rearing by a more aggressive mother did not equal the amount of aggressiveness behavior than was ordinarily exhibited by the biological offspring of the aggressive mother.

Denenberg and his colleagues (38, 39, 59, 60) examined the variables of cross-fostering both within and across strains and species upon adult aggressive behavior. They manipulated the maternal variable by rearing neonatal mice either (1) by the biological or a foster mother of the same strain, or (2) by a lactating or nonlactating rat. They reasoned that this interspecies-maternal manipulation provided for an investigation of the effects of postnatal maternal environment on adult aggressiveness, independent of the subject's genetic and prenatal history (but see Cairns, 20, for a critique of this methodology). It was assumed that if the subjects that were reared by a rat mother behaved differently from mice reared by their own or a mother of the same species, it would be possible to conclude that the postnatal maternal environment was a significant determinant of the subject's subsequent behavior (cf. 36).

In order to summarize the results of Denenberg and his colleagues, it is important to keep in mind their definition of a control group (cf. 38). A control group was defined as mice that were reared by a mouse mother, biological or fostered, and with mouse peers present before and after weaning (with the exception that each animal was placed in isolation prior to aggression testing). They found that when mice were reared with the rat mother or a rat aunt (i.e., a nonlactating adult virgin rat trained to rear mice) marked reductions resulted in intraspecific aggression in C57BL/10J mice, but not in the Swiss-albino mouse. Thus, for the C57BL/10J mouse, 82 percent of the control, 17 percent of the mice reared by rat mothers, and 36 percent reared by rat aunts (the latter two were not significantly different) exhibited aggressive behavior. Denenberg (cf. 100) concluded that the critical determinant of attenuated fighting for C57BL mice was maternal-rearing behavior of the rat mother or rat aunt (and not the milk, for example) toward the young between birth and weaning. For Swiss-albino mice, 80 percent of the control, 82 percent of the mice reared by rat mothers, and 84 percent of those reared by rat aunts fought. These differences were not statistically significant.

As noted, some of the findings of Denenberg appear inconsistent with reports from other laboratories; one important inconsistency pertains to the effects of postweaning, peer-group interaction on adult aggressive behavior. Banerjee (15), Welsh and Welsh (132), Cairns and Nakelski (23), and Cairns and Milakovih (22) have reported that post-weaning isolation intensifies aggressive behavior rather than having no effect on it. However, it should be noted that regardless of rearing conditions, Denenberg routinely employed a short-term isolation procedure prior to aggression testing. Cairns, Midlam and Sholz (21) reported that a 4-day isolation period was a sufficient condition for producing aggression in 84-day-old ICR mice that previously had been group-reared. It would appear that Cairns et al. (21) and Denenberg may be investigating factors in addition to that of isolation per se.

Interestingly, Cairns (20) has supplied evidence to suggest that isolation rearing produces, as a major behavioral outcome, increased dyadic investigatory activity and hyper-reactivity to stimulation (20, pp. 75-77). The combination of these two isolation-produced factors may account, in Cairns' opinion, for the increased aggressive behavior envinced by postweaning, isolation-reared mice (cf. 23). To test this speculation, Cairns and Scholz (24) reasoned that fighting by isolation-reared mice could be de-escalated by reducing the feedback stimuli that was normally supplied by an intact, reciprocally aggressive target subject. The procedure employed was not unlike that used by others who have been interested in the reciprocal attacker-attackee stimulus feedback effects on aggressive behavior in other paradigms (cf. 73). Several studies have shown attenuated aggressive behavior when one of a pair of partners has been disenabled in some manner from responding to the attack of the other.

Cairns and Sholz (24) "disenabled" the partner of each dyadic pair of fighting mice through injections of either chlorpromazine or pentobarbital. The probability of attack behavior was found to decrease as a function of increasing doses of chlorpromazine, and to be virtually zero when one "partner" was disenabled with lethal doses of pentobarbital. Cairns (20), in summarizing his research on the effects of ontogenetic variables on aggressive behavior, emphasized the importance of the reciprocal stimulation that is supplied by dyadic fighting and attack. If various rearing conditions attenuate adult dyadic interchange, or if the target object is not salient, there will be less of the kind of stimulation that is necessary for aggressive performance. Postweaning isolation rearing was seen by Cairns (20) to increase aggression indirectly by producing increased dyadic investigatory activity and hyper-reactivity to stimulation. These two features served to promote contact between pairs of mice which, in turn, produced reciprocal stimulation. Hyper-reactivity to such stimulation resulted in "escalation" of investigatory contact and eventual tissue injury. The latter, of course, often resulted in actual fighting and further escalation.

The mouse-mouse aggression paradigm has been well suited to the technique of *selective breeding*, as well as for studies involving strain comparisons. Selective breeding involves, initially, the use of a genetically heterogeneous group of subjects. Subjects at the extreme ends of a particular "trait" (such as aggressiveness) are then selected for inbreeding. On the assumption that the phenotypical characteristic under study has a genetic basis, the offspring of these selected subjects should show either a high- or low-profile manifestation of the selected trait. The rate at which the extreme values of the characteristic diverge over generations can be taken as a measure of the "heritability" of the trait for that particular population.

Perhaps Lagerspetz (78) has provided the most complete study of the genetics of mouse aggression utilizing the technique of selective breeding. By systematically inbreeding high- and low-aggressive mice initially selected from a heterogeneous population, Lagerspetz (78) was able to produce a relatively stable population of high- and low-aggressive mice from generation to generation. In a series of follow-through studies, Lagerspetz studied the reinforcing effect of *defeat* and *success* in aggressive encounters upon the future probable recurrence of aggressive behaviors with both of these groups. She reported an interaction between the effects of these two outcomes and strain. Whereas defeats reduced aggressiveness in both the high- and low-aggressive strains, the effect of victories increased aggressiveness only for the high-aggressive strain.

The data thus far clearly seems to indicate the presence of a genetic component that may account (partially) for individual differences in certain kinds of aggressive behaviors for certain species. McClearn and DeFries (84) have recently discussed how the reverse condition can also influence aggressive performance. Individual differences in aggressive behavior can influence the genetic constituency of the offspring of mice in given populations. DeFries and McClearn (35), McClearn, Wilson and Meredith (85), and McClearn and DeFries (84) have shown that dominant male mice (i.e., more aggressive mice) can contribute over 90 percent of the litters in a subpopulation or commune of mice. In contrast, the very submissive males may not contribute any litters. Thus, "being aggressive" apparently can increase the likelihood that the genotypical basis for such may be propagated.

There is a growing literature that deals with variables that influence *interspecies aggressive behavior*. A number of species combinations have been explored. Cairns (20) has alluded to the effects on aggression of rearing dogs by rabbit mothers, and Kuo, in a series of reports in 1960 (77), studied the effects of various rearing procedures between different species (cats and cockatoos; cats and canaries; dogs and canaries; dogs and cockatoos; cats and rabbits; cats and rats; dogs and rabbits; dogs and rats; dogs and cats) upon the development of certain "anti-social" habits such as "prey and hunting and killing of smaller animals, interspecies 'angatonism,' fighting, and domination over conspecies." His findings can be summarized by noting that, in the great majority of cases, interspecies co-rearing and other environmental manipulations could bring about tranquil and "human-like etiquette behaviors" between contraspecifics that normally have been noted for strong mutual antagonisms (cf. 77).

Probably because of the low cost of maintenance, ease of housing and related factors, the most completely researched interspecies paradigm has involved the *mouse-killing rat* (67, 68, 75, 92, 94, 95, 96, 97, 99, 101, 128). The typical scoring procedure in "mouse-killing" studies has been simply to place a rat and mouse together for a specified period (such as 24 hours) and tally whether the mouse is alive or shows signs of injury at the end of the session. Some of the variables that have been investigated in terms of the effects on mouse-killing by rats (*muricidal aggression*) have included isolation rearing (found ineffective by Myer, 94), shock-punishment (found to produce temporary suppression and also to enhance mouse-killing by Myer, 93); and various neural and hormonal physiological manipulations (68, 99).

More recently, Denenberg and his associates (40) investigated the influence of various maternal and peer-group rearing factors on muricidal aggression. Consistent with the findings of Kuo (77) regarding other forms of interspecies antagonism, they found that the post-weaning, social grouping of Wistar rats with C57BL/10 mice eliminated muricidal aggression as measured by testing the socially reared rats later with a "fresh" C57BL/10 or an Swiss-albino mouse. These data have also been confirmed by Myer (95).

CONCLUSIONS

Several factors appear to have somewhat common effects upon the rather different behaviors that have been labeled as aggressive. These factors include the genetic constituency of the subject, prior peer-group and maternal-rearing conditions, the presence and the source of aversiveness in the measurement setting, the nature and "salience" of the target object, and the particular reinforcement contingency that prevails. Although the effects of each of these factors have been investigated in somewhat different ways and with different subject populations, it can be concluded that the occurrence of either inter- or intra-specific aggressive behaviors can be due, either directly or indirectly, to (1) a high genetic loading for such activity, (2) pre- and post-weaning isolation rearing, (3) post-weaning environmental "crowding" (cf. 25), (4) maternal aggressiveness, (5) various sources of antecedent painful events including shock, thwarting, physical blows, food extinction, and high-demand reinforcement schedules, and (6) various consequent rewarding events including target contact and availability, target aggressiveness, food and so forth. All of these factors have, in one way or another, been shown to influence the occurrence of aggressive-labeled behaviors in at least one and sometimes in virtually all of the paradigms discussed in the present paper.

Unfortunately, the qualification of "in one way or another" is a major one. Much of the research on the trans-paradigm effects of the latter factors has not been systematic with regard either to the issues of ensuring the comparability of the conditions of manipulation or of the methods of recording so as to make direct comparisons possible. When a variable of known effectiveness in one paradigm has been manipulated in another, other factors also have often been allowed to co-vary across procedures and thereby obscure an interpretation of the results that have been obtained. Thus, before any solid conclusion can be made that the paradigms surveyed in this report each represent different ways of measuring the same basic behavioral form or function (as, for example, implied by Scott's use of the label "agonistic behavior"), many more investigations are needed in which better trans-paradigm control is exerted over situational, subject and measurement variables.

At present, then, the data can primarily be taken as suggestive of future directions, of variables to examine, and of needed areas of experimental control. However, until such systematic research has been conducted, care should be taken in making broad, extrapolative generalizations to other paradigms that have employed the label of "aggression." More comparison research is necessary not only between the paradigms that have been used in the study of nonhuman aggressive behavior, but also between the latter and those used with humans. It seems a safe speculation that the procedural variability between the different paradigms that have been used to study nonhuman aggressive activity is far less than that between the latter and those used to study the aggressive performances of nursery children, and college sophomores, and between nations.

REFERENCES

1. Altevogt R: Inter such ungen zur Biologie and Okologie indischer Winkerkrabben. Z. Morphal. Okol. Tiere 46:1-110, 1957.
2. Amsel A: The role of frustrative nonreward in noncontinuous reward situations. Psychol. Bull. 55:102-119, 1958.
3. Amsel A: Frustrative nonreward in partial reinforcement and discrimination learning: Some recent history and a theoretical extension. Psychol. Rev. 69:306-328, 1962.
4. Amsel A: Behavioral habituation, counterconditioning and a general theory of persistence, in Classical Conditioning II: Current Theory and Research, Black AH, Prokosy WF (eds). New York, Appleton-Century-Crofts, 1972.
5. Anderson DC, Lupo V, Cunningham C, et al: Variations in pretreatments as determinants of shuttlebox behavior and shock-induced aggression. Paper presented to the Psychonomic Society Convention, Boston, 1974.
6. Ardrey R: The Territorial Imperative. New York, Atheneum, 1966.
7. Azrin NH, Hake DF, Hutchinson RR: Elicitation of aggression by a physical blow. J. Exp. Anal. Behav. 8:55-57, 1965.
8. Azrin NH, Hutchinson RR: Conditioning of the aggressive behavior of pigeons by a fixed-interval shcedule of reinforcement. J. Exp. Anal. Behav. 10:395-402, 1967.
9. Azrin NH, Hutchinson RR, Hake DF: Pain-induced fighting in the squirrel monkey. J. Exp. Anal. Behav. 6: 620, 1963.
10. Azrin NH, Hutchinson RR, Hake DF: Extinction-induced aggression. J. Exp. Anal. Behav. 9:191-204, 1966.
11. Azrin NH, Hutchinson RR, Hake DF: Attack avoidance and escape reactions to aversive shock. J. Exp. Anal. Behav. 10:131-148, 1967.
12. Azrin NH, Hutchinson RR, McLaughlin R: The opportunity for aggression as an operant reinforcer during aversive stimulation. J. Exp. Anal. of Behav. 8:171-80, 1965.

13. Azrin NH, Hutchinson RR, Sallery RD: Pain-aggression toward inanimate objects. *J. Exp. Anal. of Behav.* 7:223-28, 1964.

14. Bandura A: Aggression a Social Learning Analysis. Englewood Cliffs, Prentice-Hall, 1973.

15. Banerjee V: An inquiry into the genesis of aggression in mice induced by isolation. *Behavior* 12:86-99, 1970.

16. Barnett SA: Rats. *Sci. Am.* 216:78-85, 1967.

17. Berkowitz L: The frustration-aggression hypothesis revisited, in *Roots of Aggression*, L Berkowitz (ed). New York, Atherton Press, 1969.

18. Berkowitz L.: Words and symbols as stimuli to aggressive responses, in *Control of Aggression*, JF Knutson (ed). Chicago, Aldine Publishing Co., 1973.

19. Boshka SC, Weisman MH, Thor DH: A technique for inducing aggression in rats utilizing morphine withdrawal. *Psychol. Record* 16:541-43, 1966.

20. Cairns RB: Attachment and dependency: A psychobiological and social learning synthesis, in JL Gewritz (ed). *Attachment and Dependency.* Washington, D.C., VH Winston, 1972.

21. Cairns RB, Medlam J., Scholz SD: The joint effects of age of isolation and length of isolation in fighting in mice. Unpublished manuscript, Indiana University, 1972.

22. Cairns RB, Milakovich JF: On fighting in mice: Is training necessary? Unpublished manuscript, Indiana University, 1972.

23. Cairns RB, Nakelski JS: On fighting in mice: Ontogenic and experiential determinants. *J. Comp. Physiol. Psychol.* 71:354-64, 1971.

24. Cairns RB, Scholz SD.: On fighting in mice: Dyadic escalation and what is learned. *J. Comp. Physiol. Psychol.* 85:340-550, 1973.

25. Calhoun, JB: Description of behavioral states as a cause of aggression. Nebraska Symposium 20:182-260, 1972.

26. Carpenter CR: Societies of monkeys and apes. Biological Symposium 8:177-204, 1942.

27. Carthy JD, Ebling FJ (eds): *The Natural History of Aggression.* New York, Academic Press, 1964.

28. Cherek DR, Thompson T, Heistad GT: Responding maintained by the opportunity to attack during an interval food reforcement schedule. *J. Exp. Anal. of Behav.* 19:113-123, 1973.

29. Cole JK, DD Jensen (eds): *Nebraska Symposium on Motivation.* Lincoln, University of Nebraska Press, 1972.

30. Cole JM, Parker BK: Schedule-induced aggression: Access to an attackable target bird as a positive reinforcer. *Psychonomic Science* 22:33-35, 1971.

31. Conner RL, Levine S: Hormonal influences on aggressive behavior, in *Aggressive Behaviour*, S Garanttini, EB Sigg (eds). Amsterdam: Excerpta Medica Foundation, 1969.

32. Crane J: Combat, display and ritualism in fiddler crabs. *Philosophical Transactions of the Royal Society*, London 251:459-472, 1966.

33. Daly HB: Learning of a hurdle-jump response to escape cues paired with reduced reward or frustrative nonreward. *J. Exp. Psychol.* 79:146-51, 1969.

34. Daly HB: Aversive properties of partial and varied reinforcement during runway acquisition. *J. Exp. Psychol.* 81:54-60, 1969.

35. DeFries JC, McClearn GE: Social dominance and Darwinian fitness in the laboratory mouse. *Am. Naturalist* 104:408-11, 1970.

36. Denenberg VH: The mother as a motivator, in *Nebraska Symposium on Motivation*, WJ Arnold and MN Page (eds). Lincoln, University of Nebraska Press, 1970.

37. Denenberg VH: Developmental factors in aggression, in *the Control of Aggression*, JF Knutson (ed). Chicago, Aldine Publishing Co., 1973.

38. Denenberg VH, Hudgens GA, Zarrow MX: Mice research with rats: Modification of behavior by early experience with another species. *Science* 143:380-81, 1964.
39. Denenberg VH, Hudgens GA, Zarrow MX: Mice reared with rats: Effect of mother on adult behavior patterns. *Psychol. Reports* 18:451-456, 1966.
40. Denenberg VH, Paschke RE, Zarrow MX: Killing of mice by rats prevented by early interaction between the two species. *Psychonomic Science* 11:39, 1968.
41. DeReuck A, Knight J (eds.): *Conflict in Society.* Boston, Little, Brown and Co., 1966.
42. Dollard J, Doob L, Miller N, et al: *Frustration and Aggression.* New Haven, Yale University Press, 1939.
43. Eibl-Eibesfeldt I: *Land of a Thousand Atolls.* New York, Holt, Rinehart and Winston, 1965.
44. Eibl-Eibesfeldt I: *Ethology: The Biology of Behavior.* Translated from the German by E Klinghammer. New York, Holt, Rinehart & Winston, 1970.
45. Eibl-Eibesfeldt I: *Love and Hate: The Natural History of Behavior Patterns.* Translated by G Strachan. New York, Holt, Rinehart & Winston, 1971.
46. Eleftheriou BE, Scott JP (eds): The Physiology of Aggression and Defeat. New York, Plenum Press, 1971.
47. Ellefson J: Territorial behavior in the common white-handed Gibbon Hylobates lar, in Jay PC (ed): *Primates.* New York, Holt, Rinehart & Winston, 1968.
48. Emley GS, Hutchinson RR, Brannan IB: Aggression: Effects of acute and chronic morphine. *Michigan Mental Health Res. Bull.* 4:23-26, 1970.
49. Feshback S: The function of aggression and the regulation of aggressive drive. *Psychol. Rev.* 71:257-72, 1964.
50. Festetics A: Ökologesche Untersuch ungen an Brutvögeln des Saser Vogelwelt 80:1-21, 1959.
51. Flory RK, Attack behavior as a function of minimum inter-food interval. *J. Exp. Anal. Behav.* 12:825-28, 1969.
52. Follick MJ, Knutson JF: Shock source and intensity: Variables in shock-induced fighting. *Behavior Research Methods and Instrumentation* 6 (5):477-480, 1974.
53. Fredericson E, Story AW, Gurney NL et al: The relationship between heredity, sex and aggression in two inbred mouse strains. *J Genetic Psychol.* 87:121-30, 1955.
54. Garattini S, Sigg EB: *Aggressive Behavior.* New York, John Wiley & Sons, 1969.
55. Gentry WD: Fixed ratio schedule-induced aggression. *J. Anal. Behav.* 11:813-17, 1968.
56. Ginsburg B, Allee WC: Some effects of conditioning on social dominance and subordination in inbred strains of mice. *Physiol. Zool.* 15:485-506, 1942.
57. Hess EH: *Ethology: An Approach Toward the Complete Analysis of Behavior.* New Directions in Psychology I. New York, Holt, Rinehart & Winston, 1962.
58. Hinde RA: Ethological models and the concept of drive. *Brit. J. Phil. Sci.* 6:321-31, 1956.
59. Hudgens GA, Denenberg VH, Zarrow MX: Mice reared with rats: Relations between mothers activity level and offspring's behavior. *J. Comp. Physiol. Psychol.* 63:304-8, 1967.
60. Hudgens GA, Denenberg VH, Zarrow MX: Mice reared with rats: Effects of preweaning and postweaning social interactions upon adult behavior. *Behaviour* 30:259-74, 1968.
61. Hutchinson RR: The environmental causes of aggression, in JK Cole, DD Jensen (eds): *Nebraska Symposium on Motivation.* Lincoln: Univ. of Nebraska Press, 1972.
62. Hutchinson, RR, Azrin NH, Hake DF: An automated method for the study of aggression in squirrel monkeys. *J. Exp. Anal. Behav.* 9:233-37, 1966.
63. Hutchinson RR, Azrin NH, Hunt GM: Attack produced by intermittent reinforcement

of a concurrent operant response. *J. Exp. Anal. of Behav.* 11:489-495, 1968.

64. Hutchinson RR, Emley G: Effects of nicotine on avoidance, conditioned suppression and aggression response measures in animal and man, in Council for Tobacco Research, *Conference on Motivation in Cigarette Smoking.* New York, Academic Press, 1972.

65. Hutchinson RR, Pierce GE: Jaw clenching in humans: Its measurement, and effects produced by conditions of reinforcement and extinction. Paper presented at the meeting of the American Psychological Association, 1971.

66. Hymowitz N: Schedule-induced polydipsia and aggression in rats. *Psychonomic Sci.* R3:226-8, 1971.

67. Karli P: The Norway rat's killing response to the white mouse: An experimental analysis. *Behavior* 10:81-103, 1956.

68. Karli P, Vergnes M, Didiergeorges F: Rat-mouse interspecific aggressive behavior and its manipulations by brain ablation and by brain stimulation, in *Aggressive Behaviour,* S Garattani, EG Sigg (eds). New York, Wiley, 1969.

69. Kaufmann H: *Aggression and Altruism.* New York, Holt, Rinehart & Winston Inc., 1970.

70. Kenney NT: Sharks: wolves of the sea. *Nat. Geog.* 133(2):222-57, 1968.

71. Klein TW, Howard J, DeFries JC: Agonistic behavior in mice: Strain differences as a function of test illumination. *Psychonomic Sci.* 19:177-78, 1970.

72. Knutson JF: Aggression during the fixed-ratio and extinction components of a multiple schedule of reinforcement. *J. Exp. Anal. Behav.* 13:221-31, 1970.

73. Knutson JF: The effects of shocking one member of a pair of rats. *Psychonomic Sci.* 22:265-66, 1971.

74. Knutson JF (ed): *The Control of Aggression.* Chicago: Aldine Publishing Co., 1973.

75. Knutson JF, Hynan MT: Influence of upright posture on shock-elicited aggression in rats. *J. Comp. Physiol. Psychol.* 81:297-306, 1972.

76. Knutson JF, Hynan MT: Predatory aggression and irritable aggression: Shock-induced fighting in mouse-killing rats. *Physiol. Behav.* 11:113-115, 1973.

77. Kuo ZY: Studies on the basic factors in animal fighting: VII. Interspecies co-existence in mammals. *J. Genetic Psychol.* 97:211-225, 1960.

78. Lagerspetz K: *Studies Upon the Aggressive Behavior of Mice.* Helsinki: Suomalainer Tredeak atemina, 1964.

79. Lehreman DS: *A critique of Konrad Lorenz's theory of instinctive behavior. Q. Rev. Biol.* 28:337-63, 1953.

80. Logan FA, Boice R: Aggressive behaviors of paired rodents in an avoidance context. *Behavior* 34:161-83, 1969.

81. Lorenz K: Uber dre Beldung des Instinktbegriffes. *Dri Naturwiss* 25:1937.

82. Lorenz K: *On Aggression.* New York, Harcourt, Brace & World, 1966.

83. Maier SF, Anderson C, Leiberman DA: Influence of control of shock on subsequent shock-elicited aggression. *J. Comp. Physiol. Psychol.* 81:94-100, 1972.

84. McClearn GE, DeFries JC: Genetics and mouse aggression, In *The Control of Aggression,* JF Knutson (ed). Chicago, Aldine Publishing Co., 1973.

85. McClearn GE, Wilson JR, Meredith W: The use of isogenic and heterogenic mouse stocks in behavioral research, in *Contributions to Behavior-Genetics Analysis: The Mouse as a Prototype,* G Lindzey and DD Thiessen (eds). New York, Appleton-Century-Crofts, 1970.

86. Miller NE: Theory and experiment relating psychoanalytic displacement to stimulus response generalization. *J. Abn. Soc. Psychol.* 43:155-78, 1948.

87. Moltz H: Contemporary instinct theory and the fixed action pattern. *Psychol. Rev.* 72:1965.

88. Montagu MFA: *Man and Aggression*. New York, Oxford University Press, 1968.
89. Moyer KE: Kinds of aggression and their physiological basis. *Communications in Behavioral Biology* 2:65-87, 1968.
90. Moyer KE: *The Psychobiology of Aggression*. New York, Harper & Row, 1972.
91. Moyer KE: The physiological inhibition of hostile behavior, in Knutson JF, *The Control of Aggression*. Chicago, Aldine Publishing Co., 1973.
92. Myer JS: Stimulus control of mouse-killing rats. *J. Comp. Physiol. Psychol.* 58:112-17, 1964.
93. Myer JS: Punishment of instinctive behavior: Suppression of mouse-killing by rats. *Psychonomic Sci.* 4:385-86, 1966.
94. Myer JS: Associative and temporal determinants of facilitation and inhibition of attack by pain. *J. Comp. and Physiol. Psychol.* 66:17-21, 1968.
95. Myer JS: Experience and the stability of mouse killing by rats. *J. Comp. Physiol. Psychol.* 75:264-68, 1971.
96. Myer JS, Baenninger R: Some effects of punishment and stress on mouse killing by rats. *J. Comp. Physiol. Psychol.* 62:292-297, 1966.
97. Myer JS, White RT: Aggressive motivation in the rat. *Animal Behavior* 13:430-33, 1965.
98. O'Kelly LE, Steckle LC: A note on long-enduring emotional responses in the rat. *J. Psychol.* 8:125-31, 1939.
99. Panksepp J: Effects of hypothalamic lesions on mouse-killing and shock induced fighting in rats. *Physiol. and Behav.* 6:311-16, 1971.
100. Paschke RE, Denenberg VH, Zarrow MX: Mice reared with rats: An interchain comparison of mother and "aunt" effects. Behavior 38:315-31, 1971.
101. Paul L, Miley WM, Baenninger R: Mouse killing by rats: Role of hunger and thirst in its initiation and maintenance. *J. Comp. Physiol. Psychol.* 76:242-49, 1971.
102. Payne R, Anderson DC, Marcurio J: Preshock-produced alterations in pain-elicited fighting. *J. Comp. Physiol. Psychol.* 71:258-266, 1970.
103. Powell DA, Creer TL: Interaction of developmental and environmental variables in shock-elicited aggression *J. Comp. Physio. Psychol.* 69:219-25, 1969.
104. Powell DA, Francis MJ, Francis M, Schneiderman N: Shock-induced aggression as a function of prior experience with avoidance, fighting or unadvoidable shock. *J. Exp. Anal. Behav.* 18:323-332, 1972.
105. Renfrew JW: The intensity function and reinforcing properties of brain stimulation that elicits attack. *Physiol. Behav.* 4:509-515, 1969.
106. Rilling M, Caplan HJ: Extinction-induced aggression during errorless discrimination learning. *Journal of the Experimental Analysis of Behavior* 20:85-92, 1973.
107. Schenkel R: Submission, its features and function in the wolf and dog. *Am. Zool.* 7:319-29, 1967.
108. Scott JP: *Aggression*. Chicago: Univ. of Chicago Press, 1958.
109. Scott JP: Agonistic behavior of mice and rats: A review. *Am. Zool.* 6:683-700, 1966.
110. Scott JP: Theoretical issues concerning the origin and causes of fighting, in BE Eleftheriou and JP Scott (eds): *The Physiology and Aggression and Defeat*. New York, Plenum Press, 1971.
111. Scott, JP, Fredericson E: The cause of fighting in mice and rats. *Physiological Zoology* 24:511-20, 1951.
112. By Sidman M: *Tactics of Scientific Research*. New York, Basic Books, 1960.
113. Skinner BF: *The Behavior of Organisms: An Experimental Analysis*. New York, Appleton-Century-Crofts, 1938.
114. Southwick CH: Effects of maternal environment on aggressive behavior of inbred mice. *Communications in Behavioral Biology* 1(A):129-32, 1968.

115. Southwick CH: Aggressive behavior of rhesus monkeys in natural and captive groups, in *Aggressive Behaviour*, S Garattini and EB Sigg (eds). Amsterdam: Excerpta Medica Foundation, 1969.
116. Southwick CH (ed).: *Animal Aggression*. New York, Van Nostrand Reinhold Co., 1970.
117. Southwick CH, Clark LH: Interstrain differences in aggressive behavior on exploratory activity of inbred mice. *Communications in Behavioral Biology 1(A)*:49-59, 1968.
118. Stachnic TJ, Ulrich RE, Mabry JH: Reinforcement of aggression through intracranial stimulation. *Psychonomic Sci.* 5:101-2, 1966.
119. Steiniger F: Revier- and A Ktionsraum bei der Wanderratte. *Z. Hyg. Zool.* 39:33-51, 1951.
120. Thompson T, Bloom W: Aggressive behavior and extinction-induced response rate increase. *Psychonom. Sci.* 5:335-336, 1966.
121. Tinburgen N: *The Study of Instinct*. Oxford, Oxford Press, 1961.
122. Tinbergen N: The functions of territory. *Bird Study* 5:14-27, 1957.
123. Ulrich RE: Interaction between reflexive fighting and cooperative excape. *J. Exp. Anal. Behav.* 10:311-17, 1967.
124. Ulrich RE, Azrin NH: Reflexive fighting in response to aversive stimulation. *J. Exp. Anal. Behav.* 5:511-20, 1962.
125. Ulrich R, Dulaney S, Arnett M, Mueller K: An experimental analysis of nonhuman and human aggression, in Knutson JF (ed): *Control of Aggression*. Chicago, Aldine Publishing Co, 1973.
126. Ulrich RE, Hutchinson RR, Azrin NH: Pain-elicited aggression. *Psychol. Rec.* 15:111-126, 1965.
127. Vernon W, Ulrich RE: Classical conditioning of pain-elicited aggression. *Sci.* 12:668-669, 1966.
128. Whalen RE, Fehr H: The development of the mouse killing response in rats. *Psychono. Sci.* 1(4):77-78, 1964.
129. Walther FR: Zum-Kampf- und Paaerungsverhalten einiger Antilopen. *Z Tierpsychol* 15:340-380, 1958.
130. Walther FR: Verhaltenstudien an der Grand Gazelle (Gayella granti Brooke) im Ngorongoro Krater. *Z Tierpsychol* 22:166-208, 1965.
131. Washburn SL: Conflict in primate society, in De Reuck, Knight J (eds). *Conflict in Society*. Boston, Little, Brown and Co, 1966.
132. Welsh AS, Welsh BL: Isolation, reactivity and aggression: Evidence for an involvement of brain catecholamines and serotonin, in BE Eleftheriou, JP Scott (eds): *The Physiology of Aggression and Defeat*. New York, Plenum Press, 1971.
133. Wilson AP: Social behavior of free-ranging Rhesus monkeys with an emphasis on aggression. Dissertation. University of California. Berkeley. Department of Anthropology, 1968.
134. Wolfe M, Ulrich RE, Dulaney S: Fighting and escape reaction in paired rats. *Psychol. Rec. 21(1)*: 59-68, 1971.

Epilepsy and Violence

DIETRICH BLUMER

With sudden, savage muscle spasms, cyanosis simulating impending death, and subsequent unresponsiveness, the generalized seizure presents a frightening sight. A naive observer is left with the impression of epilepsy as an eminently violent disease. Beyond its repetitive sudden and excessive neuronal discharges manifest as clinical seizures, violence *directed outwards* has been notoriously linked to epilepsy.

HISTORICAL REFERENCES

In antiquity, the "sacred disease" was also referred to by some as the Herculean disease. But those interpreting the Herculean disease as epilepsy had much difficulty in explaining this name (37). Hercules was said to suffer not from seizures but from attacks of fury. According to legend, Hercules returned home from Hades, upon completion of his last labor, in a confused and deluded state, to slay not only a hostile king and his henchmen but his own sons and wife; he then fell in a deep sleep from which he awakened freed from his fury and unaware of what he had done (Kerényi, 1958). The mythological hero thus suffered from a state of blind rage not unlike the rare but well-documented postictal violence for which there is usually amnesia.

While it was recognized that epilepsy tended to impair the mind,* signs and symptoms differentiating epilepsy from mental diseases were not detailed in ancient and medieval medical literature. The existence of epileptic attacks was at times overlooked, and a case considered as one of "furor," "delirium," or "mania" without reference to epilepsy (Temkin, 1971 pp. 50-51, p. 269). The psychiatric study of epileptics began in the early nineteenth century with Esquirol, and the *furor epilepticus*—preceding the fits, following them, or taking place independently of any classic fit—was henceforth considered most important among all the psychiatric complications of epilepsy and was carefully studied. Esquirol was the first of many authorities to state that the minor epileptic attack ("vertigo") had a much stronger influence upon the brain than the grand mal (Temkin, 1971 pp. 266-267). After 1850, Morel, Griesinger and Falret—three psychiatrists—developed the clinical picture of what is now termed psychomotor or temporal lobe epilepsy, with emphasis on its psychiatric aspects.

Influenced by Hughlings Jackson more than by any other single physician, modern epileptology has been neurologically oriented, and careful neuropsychiatric studies of the epilepsies have been scarce (7). Yet it appears possible, at this time, to sort out myth and fact in the relationship of violent behavior and epileptic abnormalities.

The psychiatric manifestations associated with epilepsy have changed over the first half of this century with the introduction of effective anticonvulsant medication (7). With better seizure control, the postictal confusional states, and in particular the postictal psychoses (or prolonged twilight states) which tend to follow upon a flurry of seizures have become less important. The "Herculean fury" is now rare. Instead, the interictal psychopathology is more prominent. The interictal angry irritability, the mood changes, and the alternating epileptic or "schizophrenia-like" psychoses may indeed be iatrogenic, as is evident if they resolve with decrease of anticonvulsant medication.

SOME BASIC CONSIDERATIONS

Recent reviews (36, 26) and a monograph (24) deal with the topic of aggressivity and epilepsy. Considerable public interest has been aroused, but "violence" or "aggressivity" in relation to epilepsy has remained poorly defined and many questions have been left

---

* Cf. Aretaeus: epileptics become "Languid, spiritless, stupid, inhuman, unsociable, not disposed to hold intercourse . . . (37).

unanswered. The controversy can be largely solved by a more qualitative clinical analysis (7). Szondi (35) and Geschwind (10) have given accurate descriptions of the particular setting of aggressiveness in epilepsy. Monroe's monograph on episodic behavioral disorders (27) represents a further important contribution.

From the psychiatric viewpoint, the more or less pronounced proneness toward irritable and angry-explosive behavior in certain epileptics is merely one aspect of a complex personality and behavior change which may develop after onset of overt seizures (5, 7, 9). This irritable, at times threatening and abusive behavior is episodic, and combines paradoxically with a highly good-natured (hyperethical and sometimes hyperreligious) attitude which may be almost entirely predominant. What is loosely referred to as "violence" or "aggressiveness" in epileptics represents a very real problem, but is distinctly different from the deviant aggression commonly found in passive-aggressive and antisocial personality disorders, as well as from the one less commonly found in paranoid, catatonic or manic-depressive patients (22). A certain relationship of the "aggressiveness" in epileptics with the impulsive behavior of "epileptoid" or explosive personality disorders is probable but not well established (see below). As in the general population, outwardly directed anger and aggressiveness among epileptics tends to decrease in degree and frequency of manifestation from childhood to adolescence and through adulthood, while depressive manifestations become gradually more prominent.

From the neurological viewpoint the specific association of psychiatric disorders and temporal lobe disorder remains highly plausible. Studies which compared the psychopathology in grand mal epileptics with that in temporal lobe epileptics and found in both an equally high incidence have not differentiated between the benign "pure" common generalized epilepsy and the more chronic generalized seizure disorders with primary or secondary temporal lobe involvement (28), and are open to some further criticism (10, 7). A careful analysis of the characteristics of temporal lobe seizures leads to the conclusion that aggressive acts are not likely to occur as part of a clinical seizure. The important role of subclinical (interictal or "subictal") seizure discharges and of the postictal state will be discussed below.

The manifestations of temper and violence in epilepsy can best be discussed under the traditional headings of interictal, ictal and postictal events. A fourth section will deal with the problem of violent behavior and EEG abnormalities in the absence of overt seizures.

IRRITABILITY OR VIOLENCE IN THE VARIOUS PHASES OF THE SEIZURE DISORDER

Interictal Angry-Irritable Behavior:
A Common Finding in Temporal Lobe Epilepsy

A proneness towards episodic outbursts of angry, verbally or even physically abusive behavior develops gradually in many temporal lobe epileptics perhaps a couple of years after onset of recurring seizures, or after a more prolonged latency period. These outbursts tend to be confined to periods of bad mood lasting hours or days, and contrast sharply with the usually predominant good-natured attitude. The outbursts do not occur without provocation, but are often triggered by seemingly petty issues of right-or-wrong or by overreaction to a person who is not trusted. Through a patient, considerate approach and a relationship of trust, these outbursts can be avoided, even with patients selected as "violence-prone" (8). A tactful physician will not have to witness a marked display of temper and will only hear about it if he asks those who are with the patient 24 hours a day and cannot avoid friction at a certain time. The families are acutely aware of the increased explosiveness, and tend to use "kid gloves" with the patient, particularly during those times when increasing impatience and volatility betray a state of markedly pent-up anger. In some patients, such a state of increased irritability builds up *preictally* and is resolved by the attack. The patients tend to feel remorse for their episodes of angry behavior, and if not by word then by their action usually attempt to make up for their misbehavior. This pattern accounts for the hesitation on the part of the family to insist on psychiatric hospitalization even though the family life may be markedly disturbed. It is further remarkable how even during extreme outbursts a measure of control seems to be present: the rage is frightening, furniture is destroyed, a family member is struck, but rarely is someone injured. The interictal (and preictal) violence may cause much turmoil at home and represents the prominent reason for psychiatric hospitalization of epileptics (31, 19), but only rarely will lead to criminal charges. The incidence of penal records among epileptics or of epilepsy among criminals in indeed not significantly higher than in the general population (2, 14). Where the rage is most uncontrolled and has been labeled "catastrophic rage" (29) in children, physical harm to others is again an unlikely concomitant.

Heightened angry-irritable behavior has been reported in as many as 75 percent of a series of temporal lobe epileptics (9). Among children (29) and patients who underwent temporal lobectomy for epilepsy (4,

15, 32, 36, 42), 27 to 38 percent were rated as aggressive to a socially disruptive degree. Among 700 temporal lobe epileptics from an epilepsy center, "destructive-assaultive" behavior was noted in 4.8 percent only (30), but apparently in the absence of any systematic psychiatric exploration. By English investigators a certain prevalence of aggression has been noted among temporal lobe epileptics who were male, of low class and low intelligence, had left temporal lobe abnormalities, and an early onset of epilepsy (36).

The only occasion when I witnessed a violent outburst in a temporal lobe epileptic was brought about by some mishandling on the part of the staff.

Case 1: A 23-year-old single male who worked in his father's trucking business developed temporal lobe seizures and occasional grand mals a few months after a head injury at age 17. He had been likable and eventempered, but from age 19 on his disposition changed radically. Outbursts of anger with verbal abusiveness over trivial matters became very frequent, there were occasional physical fights, and he gradually lost all of his friends. He would tease others often, but was unable to take a joke himself. His disposition would be temporarily improved following generalized convulsions. A left temporal lobectomy at age 21 left seizures and temper unchanged. When he was reevaluated on the research ward, at age 23, he resented a humorously meant remark made to him in the admitting office, that charity would take care of his hospital bill. He continually antagonized the ward staff, and on the fifth day of his stay refused to relinquish his seat on a cart which was needed by the nurses. Unwisely, the resident physician finally attempted to lift him off the cart. A violent battle ensued, which only terminated when the patient was put in restraints. Fortunately torn clothing was the only visible damage suffered by the combatants.

The following case is characteristic of the catastrophic rage of temporal lobe epilepsy in childhood, and for a dramatic improvement brought about by successful temporal lobectomy.

Case 2. At about age 2 this girl had two or three generalized "spasms" followed by slep. At age 4 she was thrown against a wall by her alcoholic father, suffering a bruise to the right side of her head. Father left the family one year later. At age 6 she began to suffer from very sporadic generalized seizures. In spite of the bad family situation she had maintained a good disposition. It was only after the onset of the epilepsy that she changed: for the slightest reasons, she would become mean, foul-mouthed and assaultive. She threw things at mother, would bite her, attacked her sisters with scissors, beat up peers with a baseball bat and lead pipe. Initially, she had been apologetic for her outbursts (which she recalled), but by age 9, when there were almost daily rages, she didn't seem to care. She was also hyperkinetic. Because of the finding of an atrophic lesion in the right temporal lobe with adjoining spike focus, a right temporal lobectomy was performed at age 10, in spite of the rarity of her seizures. The rage ceased promptly, and no further seizures occurred.

The next case shows an onset of angry-irritable behavior which was exceptionally long-delayed after first manifestation of the epilepsy. Episodic anger and rage developed concomitantly with an excessive religiosity, and on occasion an abrupt switch from one to the other would occur.

Case 3. A 40-year-old male had suffered from temporal lobe seizures since puberty. When he finally married, at 37, he showed no sexual interest, but became increasingly more religious, and every few weeks suffered periods of marked moodiness lasting several days. Although he was usually gentle, friendly and deferent, he could be sarcastic, hostile and arrogant during his bad days. The following incident led to his first psychiatric hospitalization: He had spent a weekend in the country in the company of his wife and stepson, listening all day to a radio station which continuously transmitted religious sermons. On the way home he debated with his wife, arguing that she was not saved, whereas his soul was saved. When his stepson asked him how this was possible, he slapped both the youngster and his wife, shouting: "For a nickel, I will kill you both!" His angry outbursts, though usually limited to verbal threats and hostile glares, were always frightening, but within days he would revert, without explicit apologies, to his usual self.

It has to be emphasized that many patients become not aggressive but merely impatient, easily angered and contrary on certain days, some time after onset of the temporal lobe attacks. Others show not the slightest trace of irritability. If temporal lobe patients are approached with patience and consideration, they will almost invariably respond good-naturedly and will be very cooperative.

Ictal Violence: A Myth?

The interictal outbursts of anger and rage tend to occur in a paroxysmal fashion, are sometimes referred to as "fits" by relatives, and are often not clearly differentiated from the clinical seizures. It has been shown that aggressive rage may occur concomitantly with increased electroencephalographic seizure discharges (24). The not-uncommon finding of increased preictal petulance or explosiveness may be likewise related to an increased, but still subclinical, build-up of seizure activity.

The common outbursts of anger among epileptics occur upon at least some provocation, are directed toward the environment, are not recurrent in a stereotyped form, are not associated with characteristic seizure phenomena, are recalled (though amnesia may be alleged), and last longer than a couple of minutes. Thus, they lack all the criteria of a clinical temporal lobe seizure (see Table I). Sexual climax occurs, in contrast to the paroxysm of rage, as a brief stereotyped ictal event,

Table I.
SYMPTOMATOLOGY OF TEMPORAL LOBE SEIZURES

A. ICTAL PHENOMENA

Stereotyped sequence of events: expressionless stare, passive experience, not related to environment. — Duration seconds to 1½ minute.

I.   PRIMICTAL EVENTS (AURA) — recalled.

"Dreamy state":	déjà-vu, jamais-vu, illusions, hallucinations, mood changes, fear
"Oral-digestive type":	visceral sensations, olfactory-gustatory sensations
"Adversive type":	dizziness, crescendo sensations, auditory or visual hallucinations.

II. ICTAL EVENTS — not recalled.

"Oral-digestive type":	oral-alimentary and respiratory automatisms
"Adversive type":	supple turning of eyes, head or trunk
"Speech utterances":	euphasic or dysphasic
Other phenomena:	repetitive motions, autonomic changes, tonic-atonic alterations.

B. POSTICTAL PHENOMENA

Increasingly more variable and more complex events: looking about, more active, more related to environment; usually not recalled. — Duration 2-10 min. (0-60 min.).

I.   SIMPLE REPETITIVE MOTIONS

II. SCENIC BEHAVIOR

III. ATTEMPTS AT RE-ORIENTATION

combined with other seizure phenomena, and in the absence of interaction with the environment (7). Fear is the most common ictal emotion, with depression, pleasure and displeasure occurring much less often. Among 100 patients who reported ictal emotions, only one patient reported feeling "furious" and having "an unpleasant abdominal sensation, then a sense of terrific release, of elation"; during this experience he would not attack people although he had a pathological temper in between his seizures (44). We conclude, with Gloor (11), that clinical seizures of violence are most unlikely events. I have seen a few patients who alleged amnesia for their outbursts of rage and felt entitled to a diagnosis of epilepsy; but true ictal events could not be documented in these cases.

Postictal Violence: A Rare Event

As a rule, the confusional-amnestic postictal phase tends to be more prolonged than the ictal phase proper. Following the brief stereotyped sequence of seizure events which was passively endured, the patient now begins to look about and gradually interacts more with the environment. The amnesia may last longer than the confusional phase, covering periods of relatively coherent and appropriate responses. (Table I) The postictal period following temporal lobe seizures and generalized seizures is similar. With the latter, however, a certain exhaustion of the motor system is naturally present, and consequently the ambulatory automatisms are perhaps more characteristic for the postictal phase of the temporal lobe seizure.

In the postictal phase of a generalized seizure, restlessness and agitation are rather common, but hostile acts are extremely unusual, especially if the patient remains unrestrained (1). In a series of 43 patients with postictal automatisms (17), 21 were considered to have temporal lobe epilepsy. Six patients resisted attempts to restrain them but could not be considered as behaving violently. There was but one patient who would react with violence, was considered a homicidal risk, and later required psychiatric hospitalization:

Case 4. (Case 33 of Knox): A 50-year-old male with temporal lobe epilepsy would experience, as his seizure, a peculiar rhyme going through his head. The following postictal behavior was reported: He has lifted kettle of boiling water and poured it over his arm. Several episodes of automatism observed in hospital during investigation. Staggers about. When assisted may shout "Leave me alone." Caught orderly by throat and held him for 2-3 minutes. Shouted "I'll kill you." Kicked out at doctor. Family very afraid of him in automatism on account of violence. Has struck out at them. Patient says that if he has attack at work his colleagues know not to approach him—"It seems I don't attack them if I'm not touched." No memory of the automatism. He is very concerned after the attacks, lest he might have injured someone.

I have never observed any postictal violence and personally know of only one patient (a temporal lobe epileptic with chiefly generalized seizures) who would fight with his parents after his attacks, apparently because they considered it their duty to hold him down as soon as he suffered an attack.

Savage acts of unchecked violence among epileptics are very rare, and are most likely to occur in the confusion of the postictal phase. Walker (40) reviewed the topic of murder and epilepsy, reported illustrative cases, and postulated the following criteria to be considered in attributing a crime of violence to an epileptic state.

1. That the patient was subject to *bona fide* epileptic attacks.

2. That the spontaneous attacks of the individual are similar to the one which allegedly occurred at the time of the crime.

3. That the period of loss of awareness alleged to have been present is commensurate with the type of epileptic attack the individual had.

4. That the degree of assumed unconsciousness is commensurate with the degree of unconsciousness the patient has had in previous attacks.

5. That the EEG findings are compatible with the type of clinical disorder assumed to be present. Repeated normal EEG's should be construed as decreasing to a one-to-twenty chance the possibility of epilepsy.

6. That the circumstances of the crime are compatible with the assumption of a lack of awareness of the individual at the time of the crime. This implies that obvious motives were not present, that the crime appeared to be senseless, that the mutilation was unnecessarily violent and extensive, and that the murderer did not attempt to escape, that he acted as if the act was foreign to him, and that he had given no evidence of premeditation.

The nature of the memory impairment following seizures (6) may account for instances where a murderer was found next to the body of his wife, muttering that he had killed her, yet later claiming amnesia. It is a fact that, postictally, awareness of an act may be protracted, yet with no memory trace retained as soon as distraction has occurred.

Violence and Epileptic EEG Abnormalities: An Important but Unclear Issue

A very high incidence of abnormal EEG's in psychopathic personalities and prisoners has been frequently confirmed (33, 34, 44). The role of epileptic EEG abnormalities, generalized or temporal, *in the absence of clinical seizures* is more germane to our topic. Temporal lobe spiking and sharp waves may be the more pertinent for abnormal behavior, but we again have to assume that a detectable generalized epileptic EEG abnormality may be either secondary to a primary (nondetectable) temporal lobe abnormality or may be primary but associated with a secondary (nondetectable) temporal lobe abnormality.

Individuals who come to a medical facility (emergency room, violence clinic) complaining of fear of going out of control and injuring someone, of homicidal ideation, repetitive aggressive behavior under the influence of alcohol, impulsiveness, rage outbursts, dangerous use of the automobile, or of repeated arrests for violent acts, have been carefully examined (3, 21). In one series, 37 of 79 who were given an EEG showed abnormalities, with 20 out of the 37 having temporal lobe spikes. Other studies raise more doubts about any relationship of epileptic temporal lobe abnormalities, in the absence of clinical seizures, and episodic loss of control over violent impulses (13, 25).

The problem obviously needs to be studied further. Based on the experience with careful individual neuropsychiatric case studies, well-defined case groups need to be investigated and compared. A most interesting hypothesis, however, has already been suggested (27, 38): that individuals with the epileptic EEG abnormality and no overt seizures may be prone toward more harmful outbursts of violence than patients with clinical seizures. This hypothesis is in keeping with the clinical observation of the "tension-releasing property" of overt generalized seizures (and occasionally of minor seizures) in certain patients. The well-accepted therapeutic use of seizures in psychiatric patients clearly attests that a seizure is not merely a neurological phenomenon, but also a mechanism for abnormal instinctual discharge.

Van der Horst (39) has reported the case of a very conscientious worker and devoted family man, who had become aggressive on two or three occasions in the past when he had been wronged, and who abruptly decapitated his superior (a man he had judged incompetent, but whom he had always obeyed), when this superior had repeatedly refused to listen to him (he wanted permission to leave work 10 minutes early so he wouldn't have to wait two hours for the next train). The crime was well recalled by its perpetrator, who was found to have a clear left temporal lobe abnormality in EEG and a marked deformation of the left temporal horn. Van der Horst speculated that this man might never have committed the crime had he been able to experience a clinical seizure.

The following case further illustrates a dangerous degree of violence-propensity in a woman with EEG abnormality without clinical seizures.

Case 5. A 30-year old mother of two came for consultation accompanied by her husband. She revealed for the first time that she had experienced a frightening problem with her impulse control towards the infant she cared for during the day. She had at times hit the infant, in particular when it was crying. On the most recent occasion, which prompted her to seek help, she had struck the child, then silenced the screaming by pressing her hand over the baby's face. Suddenly she realized that it had stopped breathing. Fortunately, the child was revived.

An EEG showed a left temporal lobe abnormality in the form of sharp waves. She was treated with psychotherapy and anticonvulsants. An early history of being frequently left alone by her parents and of cruelty toward animals was elicited. Further investigation revealed that she had experienced brief episodes of heart palpitations and "fuzzy" feelings, but it was not clear if these events represented abortive temporal lobe seizures. The anticonvulsants seemed to play less of a therapeutic role than did frank discussion of the situation with her husband which led to her getting more support from him.

Excessive violence in a state of clear consciousnesss thus appears to be more characteristic for some individuals without seizures but with an EEG seizure focus, and less characteristic for chronic temporal lobe epileptics with their common (interictal or preictal) outbursts of temper. As in temporal lobe epilepsy, these outbursts of excessive violence tend to contrast with the usual personality of such individuals. The presence among explosive epileptoid individuals of a hyperethical and hyperreligious attitude, of "viscosity," and hyposexuality—traits characteristic of many chronic temporal lobe epileptics (7)—needs to be investigated.

THERAPEUTIC CONSIDERATIONS

It is merely stating the obvious to point out that individual psychological conflicts and situational factors are important precipitants of the angry-irritable or violent behavior in certain epileptics or epileptoid individuals. These precipitants are important factors in the pathogenesis of any of the multitude of psychiatric abnormalities, and need to be considered in all psychiatric treatment. Some relatively specific dynamic factors involved in human violence need particularly to be considered, such as abandonment, helplessness and intolerance of depression (22, 20).

We have emphasized the specific nature of the psychopathology which has been losely referred to as violence or aggressiveness of epileptics, and have outlined the relationship of this psychopathology to the seizure disorder. The impact of social deprivation, a learning defect, or a maturity lag is frequently invoked to explain many conditions, from hyperkinesis to heroin addiction. The peculiarities of the seizure disorder have to be recognized as the specific etiologic factors (41). If a specific etiology is postulated, we need to be able to outline specific therapeutic approaches.

Interictal Angry-Irritable Behavior

The initial therapeutic effort is directed at the control of the seizure activity which, if achieved, may also improve the interictal impulsive-irritable behavior. But temporal lobe seizures are often resistant to therapy, and control of the (tension-releasing) overt seizures by means of medication, with persistence of subclinical epileptic potentials, may lead to a worsening of the behavior disorder in epilepsy, and to prolonged periods of heightened irritability. This is well known in children (23), but also occurs in adults. It may sometimes be necessary to lower the dose of anticonvulsants and to sacrifice seizure freedom to improve behavior. Such a procedure must be carefully explained to the patient and those about him. A need for occasional seizures in the interest of emotional well-being is apparent in patients who display a protracted prodromal phase marked by increasing angry explosiveness terminated by a seizure. Major seizures tend to have a more beneficial effect on behavior than minor seizures, as can be observed with ECT. Successful anterior temporal lobectomy (for intractable, chiefly unilateral seizure disorders) may sometimes improve this behavior dramatically and immediately following surgery; more often there will be only a gradual improvement of the heightened irritability following surgery (15, 32, 42).

Prior to a lowering of the anticonvulsant medication, a trial with tranquilizing drugs should be undertaken. Phenothiazines are not contraindicated for epileptics and may be helpful in some violence-prone cases. Tegretol is an interesting anticonvulsant drug, effective in temporal lobe epilepsy and sometimes having a beneficial psychotropic effect.

Postictal Violence

Epileptics in the confused postictal state need to be allowed to recover on their own. If restraint is necessary (e.g., if the patient moves toward traffic or another danger area), it must be gentle.

Violence with Epileptic EEG-Abnormality

The use of anticonvulsants to change behavior may be more effective in this group with relatively minor seizure abnormalities; Dilantin, phenobarbital, Mysoline and Tegretol should be all given a trial, if necessary. While one obviously does not need to be concerned here about a worsening of the mental state through suppression of overt seizures, a possible paradox-effect of the drugs, and of phenobarbital in particular—heightened impulsive and aggressive behavior—may occur. One also needs to consider that some patients may be better off mentally as long as their EEG is abnormal, and more disturbed upon "forced normalization" of the EEG (18). Much needs to be clarified in this area.

CONCLUSION

The time-honored relationship of epilepsy to violence needs to be reassessed and can be reasonably well defined if proper methodology is employed. Time-consuming psychiatric study is required: one needs to establish rapport with patient and family, inquire about past and present, assess individual reliability, get an understanding of how the individual functions in all areas, and explore possible relationships between personality, behavior and the seizure disorder.

The fashionable reliance on elegant statistical methods of analysis has been combined all too often with neglect of the clinical complexities; rare syndromes have been altogether ignored. In an area which requires both psychiatric and at least some neurological sophistication, controversy has been rampant and seemingly irreconcilable. Thus, Mark and Ervin (24) emphasized the relationship between violence and temporal lobe epilepsy, while a National Institute of Neurological and Communicative Disorders and Stroke panel recently concluded that epilepsy appeared to be a rare cause for violent and aggressive behavior, and that most neurologists believed that the association between temporal lobe epilepsy and violent behavior was equal to or only slightly higher than in the nonepileptic population (12).

The important concern about the public's prejudice against epileptics has undoubtedly been a potent factor in the debate and appears to be reflected in the NINCDS panel's conclusions.

A summary of the topic "epilepsy and violence" can be detailed as follows:

1. Angry-irritable behavior during the *interictal* phase (and sometimes accentuated preictally) is commonly found among chronic temporal lobe epileptics. It can reach threatening and violent proportions in some of them, but physical harm is rarely inflicted. This behavior is episodic and combines with a usually predominant good-natured (hyperethical and sometimes hyperreligious) attitude. Seizures may serve as a safety valve for the discharge of pent-up crude affects. The outbursts of temper can cause serious problems in the domestic sphere or in institutions, but are not a threat to the public safety.

2. *Ictal* violence is a most unlikely event, if it occurs at all. It is suggested, however, that outbursts of anger may occur in association with a build-up of subclinical seizure activity.

3. In rare cases, unchecked violence may take place in the con-fusional-amnestic *postictal* state when an individual meets with some

interference. The importance of these states has decreased with modern seizure control.

4. Some individuals who are not epileptic but have *paroxysmal EEG abnormalities* (temporal lobe sharp waves or spikes in particular) seem to be more prone to react with excessive violence than patients with overt seizures. The syndrome, however, is not well outlined and needs further investigation.

REFERENCES

1. Ajmone-Marsan C, Ralston BR: The epileptic seizure: Its functional morphology and diagnostic significance. Springfield, Ill., Charles C Thomas, 1957.
2. Alström CH: A study of epilepsy in its clinical, social and genetic aspects. *Acta Psychiat Scand* Supp. 63, 1950.
3. Bach-y-Rita G, Lion JR, Climent CE, et al: Episodic dyscontrol: A study of 130 patients. *Am J Psychiatry* 127: 1473-1478, 1971.
4. Blumer D: The temporal lobes and paroxysmal behavior disorders. Beiheft *Schweiz. Zeitschrift Psychol und Anwendungen* (Szondiana VII) 51: 273-285, 1967.
5. Blumer D: Organic personality disorders, in Lion J: *Personality Disorders*. Baltimore, Williams and Wilkins, 1974.
6. Blumer D, Walker AE: Memory in temporal lobe epileptics, in Talland GA, Waugh NC (eds): *The Pathology of Memory*. New York, Academic Press, 1969.
7. Blumer D: Temporal lobe epilepsy and its psychiatric significance, in Benson F, Blumer D (eds): *Psychiatric Aspects of Neurologic Disorders*. New York, Grune and Stratton, 1975.
8. Blumer D, Williams HW, Mark VH: The study and treatment, on a neurological ward, of abnormally aggressive patients with focal brain disease. *Confinia Neurologica* 36: 125-176, 1974.
9. Gastaut H, Morin G, Lesèvre N: Étude du comportement des épileptiques psychomoteurs dans l'intervalle de leurs crises; les troubles de l'activité globale et de la sociabilité. *Ann Méd Psychol* 113: 1-27, 1955.
10. Geschwind N: The clinical setting of aggression in temporal lobe epilepsy, in Fields WS, Sweet WH, (eds): *The Neurobiology of Violence*. St. Louis, Warren H. Green, 1975.
11. Gloor P: Discussion, in Clemente CD, Lindsley DB (eds), *Aggression and Defense*. Los Angeles, University of California Press, 1967 (pp 116-124).
12. Goldstein M: Brain research and violent behavior. *Arch Neurol* 30: 1-35, 1974.
13. Green JB: Association of behavior disorder with an electroencephalographic focus in children without seizures. *Neurology* 11: 337-344, 1961.
14. Gunn J: Criminality and violence in epileptic prisoners. *Br J Psychiat* 118: 337-343, 1971.
15. James IP: Temporal lobectomy for psychomotor epilepsy. *J Ment Sci* 106: 543-558, 1960.
16. Kerényi K: *Die Heroen der Griechen*. Zürich, Rhein-Verlag, 1958.
17. Knox SJ: Epileptic automatism and violence. *Med, Sci Law* 8: 96-104, 1968.
18. Landolt H: Serial electroencephalographic investigations during psychotic episodes in epileptic patients and during schizophrenic attacks. *Folia Psychiat Neurol Neurochir Neerland* Suppl 4: 91-133, 1958.

19. Liddell DW: Observations on epileptic automatism in a mental hospital population. *J Ment Sci* 99: 732-748, 1953.
20. Lion JR: The role of depression in the treatment of aggressive personality disorders. *Am J Psychiat* 129: 123-125, 1972.
21. Lion JR, Azcarate C, Christopher R, Arana JD: A violence clinic. *Md St Med J* 2:453-48, 1974.
22. Lion JR, Penna M: The study of human aggression, in Whalen R (ed): *Neuropsychology of Aggression*. New York, Plenum Press, 1975.
23. Livingston S: *Comprehensive Management of Epilepsy in Infancy, Childhood and Adolescence*. Springfield, Ill. Charles C Thomas, 1972.
24. Mark V, Ervin F: *Violence and the Brain*. New York, Harper & Row, 1970.
25. Milstein V, Small JG: Psychological correlates of 14 and 6 positive spikes, 6/sec. spike wave, and small sharp spike transients. *Clin EEG* 2: 206-212, 1971.
26. Mirsky AF, Harman N: On aggressive behavior and brain disease—some questions and possible relationships derived from the study of men and monkeys, in Whalen R (ed): *Neuropsychology of Aggression*. New York, Plenum Press, 1975.
27. Monroe R: *Episodic Behavioral Disorders*. Cambridge, Harvard Univ. Press, 1970.
28. Niedermeyer E: *The Generalized Epilepsies*. Springfield, Ill., Charles C Thomas, 1972.
29. Ounsted C: Aggression and epilepsy—rage in children with temporal lobe epilepsy. *J Psychosom Res* 13: 237-242, 1969.
30. Rodin EA: Psychomotor epilepsy and aggressive behavior. *Arch Gen Psychiatry* 28: 210-213, 1973.
31. Roger A, Dongier M: Corrélations électrocliniques chez 50 épileptiques internés. *Rev Neurol* 83: 593-596, 1950.
32. Serafetinides EA: Aggressiveness in temporal lobe epileptics and its relation to cerebral dysfunction and environmental factors. *Epilepsia* 6: 33-42, 1965.
33. Small J: The organic dimension of crime. *Arch Gen Psych* 15: 82-89, 1966.
34. Stevens JR, Sachdev K, Milstein V: Behavior disorders of children and the EEG. *Arch Neurol* 18: 160-177, 1968.
35. Szondi L: *Triebpathologie*. Berne, Huber, 1952.
36. Taylor DC: Aggression and Epilepsy. *J of Psychosom Res* 13: 229-236, 1969.
37. Temkin O: *the Falling Sickness* (2nd ed). Baltimore, Johns Hopkins Press, 1971.
38. Treffert DA: The psychiatric patient with an EEG temporal lobe focus. *Am J Psychiatry* 120: 765-771, 1964.
39. Van der Horst L: Epilepsie mentale. *Riv Neurol* 10: 1109-25, 1964.
40. Walker AE: Murder or epilepsy? *J Nervous Mental Dis* 133: 430-437, 1961.
41. Walker AE: Man and his temporal lobes (John Hughlings Jackson Lecture). *Surg Neurol* 1: 69-79, 1973.
42. Walker AE, Blumer D: Long-term effects of temporal lobe lesions on sexual behavior and aggressivity, in *The Neurobiology of Violence*, WS Fields, WH Sweet (eds). St. Louis, Warren H. Green, 1975 .
43. Williams D: The structure of emotions reflected in epileptic experiences. *Brain* 79: 29-67, 1956.
44. Williams D: Neural factors related to habitual aggression. *Brain* 92: 503-522, 1969.

Treatment of the
Aggressive Patient

FRANCIS L. CARNEY

There are a number of questions that arise when we speak of "the aggressive patient." First, who is he? Displaced aggression forms the psychodynamic basis for many psychiatric illnesses, and aggressive behavior might be a part of a psychotic, neurotic or organic illness. Second, what is he? He is aggressive, no question, often violent and dangerous, but there has to be more to him than just that. Third, how can a clinician treat him and still retain a sense of his own safety and well-being? Fourth, what is the clinician's responsibility to the community? To put it another way, should the aggressive patient be treated at all or should he be locked up and forgotten, or given that he is locked up and treated, when is it safe to return him to society? Finally, if you do treat him, how do you treat him? This chapter will address itself to these questions.

DEFINING THE AGGRESSIVE PATIENT

For purposes of this chapter I shall consider the aggressive patient to be one who is suffering from a personality disorder as defined in DSM-II. However, as Lion (27) points out, these patients do not easily fall into categories, nor is it unusual for a personality-disordered individual to develop a neurotic or psychotic illness. Within the general grouping, acting-out tends to be a primary mode of defense, and for this reason these are the patients who most often tend to come into conflict with society and thus require such affirmative restraints as imprisonment or involuntary hospitalization. While the antisocial personality (or sociopath or psychopath) has a reputation for being the most dangerous, Cleckley (15) suggests that these individuals are most often a nuisance in their communities and to their families, that their irresponsible behavior leads to minor crimes, but that they are rarely involved in such things as rape, murder and aggravated assault. Cleckley also makes a clear distinction between the sociopath and the "ordinary" criminal, especially in that the criminal's behavior is orderly and well planned rather than impulsive, and in that the criminal can be loyal to friends, family and groups. I, too, have suggested that on a psychodynamic basis there is a distinction between criminality and sociopathy (11). There is also some evidence to suggest that violence cuts across diagnostic categories, and the most disturbing thing about this evidence is that there seem to be no clear-cut predictors of violent behavior. In fact, the best predictor of violent behavior is a history of violent behavior (18, 23).

The personality disorders form a large diagnostic classification, and while there are enough differences among them so as to define a paranoid personality, a passive-aggressive personality, an antisocial personality, and so forth, there are also enough similarities in their functioning so as to make possible some fairly specific statements about their treatment. But first I wish to consider two instances of personality disorder which have special treatment implications: (1) episodic dyscontrol and the explosive personality, and (2) the sexual offender.

Episodic Dyscontrol

Among the most violent individuals are those who suffer from episodic dyscontrol. Though not always clearly labeled as such, discussion of these patients can be found in Greenland (18), Sturup (47), and Monroe (35). The distinctive feature is that these patients tend to live lives not too far out of the ordinary until one day they commit some irrational and horrendous act. They are most often found "not guilty by reason of insanity" and committed to hospitals for the criminally insane. At this time a closer look at the life history of the patient reveals that there were plenty of warning signs had anyone bothered to notice, including such things as a history of enuresis, sexual dysfunction, moodiness, etc., and an exacerbation of these "minor" symptoms just prior to the violent act. The act itself is a release, and is followed by almost immediate remission of symptoms. Many institutions now release these most violent offenders in a very short time (two or three years) and with very good results.

It has been suggested that episodic dyscontrol is associated with psychomotor or temporal lobe epilepsy, but the data are controversial. Also open to some question is the differential diagnosis between "episodic dyscontrol" and "explosive personality," and whether or not the explosive personality should be a diagnostic entity separate from the other personality disorders. Pasternack (36) describes the explosive personality as follows: ". . .[he] often resorts to physical threats; he breaks furniture, throws objects, strikes his adversaries. He can be brutally sadistic . . . [he] takes major offense at minor insult; he reacts defensively when there is no need to defend." The distinction seems to be that the explosive personality has adopted a relatively enduring life pattern of more or less minor violence, while in episodic dyscontrol the patient has infrequent episodes of truly terrifying rage. No distinction between the two can be made with respect to organicity, and either, both, or neither can have an organic basis.

This brings us to one of the more controversial ways of treating violent behavior: psychiatric neurosurgery (14). A full discussion of this treatment is beyond the scope of this chapter, but it is important to note that it is a method again coming back into vogue. From the mid-thirties to the mid-fifties pre-frontal lobotomies were in fashion, but after twenty years of lobotomizing patients with all kinds of disorders, the results were so inconclusive—even disheartening—that psychosurgery acquired a bad reputation and was largely discontinued. However, in the 1960's, with advances in surgical technique and as experimental surgery taught more about the relationship of specific behavior to brain function, there came a resurgence of interest in the control of behavior through surgery. Mark and Neville (33) state that no human behavior is the consequence of just the brain or just the environment, and for the cause of violent behavior one must look to both. While they admit that psychiatric neurosurgery is still experimental, they also say that there is solid medical evidence to link aggressive behavior to focal brain disease. However, the new interest in psychiatric neurosurgery is prompted as much by social conditions as it is by advances in medicine, and there are those in our society who advocate massive surgical intervention to control the most violent people in our institutions. These surgical techniques have already been used injudiciously and have generated civil suits in several parts of the country, and several organizations have sprung up to protect the rights of patients and prisoners. Psychiatric neurosurgery has the potential to become a political tool, and Mark and Neville state unequivocally that it *"should never be performed on per-*

sons in any context in which they are under the jurisdiction of a court as the result of alleged criminal activity." (Italics in the original.)

The results of psychiatric neurosurgery are still controversial and still not encouraging. When we consider that diagnosis of organicity in conjunction with explosive and violent behavior is the exception and not the rule, and when we consider the irreversible effects of neurosurgery, it must be concluded that this is a heroic form of treatment which is justified in only the most exceptional circumstances.

On the other hand, behavior which is characterized by periodic explosiveness does particularly lend itself to medical intervention. Most psychiatrists do make use of the psychotropic drugs in conjunction with their psychotherapy of violent patients, and some, Maletzky (29), for example, have reported dramatic results when they have treated explosive patients with Dilantin. However, no one suggests that medication alone is enough, and psychotherapy is a part of every treatment.

The Sexual Offender

There is reason to question the dangerousness of sex offenders (18,19,43). There are apparently two predominant myths both in psychiatry and among the general public: (1) the sex offender moves from less violent to more violent crimes, i.e., the exhibitionist of today is the rapist of tomorrow; and (2) incalculable psychological harm is done to the victim. There is no evidence to support either of these statements. In fact, the exhibitionist is likely always to be an exhibitionist, the voyeur a voyeur, and so forth; and not only is there no evidence to suggest that adults are damaged psychologically by sexual attack, there is also no evidence to suggest that children suffer lasting psychological harm as the result of pedophiliac attack. Sex offenders, as a class, cannot be considered dangerous, but they do offend against public morality, and they do frequently end up in jails and in hospitals. *Some of them* act-out violently. There is some question, too, that sexual deviation per se is a personality disorder. As an illustration one need only think of the recent controversy in the American Psychiatric Association over homosexuality. There is probably less question about the sexual *offender* having a personality disorder in that in order to be an offender the individual has to bring his deviation to public attention. Studies of sex offenders generally reveal in them characteristics of the personality disorders as a whole, and their psychotherapy does not differ markedly from the other personality disorders. I include them as a group apart from the others because they are subject to two unique treatment techniques.

The first of these is castration. The last Western nation to judicially impose castration as a "treatment" was Nazi Germany, and the magnitude of the abuses under that system dramatically illustrate the more subtle abuses which occurred in other countries at other times, and most modern nations did judicially impose castration as a treatment at one time or another. In the United States such laws have been declared unconstitutional. The newer approach is to give legal sanction for the castration *when the patient volunteers*, though some might question how "voluntary" it is when the alternative is possibly long years of imprisonment. Several European countries do now have laws which allow patients to volunteer for castration under certain circumstances. In Denmark, for example, persons coming under that law include those who have offended against women, including rapists, those who threaten rape, and those who abuse females who are incompetent by reason of psychosis or mental deficiency; those who sexually abuse children; persons convicted of incest; and persons who offend against public morality, such as exhibitionists. When application is made for the castration, there is a careful psychiatric review before the surgery is performed. Sturup (48) believes that only a small number of dangerous sex offenders are amenable to any form of psychotherapy, and he feels that the only hope of helping the greater number is by reducing both their libido and potency through removal of the sex-hormone-producing glands. He says that studies of recidivist rates of sex offenders in Denmark and in other European countries demonstrate that castration is an effective technique for the control of aggressive sexual acting-out.

The second unique treatment technique is the administration of a wide variety of hormones and/or sex suppressant drugs. Chatz (13), for example, recommends the following in the treatment of sexually aggressive adolescents: Thioridazine, 20 to 50 mg. three times a day, which has the side effect of producing impotence; an estrogen such as Stilboestral, 0.5 to 4 mg. per day; or Cyproteran which has an antiandrogenic effect. This is one of many therapies, and it is enough to indicate here that these therapies have proliferated, that the drugs used are often experimental, and that the results have been mixed.

There is no doubt that both surgery and medicine have their place in the treatment of aggressive behavior. But one should consider carefully before using any technique that will bring about structural change in order to bring about behavioral change, especially if that structural change is irreversible as in the case of surgery. Every practitioner indicates that both medicine and surgery are ancillary to the primary treatment mode, psychotherapy, and that psychotherapy is the cornerstone of any successful treatment of violence, and so we turn our attention to that now.

PERSONALITY DYNAMICS AND THEIR RELATION TO PSYCHOTHERAPY.

It is not enough to say a patient is violent, aggressive and explosive, nor is it enough to label him as one with a "personality disorder" or even to refine the diagnosis down to antisocial personality or passive-aggressive personality. Patients are something more than labels, and the labels themselves are often misleading. For psychotherapy to be effective one must get beyond the often pejorative labels to describe the human process. What is the aggressive patient? The literature answers this question with remarkable consistency. In the following sections I shall attempt a synthesis of current research, opinion and experience, with particular emphasis on the work of Adler and Shapiro (1,2), Kozol (22), Lion (25), Manne (31), Schmideberg (42), Sturup (46,47) Teitelbaum (49) and Vaillant (50). With this as a foundation I shall try to describe the aggressive patient as one who has four specific inabilities: (1) the inability to trust, (2) the inability to feel, (3) the inability to fantasize, and (4) the inability to learn. We shall see that a number of personality traits arise from each inability and that each poses its own problems for therapy.

The Inability to Trust

There is virtually unanimous agreement that this is the core issue in the treatment of the personality disorders. In some instances it is expressed as "the inability to form object relationships," which may be a better description of the pervasive distortions in the interpersonal relationships of all these patients. Since the patients accept nothing at face value, every meeting with them becomes a confrontation, and their "game" is to ferret out the therapist's "con" while at the same time giving the therapist a "con." They have no willingness—perhaps not even the capacity—to believe that other human beings can be sincere.

The game that they take into therapy is an extension of the game they play in all life situations. Somewhere in their life histories they have learned that honesty and sincerity don't pay, that their needs are fulfilled more readily when they play some prescribed role. Whatever real feelings they might have they have long ago learned to repress or displace, and whatever dreams, hopes, values they may have they have learned to deny. They are what some other person makes of them. By themselves they are never complete human beings—perhaps one reason why their inappropriate behavior almost always occurs in a social context. Unlike the psychotic, they cannot withdraw and hallucinate, and unlike the neurotic, they cannot fret in self-imposed loneliness; in fact, they are recognized as disturbed human beings because of their acts against particular others or against society in general. Because they are incomplete they are often described as infantile or immature, and while this may be an apt description of their functioning at any given time, one rarely finds an all-inclusive immaturity; rather, it's as if there were curious maturational lacunae in an otherwise mature individual. One of the more frequent lacunae concerns sex role behavior, so it isn't at all unusual to see them indulging themselves homosexually as well as heterosexually or to find them easily making a shift to homosexuality when confined.

However, the point is that they do not have any true sense of self, i.e., a self-concept which endures from situation to situation. Rather, in each new situation they are a new person. This is akin to the social psychologist's concept of "role playing"; the difference is that the normal individual brings to each role a consistent set of values, thoughts and feelings which he imposes on the situation so that whether he is employer or employee, father or husband, he is always basically the same person, while the personality-disturbed individual enters each new situation like a blank tape ready to record the expectancies of others and then to play back. One individual easily assumes the role of the weeping and repentant son, the high-stepping dude of the street gangs, the callous inmate, the political prisoner, the sick patient, and the sincerely motivated object of the therapist's concern. Through all of these roles there is no real person, only a reacting organism.

If the gaming was so blatantly obvious, there might not be too much trouble in treating these individuals, but it is an incredibly subtle game. These patients have an amazing capacity to sense even the secret needs of others, and they then respond in such a way as to fulfill those needs. We have only to remember how parents, spouses and lovers time and again gave these people a "second" chance even though time and again they suffered frustration and disappointment. Therapists, too, become fooled by patients who say the right thing with the appropriate affect at the right time, patients who develop astounding insights, never realizing that over a period of months they have provided the patients with all the cues they need to work the successful con.

One ordinarily thinks of the personality-disordered individual as one who uses others to satisfy his own hedonistic needs. It might be more realistic to conceive of him as one who has been used by others and whose behavior is a defense against being used again. He doesn't trust because at some point in time his trust was betrayed; thereafter, in an almost compulsive way, he sets up situation after situation in which he can reexperience the original betrayal, thereby reinforcing his conception of an unfriendly world inhabited by selfish, uncaring people. He does not believe that anyone can sincerely care for him, especially not some alien therapist who most often is an agent of the same state that is prosecuting him.

If a major task in therapy is to win the trust of the patient, then there are many roadblocks in the way of successful therapy with the aggressive behavior disorders. By the very nature of the disorder these patients most often come to therapy by way of the courts, either as a condition of probation or while being confined in a security institution. Their potential for violence can be frightening, and it is the rare therapist in the outpatient setting who does not experience some personal apprehension when treating them, while in an institution the therapy takes place in an atmosphere of locks and guards. And the therapist, whatever his personal commitment to the patient, is an agent of the state, and he does have to be concerned with the safety of society. This is the person who says to the untrusting patient, "Trust me."

There is perhaps one specific technique which facilitates the winning of trust: honesty on the part of the therapist. By this I mean direct, open, forthright dialogue with the patient. In the treatment of the behavior disorders there is no room for the analyst's couch, nor even room for the reflecting and interpreting of the Rogerian. The therapist must be willing to be a real person, one who has his own thoughts, feelings and values, one who is not afraid to express them and take responsibility for them. Therapists must be able to say to patients, "You're making me angry," or "You're making me afraid." They must be able to say, "I don't like what you did," or "What you did really pleases me." From the very beginning the therapist must structure with the patient just how he sees his responsibilities—to the patient, to legal authorities and to society. If there are limits to the confidentiality of therapy, the patient must know them. Having set the limits, the therapist must never violate them. In some ways the therapist must be more human—he can't tell a "little white lie," he can't evade, he must always be cognizant of the feelings the patient generates in him, he must never promise more than he knows he can deliver, and he must openly take responsibility for any mistake or failure, for the patient will seize on anything to convince himself that the betrayal has occurred again. The patient will attempt to induce the rejection; his experience tells him it has always happened before, and it is all that he expects.

The Inability to Feel

Personality-disordered individuals are often characterized as being callous and free from anxiety and depression. Their very inability to feel remorse or to suffer pain is often given as the reason why they do not learn from experience and why punishment has no effect on them. Having no sense of psychic discomfort, they have no motivation to be treated, and, if forced into treatment, they have no idea of what is expected of them nor any willingness to learn. They enter therapy most often because (1) they are experiencing some physical discomfort in the sense of being locked up or faced with a long prison term unless they "volunteer" for treatment, or (2) they find themselves in a psychiatric institution which requires therapy as a condition for release. In both instances there is an element of coercion; in both instances the patients enter into a game with the hope of winning some reward.

As I've indicated, the individual then begins to play the "patient role," eventually giving the therapist everything the therapist hoped to see. The patient is only too willing to feed the therapist's expectations, to be suitably depressed, anxious, angry, or to generate any other feeling he thinks the therapist thinks is appropriate. Yet every actor eventually steps offstage, and every actor is then confronted with the reality of himself. Our patients do not confront this reality long before they take on another role: the reality of self is too upsetting, it awakens too much anxiety, and it brings on feelings of depression. For however brief a time our patients do have real feelings, and their escape to a new role is a defense against them. In short, each of the "inabilities" is not so much a real inability as it is a brick in a defensive wall, a wall behind which the individual crouches in terror of both his internal and external environment. Through his acts he makes himself visible in society and so he seems more accessible than the isolated neurotic or the withdrawn psychotic, but in fact he is more isolated and withdrawn than the regressed schizophrenic on the hospital's back ward. Perhaps it is this very gap between the illusion and the reality which contributes so much to therapist frustration with these patients: they look as if they'd be so easy to treat; perhaps if they looked more like the regressed schizophrenic, one could better appreciate the treatment task and wouldn't look for easy cures.

It is not that these patients cannot feel; they will not feel because the pain is too great. To defend against feeling they have a number of maneuvers, two of which are particularly predominant. The first is acting-out, which is universally characteristic of the group. Action relieves tension, and so long as one is doing, one doesn't have time to think, feel or introspect. Acting-out is antithetical to therapy, in which awareness rather than doing is the key, so one of the first tasks of the therapist is to prevent acting-out. This is generally not possible in the outpatient clinic. The patient characteristically will experience just so much tension before he leaves therapy, even if this means a violation of his probation or other court order. Even in an institution—unless there is a commitment for an indeterminate period—the tendency is for the patient to leave therapy when his anxiety hits a certain level. It is also characteristic of these patients to create conditions which require their removal from therapy—by violating laws and going to jail, an effective way of ending outpatient treatment; by grossly inappropriate behavior in an institution so as to require their segregation; or by awakening so much fear in the therapist that the therapist terminates them—in this way achieving the desired end while avoiding the responsibility for it. To control acting-out some affirmative restraints are required, though most often it is some agent other than the therapist who imposes them. The therapist, however, must define the limits of acceptable behavior within the therapy session.

It is easier to describe the second maneuver than to name it. When the patient has a feeling he doesn't care to experience, he elicits the same feeling from some other in his environment; in this way the other experiences the emotion and the patient doesn't have to. By way of example, we almost always find that the relatives of these patients are terribly worried and concerned; the patients aren't. Another example: it is not unusual to find a physician prescribing for these patients a wide variety of medication to control their anxiety; we might wonder who is the more anxious. The empathetic therapist does become aware of the intense pain his therapy will uncover, and too often he responds to the patient's plea to spare him. Because the therapist does care, he can be too willing to accept the sham feelings the patient is willing to give, too hesitant to let the patient hurt.

It follows, therefore, that a major technique of therapy is to let the patient hurt. On the one hand, it is the therapist's task to take responsibility for everything he thinks and feels, but on the other, he must insist that the patient take full responsibility for his own feelings and his own actions. Most often the patients attempt to use the therapist as a tool, sometimes casting him in the role of advocate, sometimes in the role of scapegoat, but always the aim is to arouse strong feelings in the therapist, to force him to do the worrying, to impel him to take the action that will make everything right again. Most therapists don't like to see their patients hurt, yet there are times when pain has curative power and when the absence of pain perpetuates disease. Inevitably we must deal with the patients' fear of feeling, and no therapy with this group can be successful until that has been accomplished.

The Inability to Fantasize

Acting-out—to solve problems and relieve tensions by doing rather than by thinking—is characteristic of the group. The idea is the father of the deed and there are no intervening processes, no thinking through, no wondering what would happen if . . . In the normal individual, fantasy can serve a useful defensive function. The normal can and does permit in fantasy expression of behavior which might be illegal or immoral or highly self-defeating. The normal may use fantasy to win otherwise unattainable success or fame or glory, perhaps in this way solving unsolvable problems or easing the depression of an existence which for the moment has become tedious. Also, through fantasy the normal can anticipate a situation and work out "in his mind" alternative responses before he ever enters the situation in reality, in this way avoiding "spur of the moment decisions" and controlling potentially impulsive behavior. All of these things the normal can do; the personality-disordered individual cannot, and as a consequence it is said that he is impulsive, that he has little ability to plan, and that his judgment is poor.

There is also another aspect to this deficit in the personality, the inability to empathize. At first this might seem more related to the inability to form object relationships, but at this point I am speaking of a real inability "to put yourself in the other guy's place." As these patients relate their crimes, especially some particular act of violence, one is struck by the fact that they really don't comprehend the pain they were inflicting, and they are often genuinely surprised that the victim has experienced injury or death. In their thinking, a violent confrontation is much like little boys playing war: lots of sound and histrionics, but at the end the "dead" soldiers get up and go home to dinner. Even with regard to minor crimes they truly do not understand why the victim is angry. Certainly, they do not comprehend the measures society takes to punish and contain them. And from this inability to empathize we tend to infer about them two more traits: a fantastic ability to rationalize, and a callous disregard for the rights of others.

The above might seem at variance with my previous comment that the ability of these patients to work a successful con is linked to their acute sensitivity to the feelings of others. However, to intellectually know how another is feeling is not to feel along with him. Also, the patients' sensitivity is selective: they tune in when they have something to gain; while they are acting-out, the only concern is the release of tension.

Some therapists feel that, after trust, this should be the major area of intervention, that the patients should actually be taught to fantasize. One can't argue with the theory. As I've indicated, fantasy properly used has both a defensive and problem-solving function, and it can help to bring about such things as impulse control, relief of tension and anxiety, the ability to plan actions and anticipate consequences, and could possibly lead to an increased ability to empathize. There seem to be two specific techniques, the first of which is psychodrama. The literature suggests that this is a technique which has not been used too often with this group, and the best success seems to have occurred with acting-out adolescents. The more frequent technique is used in conjunction with traditional group and individual psychotherapy: the therapist stays attuned to say such things as, "What do you think will happen when you . . ." "When you did that, what do you suppose the other guy thought?" "What do you suppose would happen if you didn't do that but instead you . . ."

As we shall see later, no one technique of therapy is superior to any other in the treatment of this group, given that the therapist is open and accessible, and in the end no therapy has succeeded in turning out whole human beings in the sense of making these patients able in every area in which they were once disabled. The inability to fantasize seems particularly resistive to psychotherapy, perhaps because fantasy, as a defense, is so closely linked to psychosis. Over the years many people have suggested that there is a close link between the severe personality disorders and schizophrenia, and it has been hypothesized that acting-out does serve as a defense against a psychotic break. In any event, our patients, even as they become more and more socialized, do not give up acting-out as a defense, and their ability to fantasize remains at a rudimentary level.

The Inability to Learn

In most descriptions of the personality disorders, perhaps no phrase appears more frequently than this: they are unable to profit by experience. This is essentially what I mean by inability to learn, for we already know that these patients are quite capable of learning role expectations within a given situation, but no transfer of learning seems to take place. The discussion so far indicates why this is so. If each experience is a new experience, then there can be no generalizing from one situation to another.

Let us consider for a moment the role of behavior therapy in the treatment of the aggressive behavior disorders. Behavior therapy is based on learning principles, and according to Schwitzbebel (44), "The primary focus of learning theory approaches to behavior change is the modification of the environment of the patient or subject. Internal feelings, thoughts, or states of the person are not necessarily ignored but they are not usually the major objects of intervention." The major techniques used are aversive conditioning (e.g., treating alcoholics with antibuse), punishment, modeling (which is very similar to transference), and operant conditioning. It is the last which has been used most frequently in institutions, and it generally takes the form of some "token economy." Essentially this means that the patients earn rewards by engaging in certain specific behaviors, such as by going to school or to work, or by keeping the ward clean, or by keeping appointments on time, and so forth. These token economies have been used extensively now in psychiatric hospitals, training schools, institutions for the mentally retarded, and some prisons, and almost always there are glowing reports of remarkable behavioral change in the subjects. It is always emphasized that as a result the institution is a much easier place to manage. But when it comes to follow-up studies, and there aren't many of them published, we find that the behavioral change is rarely permanent. The best results seem to occur with regressed schizophrenics and mental defectives; the worst results occur with the personality disorders. This could certainly have been predicted. Our patients are master game players, and token economics arc just new games to challenge their skills.

The failure of token economies with the personality disorders is in itself evidence of the inability of these patients to generalize from experience and to transfer learning from one situation to another. But we've had other evidence for a long while. Long before there was a science called behavior modification, society sent behaviorally disturbed children to training schools and behaviorally disturbed adults to prisons with the firm expectation that their behavior would be modified, if not by the punishment of imprisonment then by the various rehabilitation programs which became a part of institutional existence. Like the theorists, society placed its focus on the disruptive behavior rather than on the internal state of the individual, and society has learned—though the theorists may not yet have—that this approach rarely brings about any permanent behavior change, and it has become an accepted "fact" that behaviorally disordered individuals do not learn from experience.

However, we do know that our patients do learn within any given situation; it is the transfer of learning that is the problem. It's as if the patients have become fixed at some moment in time, with no awareness of past experience and no expectations for the future. They are present-oriented and so require satisfaction of needs in the here and now. This has led to such descriptive labels as narcissism, hedonism and inability to delay gratification. Yet it is possible that each of these behavioral traits grow out of the patients' warped sense of time. If there is no future, then who can be blamed for grabbing what he can now? If there is no future, there is hardly any sense to make sacrifices to prepare for it, and given a deficit in the fantasy function, one can't even image what might happen next. However, I don't mean to imply that their time sense is totally warped, as in depersonalization for example; rather, there is some disturbance in the perception of time which does have behavioral consequences.

It follows that one technique of therapy is to delay rewards and to assist the patients to make plans for the future, to help them set goals and then work toward the attainment of the goals. The patients will always be concerned with the immediacy of their situation, but the therapist at least can take a wider view. Perhaps one advantage a total institutional program has over outpatient therapy is that the therapist can take the initial responsibility for getting the patients into work or school programs, and the therapist can indicate that success in these programs is part of the treatment goals. But it can never be assumed that good work performance is itself a sign of successful treatment; it may only mean that the patients have learned a new role to play at this moment in time.

THE ROLE OF THE THERAPIST

I've already indicated that psychotherapy with the aggressive patient probably should not follow traditional patterns. In order to emphasize this point let me quote Schmideberg (42): "Clinically oriented psychotherapy [with offenders] is based on empirical assessment of the patient's mentality and the current situation; it stresses the present and is geared toward the future; it tries selectively to reinforce desirable attitudes and influences while countering others. It relies on the personal relation, . . . [and] it is in stark contrast to orthodox analysis."

Given this particular form of therapy with its emphasis on the personal relationship, and given the particular personality characteristics of this kind of patient, the therapist is likely to encounter problems different from those he might encounter in more traditional practice. These include: (1) fear of the patient, (2) feelings of omnipotence, and (3) responsibility to society. All of these, even the last, could be considered to be aspects of countertransference, and it would not be unfair to say that when we deal with aggressive patients countertransference reactions tend to be extreme, and psychotherapy with this group, perhaps more than with any other, requires that the therapist be continually aware of himself.

I wish to consider each of the problems separately, and the discussion here is based mainly on the work of Adler and Shapiro (1,2) and Lion and Pasternak (26).

Fear of the Patient

A therapist who deals with patients who have a history of violence has a legitimate concerr about his own safety, but as Lion and Pasternak say, " . . . we have observed that anxiety concerning the patients' dangerousness often gets out of hand." Part of the problem undoubtedly lies in the therapist and the characteristic ways he has of handling his own aggressions. The hostility of the patient is likely to awaken hostility in the therapist, and we find therapists who, quite unaware, move from a treatment to a punitive mode, the likely result being that the patient will become even more hostile. Therapists may feel helpless in the face of the violence or it may awken old fears, and this may lead to a distorted perception of the patient and a consequent distortion of treatment methods and goals.

Feelings of fear are intimately related to the whole issue of trust, and in the therapist-patient relationship there might be some question of who fears whom more. The patient enters the situation suspiciously in the first place and with a host of personality characteristics which militate against the formation of a therapeutic relationship. All object relations are dangerous, and his anger can be seen as a defense against the threatening therapist. If the therapist responds with fear, his fear combines with that of the patient, and the whole situation is soon out of control. If the therapist attempts to minimize aggression by vacillating and conciliating, the patient seizes control of the therapy and does in fact dominate the relationship in a bullying kind of way. On the other hand, if the therapist attempts to control aggression by smothering the patient with kindness and reassurance, the patient will likely play the passive role and wait for the therapist to treat him and cure him. In short, one of the major symptoms bringing the patient into therapy is aggression and the therapist can neither ignore it nor flee from it. It must be handled as directly and reasonably as any other symptom, and the therapist who conveys a feeling of confidence and stability is the one who will help the patient most. It would be unrealistic to say that there are not real dangers in the situation, but nothing will cause a patient to lose control faster than loss of control in the therapist.

Feelings of Omnipotence

One important way to help the patient keep control is to set limits. This occurs within the therapeutic setting itself, but with these patients it frequently occurs within an institutional setting as well. Like it or not, the therapist is usually more than just a symbollic authority figure; society delegates to him real power and control over significant aspects of the patient's life. This is necessary, for without affirmative restraints the patients wouldn't sit still long enough for any therapy to take place. To keep his patients the therapist pays a price. He is first of all a target, since he is the embodiment of hated authority, but as therapy proceeds he becomes something more: he becomes omnipotent. The patient begins to invest him with a power and authority which he does not have, and this can be so pleasing to the ego of the therapist that his reality testing goes awry, and he can find himself in the role of white knight on a charger championing the cause of his patients.

This is not an easy problem to either avoid or solve. A goal in most psychotherapies is to help the patient make decisions and choices and then to act on them. Our patients are most often in a situation where they cannot make a free choice, or having made choies, are not free to act on them. Consider a man in prison: after months of therapy he may decide that his best vocational choice is a job as a lathe operator, but the prison shop won't take him because of his past behavior. Is it the therapist's function to go to the shop and convince the instructor that his patient is now ready and the timing is right, or should he counsel his patient to wait longer and improve his behavioral record in the meantime? One could find arguments for either course. Consider the same man when the therapist feels he's ready to go back into society. Does the therapist speak up for him at a parole hearing, or does he allow the man to present himself and take his chances? In most settings the therapist cannot avoid being the agent of his patients, and after months of close personal involvement it is a very difficult thing to be perfectly objective about the patient, and it is often difficult to determine what the patient can logically do for himself and what the therapist must do for him. As I mentioned above, there is no way to solve the problem except by being continually aware, accepting nothing at face value, not even internal feelings, and questioning everything. When the therapist loses touch with reality, the therapy is doomed.

Responsibility to Society

Perhaps nothing awakens more conflict in therapists than this: when we deal with the aggressive patient we must continually weigh the welfare of the individual against the best interests of society, and we must make a choice. At the beginning we make choices between outpatient and inpatient treatment, we choose between punishment and rehabilitation, between hospital and jail, and later we make choices between freedom and continued incarceration. We make these choices for others; to a large degree, society has turned us into judges and in some ways has given us even more authority than wardens and parole boards. We have the right of law behind us, but no one as yet has legislated us into responsibility, which remains unique and individual, and each therapist assumes or denies the responsibility in his own unique way.

There are those among us who feel that certain categories of violent individuals should never be treated, that they should be destroyed or sent to institutions for long, long periods of time. Others are willing to admit the possibility of treatment as long as some punishment is involved, while still others feel that punishment is a waste and that all violent individuals should be treated. Some feel that a violent person should never be returned to society unless there is an almost iron-clad guarantee that he will not act-out again; others are willing to go with a 50-50 or 60-40 or 70-30 gamble that society will be safe; while still others focus entirely on the individual and pay scant attention to the demands of society. Every therapist has an opinion and a philosophy, and they do play a role in the therapist's decision-making process.

When a therapist deals with violent individuals, he is most often a part of a team, which may include co-professionals but which may also include police officers, lawyers, judges, probation officers, wardens, correctional officers and parole boards. Not only do his patients have less freedom of choice, the therapist himself has less freedom of choice. Whatever philosophy he brings to the situation, whatever decisions he deems best, his action are likely to be tempered by the philosophies of other team members. However frustrating his patients may be, he may find the frustration of dealing with officialdom greater still. Therapist and patient both are required to deal with a real world that neither may like. It is only too easy for the therapist and patient to form a team that does battle against reality, and that was the patient's problem in the first place. If it should happen—and it happens frequently—one might say that the patient has won the "therapy game," that he has convinced the therapist that the world is hostile and uncaring and that the best defense is an offense.

There is much more to this, the therapist's perception of his role with respect to patients and society, but space does not permit me to consider it in more detail. Suffice it to say that in this directive kind of therapy the therapist is called upon to make many decisions, and each decision occurs in the context of the therapist as a total person. Neither the permissive nor the punitive therapist is likely to be too successful, but there is a world of interpsonal processes between these extremes.

RESULTS OF TREATMENT

Behavior Modification

We can discuss behavior modification very quickly: there is nothing in the literature to suggest that behavior modification techniques used with the personality disorders have ever led to enduring behavioral change, at least not in a statistically significant way, though there may be isolated cases of success. The literature is replete with studies of in-house token economy or other conditioning techniques which did bring about significant behavioral change, but these changes never generalized beyond the immediate situation. Kazdin and Bootzin (22) point out that in token economy programs there have been few studies on generalization and resistance to extinction, few attempts to control complex social behaviors, and that the stability of change is just not known. Levine and Fasnacht (24) express concern at the proliferation of token economy programs, and they say, "Based both on theoretical considerations and on practical experience, we feel that token approaches will do more harm than good when applied in what is an increasingly promiscuous manner."

In spite of the warning voices from their own ranks, the behaviorists have pushed ahead with behavior modification programs in the nation's prisons, and they've run into trouble. An article in the *Monitor* of the American Psychological Association (3) comments on the "sweeping ban of behavior modification" imposed by the Law Enforcement Assistance Administration, and Berwick and Morris (6) discuss the implications of recent court decisions with regard to the civil rights of inmates who are subjects of behavior modification experiments, agreeing that the continued use of traditional reinforcers and punishments might indeed violate the rights of the individuals. Possibly many of the programs now in operation will have to cease, and there will probably be fewer behavior modification programs in institutions in the future, but all for the wrong reason. The ban has been ordered by public agencies; behaviorists are still reluctant to admit that their present techniques don't work.

But all is not gloomy on the behavioral scene. There is reason to believe that behavioral modification techniques used in conjunction with other approaches can have a significant impact. Sage (41), while attacking most behaviorists and their techniques, speaks quite favorably of a program at Atascadero State Hospital in California, which attempts to reeducate homosexual pedophiles. Essentially, the idea is to bring these homosexual men into the homosexual mainstream, making no attempt to change the same-sex preference, but teaching them how to feel comfortable with adult "gays" and even how to "cruise" a "gay bar" in order to find an adult companion. Though there are some holdouts, there seems to be a growing number of behaviorists who have come to realize that they must treat their subjects as complex social beings who operate in a world wider than the ward or the institution, and their new learning, if it is to endure, must be meaningful in the wider world.

Individual and Group Psychotherapy

There is almost universal agreement that group psychotherapy works best, though different people have different reasons for saying so. Most therapists settle on the group after trying both, and their choice is based on the experience of what works best. The above discussion of transference and countertransference problems perhaps suggests why this might be so. The nature and intensity of feelings generated almost require that they be somewhat dispersed. On another level, a patient has less opportunity to work his "con" if there are other patients present to keep him honest. In any event, group therapy is the preferred method.

Outpatient Psychotherapy

In working with aggressive patients the principles and techniques of psychotherapy do not differ markedly whether the setting be inpatient or outpatient. What is apt to differ most is the personality structure of the patient, and it can be assumed that any patient who lasts in outpatient therapy had a more intact ego structure to begin with. The more severe the deficit of ego controls the higher the probability of acting-out and the greater the likelihood of eventual incarceration. Outpatient treatment of this less disturbed group has generally been successful.

Lion et al. (28) report on a violence clinic which has many of the features of a crisis intervention center. Lion, in another article (26), says of his outpatients: "Patients who experience violent impulses desperately want help in curbing such urges." Peters and Roether (37) discuss group psychotherapy for probationed sex offenders. Using a matched control group of nontreated offenders, they report that on two-year follow-up 27 percent of the nontreated group had been rearrested for sex-related crimes as opposed to only 3 percent of the treated group.

Sadoff et al. (40) provide some interesting insights into the dynamics when patients are forced into outpatient treatment. The patients were convicted sex offenders who, as a condition of probation, were required to attend group psychotherapy. After forty weeks of treatment each patient was rexamined by an independent psychiatrist who, at the same time, also administered a questionnaire designed to assess the patient's attitude toward therapy. The psychiatrist was asked to predict the recidivists. At the end of treatment, the treating psychiatrist was also asked to predict the recidivists. The first finding was that patients who expressed the most positive attitudes about therapy were those most often rearrested, while those who expressed negative attitudes were not rearrested. Secondly, the treating psychiatrist more accurately predicted recidivism than the examining psychiatrist. The results might be explained as follows: patients who express positive attitudes are probably "conning," and while the treating psychiatrist has ample opportunity to see through the con, the examining psychiatrist does not; on the other hand, the expression of negative attitudes can be an indication that the patient feels free to express feeling, but the examining psychiatrist is apt to see it as an expression of hostility.

This study certainly has implication for court psychiatrists, who most often are the ones responsible for recommending either outpatient treatment or incarceration, but in practice the selection of outpatients is a trial-and-error process. If an outpatient continues to commit crimes while he is in treatment, or if he absconds from supervision or avoids treatment, obviously he shouldn't have been selected in the first place. Those who complete treatment are those who had the best prognosis from the beginning, so it isn't surprising that treatment results are generally good.

Inpatient Psychotherapy

From the above it follows that the most severe of the personality disorders are treated while in institutions. Most authorities believe that a "whole person" approach is required, such as that described by Sturup (47) and which is implemented at the Herstedvester Detention Center in Denmark. This means that in addition to formal psychotherapy the therapist has some direct participation in helping the patient to choose and attain vocational and educational goals, that he is involved with the day-to-day management of the patient in his living situation, that he acts as consultant to custodial and other personnel concerned with the patient, and that he directly participates in all major decisions regarding the patient from the moment he enters the institution until the day he leaves and even beyond. However, there are few institutions in which this major effort is being undertaken.

Borriello (7) reports on his work with thirty-nine patients in a psychiatric hospital, most of whom had committed violent crimes and had been found "not guilty by reason of insanity." These patients were in group psychotherapy three days a week over a period of about two years before they were released into the community. A two-year follow-up indicated that the recidivist rate was only 20 percent. This is an exceptional finding and is perhaps a good indication that the patients did actually have a psychiatric illness other than a personality disorder, and it may also say something about treatment in a hospital as opposed to treatment in a prison.

Within the prison system, Fink et al. (17) report on a total team approach in Dannemora prison. They were quite gratified with the improvement in their patients, but they offer no follow-up data. Morris and Conway (32) discuss the problems of psychotherapy in a prison climate, but they too feel there was general improvement in their patients even though no follow-up data are given. Rappaport (39), too, has not done a follow-up study of his prison groups, but he makes the important comment that paroled men, given the opportunity to return and continue in the group, did so, and these men continued to use the group to help solve problems outside of prison. Brancale et al. (8) give a rather detailed report on the kind of therapy they use with committed sex offenders, a therapy which utilizes the "whole man" concept, provides direct sex education, and emphasizes emotional release during marathon groups.

Kozol et al. (23) discuss their work at the Center for the Care and Treatment of Dangerous Persons in Massachusetts. They state that the object of treatment is to modify the patient's dangerous potential, and "individualization is the essence of treatment." Individual treatment does not mean individual therapy, and, in fact, a combination of individual and group therapy was found to work best. Their whole approach to psychotherapy was largely experimental. For example, it was found that a group of highly verbal "good treatment prospects" were more impressive than sincere, while a group of "least treatable" patients made surprising progress. Other treatment groups were of essentially neurotic patients, who made rapid therapeutic progress; psychopathic patients, who made little progress at all; and patients convicted of the same crime, who made progress regardless of diagnosis. However, the emphasis was always on individualization, and sometimes this meant no more than a supportive case work approach. Their results indicated that when patients were released into the community by the courts but against the advice of the Center, the recidivist rate ranged between 30 and 40 percent. When patients were released after being fully treated, the recidivist rate dropped to about 6 percent.

Carney (9) also provides us with a detailed report of his work in the Mental Health Unit at Walpole State Prison. The Unit comprised 15 percent of the inmate population and was staffed by two psychologists, three psychiatric social workers and one psychology assistant, all of whom were involved in group or individual psychotherapy. All of the patients in treatment were voluntary. For the study, Carney used a sample of 115 patients who had at least twenty-five weeks of psychotherapy and who had been out of the prison for at least four years; they were matched with a control group of 138 inmates who had never received psychotherapy. Statistically, he determined that the expected recidivist rate for the groups would be 68 percent; the actual recidivist rate for the treated group was 53 percent, which was found to be a statistically significant difference, while the actual recidivist rate for the control group was 69 percent. However, in order to make these findings more meaningful, Carney considered another group: this was a group of men who had volunteered for therapy but who, for one reason or another, were never actually treated before their release. The expected recidivist rate for this group was 65.5 percent; their actual rate was 52.5 percent, another statistically significant difference. Carney concluded that the decision to volunteer for therapy was a quite important factor in eventual success. Among his other findings: (1) men with shorter records tended to benefit most from therapy; (2) older inmates with long records also benefited; (3) the longer 1 and 2 above were in therapy, the more positive the results; (4) young inmates with long records did not benefit, and the longer they were in therapy the higher their recidivist rate; (5) individual therapy seemed best when treatment was short-term, while group therapy was best when treatment was long-term; (6) treated recidivists were generally arrested for less serious crimes.

A most important study was made by Jew et al. (21), which perhaps sheds some light on why prison psychotherapy programs are not especially successful. The patient sample was selected from the therapy groups of six therapists between 1958 and 1962. These six included two psychiatrists, two psychologists and two correctional counselors. The patients had at least one continuous year of therapy with the same therapist, averaging eight hours of therapy per month. The final size of the sample came to 257. There was a carefully matched comparison sample of inmates from other correctional institutions who had not been in psychotherapy. The criterion used in assessing the degree of social adaptation and functioning of the patient upon his release from prison was whether or not he returned to prison. The results indicated that during the first year of parole the treated group maintained a significantly better adjustment rate than the untreated group. However, beginning in the second year, the gap between the two groups started to close, and by the fourth year of follow-up there was a negligible difference between the groups. The findings of the study suggest that there is some initial transfer of effects from prison therapy to the parole situation but that, at best, psychotherapy in prison does little more than delay a man's return to prison. The authors felt that psychotherapy should be a process that continues after a man is released from prison and that it should be an integral part of the parole program.

For contrast, compare the results from Patuxent Institution (34). Patuxent is the only institution in the United States which provides for both an indeterminate sentence and parole supervision by the professional staff of the Institution. Patuxent reports that in the first ten years of operation 794 men were recommended for commitment and treatment. Of these, 156 men were not committed by the courts and so returned to the Department of Corrections. A follow-up (anywhere from seven to seventeen years later) disclosed that this "untreated group" had a recidivist rate of 81 percent, considerably higher than the national recidivist rate of 65 percent, but not surprising when one considers that Patuxent recommends for treatment only the most severely disturbed individuals who already have a history of recidivism. Of the 638 men who were committed, 186 received only in-house treatment; without ever having been on parole, they were at some point released from the Institution by the courts against the advice of the Institution; this group was found to have a recidivist rate of 46 percent. There were 100 men who received treatment both in the Institution and while on parole before they were released against advice; the recidivist rate for this group was 39 percent. And there were 135 men who had both in-house treatment and treatment while on parole for at least three years and who were recommended for complete release by the Institution; their recidivist rate was only 7 percent.

Both the study by Jew and the report from Patuxent point out one very important thing: for these most behaviorally disturbed patients the treatment process cannot end in the institution. All of the reports from institutions indicate that psychotherapy can bring about dramatic improvement while the patient is incarcerated, but the traditional psychotherapists are faced with the same problem as their behavior modification colleagues: these patients seem unable to transfer their learning from one situation to another. For any psychotherapy to be effective with them, it must follow them out into the community.

CONCLUSION

There is no question that patients with personality disorders, aggressive patients, are extremely difficult to treat and that most traditional forms of psychotherapy have no impact on them. However, as we come to understand more the dynamics of their disorder, treatment methods can be devised, and have been devised, to interfere with the pathological progresses. Society is beginning to believe more and more that its own interests are served best when violence is treated rather than punished, more specialized institutions for the treatment of violence are being legislated, and more specialized programs within existing institutions are coming into being. At this point no one knows exactly what the best approach is, and many programs are still in their initial and experimental stages. We cannot discount medical and surgical treatments, nor can we say that dynamically oriented psychotherapy is superior to behavior modification. We can say it's all being tried and the results aren't in yet. The literature seems to indicate that the "whole man" approach to therapy promises the most success, and it indicates that unique institutions such as Herstedvested and Patuxent have had the greatest impact, but these institutions are very expensive and they require special laws, and in spite of their success there are many professionals who look askance at them on both legal and moral grounds. It can only be concluded that the aggressive patient is just beginning to receive considerable attention from the mental health community and that more consistency in treatment approaches will have to await further developments in research and experience.

REFERENCES

1. Adler G, Shapiro LN: Psychotherapy with prisoners. Current Psychiat Therapies 9: 99-105, 1969.
2. Adler G, Shapiro LN: Some difficulties in the treatment of the aggressive acting-out patient. Amer J Psychother 27: 548-556, 1973.
3. APA Monitor 5 (no8): 1974.
4. Anonymous: APTO in the fifties. Int J Offender Ther and Comparative Criminol 15: 88, 1971.
5. Arnold WR, Stiles B: A summary of increasing use of "group methods" in correctional institutions. Int J Group Psychother 22: 77-92, 1972.
6. Berwick PT, Morris LA: Token economies: are they doomed? Professional Psychology 5: 434-439, 1974.
7. Borriello JF: Patients with acting-out character disorders. Amer J Psychother 27: 4-14, 1973.
8. Brancale R, Vuocolo A, Prendergast WE: The New Jersey program for sex offenders, in Sexual Behaviors: Social, Clinical, and Legal Aspects, Resnik HLP, Wolfgang ME (eds). Boston, Little, Brown and Company, 1972, pp 331-350.
9. Carney FJ: Evaluation of psychotherapy in a maximum security prison. Seminars in Psychiatry 3: 363-375, 1971.
10. Carney FL: Some recurring therapeutic issues in group psychotherapy with criminal patients. Amer J Pschother 26: 34-41, 1972.
11. Carney FL: Three important factors in psychotherapy with criminal patients. Amer J Psychother 27: 220-231, 1973.
12. Carpenter P, Sandberg S: "The thing inside": psychodrama with delinquent adolescents. Psychotherapy: Theory, Research and Practice 10: 245-247, 1973.
13. Chatz TL: Recognizing and treating dangerous sex offenders. Int J Offender Ther and Comparative Criminol 16: 109-111, 1972.
14. Chorover SL: The pacification of the brain. Psychology Today 7: 59-69, 1974.
15. Cleckey H: The Mask of Sanity (4th edition). St. Louis, Mosby Co., 1964.

16. Covi L, Alessi L: Pharmacological treatment of personality disorders, in *Personality Disorders: Diagnosis and Management*, Lion JR (ed),. Baltimore, Williams and Wilkens Company, 1974, pp 406-418.

17. Fink L, Martin JP, Burke G: Correctional treatment of offenders in the USA: its possibilities and limitations. *Int J Offender Ther and Comparative Criminol* 16: 35-43, 1972.

18. Greenland C: Evaluation of violence and dangerous behavior associated with mental illness. *Seminars in Psychiat* 3: 345-356, 1971.

19. Halleck S: The therapeutic encounter, in *Sexual Behavior: Social, Clinical, and Legal Aspects*, Resnik HLP, and Wolfgang ME (eds). Boston, Little, Brown and Company, 1972.

20. Hodges EF: Crime prevention by the indeterminate sentence law. *Amer J Psychiat* 128: 291-295, 1971.

21. Jew CC, Clanon TL, Mattocks AL: The effectiveness of group psychotherapy in a correctional institution. *Amer J Psychiat* 129: 602-605, 1972.

22. Kazdin AE, Bootzin RR: The token economy: An evaluative review. *J Appli Behav Anal* 5: 343-372, 1973.

23. Kozol HL, Boucher RJ, Gorofolo RF: The diagnosis and treatment of dangerousness. *Crime and Delinquency* 18: 371-392, 1972.

24. Levine FM, and Fasnacht G: Token rewards may lead to token learning. *Amer Psychol* 29: 816-820, 1974.

25. Lion JR: The role of depression in the treatment of the aggressive personality disorders. *Amer J Psychiat* 129: 123-125, 1972.

26. Lion JR, Pasternak SE: Countertransference reactions to violent patients. *Amer J Psychiat* 130: 207-210, 1973.

27. Lion JR: Diagnosis and treatment of personality disorders, in *Personality Disorders: Diagnosis and Management*, Lion JR (ed). Baltimore, Williams and Wilkins Company, 1974.

28. Lion JR, Azcarate C, Christopher R, Arana JD: A violence clinic. *Maryland State Med J* 23: 45-48, 1974.

29. Maletzky BM: Treatable violence. *Medical Times* 100: 74-79, 1972.

30. Mann RA, Moss GR: The therapeutic use of a token economy to manage a young and assaultive inpatient population. *J Nerv Ment Dis* 157: 1-9, 1973.

31. Manne SH: A communication theory of sociopathic personality. *Amer J Psychother* 21: 797-807, 1967.

32. Marcus AM, Conway C: A Canadian group approach study of dangerous sexual offenders. *Int J Offender Ther and Comparative Criminol* 15: 59-62, 1971.

33. Mark VH, Neville R: Brain surgery in aggressive epileptics. *JAMA* 226: 765-772, 1973.

34. *Maryland's Defective Delinquent Statute: A Progress Report*. Patuxent Institution, Jessup, Maryland, 1973.

35. Monroe RR: The problem of impulsivity in personality disturbances, in *Personality Disorders: Diagnosis and Management*, Lion, JR (ed). Baltimore, Williams and Wilkins Company, 1974, pp 16-33.

36. Pasternack SA: The explosive, antisocial, and passive-aggressive personalities, in *Personality Disorders: Diagnosis and Management*, Lion, JR (ed). Baltimore, Williams and Wilkens Company, 1974, pp 45-69.

248 F.L. CARNEY

37. Peters JJ, Roether HA: Group psychotherapy for probationed sex offenders, in *Sexual Behaviors: Social, Clinical, and Legal Aspects*, Resnik HLP, Wolfgang ME (eds). Boston, Little, Brown and Company, 1972, pp 255-266.

38. Pieczenik S, Birk L: Behavior therapy of personality disorders, in *Personality Disorders: Diagnosis and Management*, Lion JR (ed). Baltimore, Williams and Wilkens Company, 1974, pp 352-367.

39. Rappaport RG: Group therapy in prison. *Int J Group Psychother* 21: 489-492, 1971.

40. Sadoff RL, Roether HA, Peters JJ: Clinical measure of enforced group psychotherapy. *Amer J Psychiat* 128: 224-228, 1971.

41. Sage W: Crime and the clockwork lemon. *Human Behavior* 3: 16-23, 1974.

42. Schmideberg M: Offender therapy as a tool of research. *Int J Offender Ther and Comparative Criminol* 16: 61-65, 1972.

43. Schmidt CW, Meyer JK, Lucas J: Sexual deviations and personality disorders, in *Personality Disorders: Diagnosis and Management*, Lion JR (ed). Baltimore, Williams and Wilkens Company, 1974, pp 154-177.

44. Schwitzgebel RK: Learning theory approaches to the treatment of criminal behavior. *Seminars in Psychiat* 3: 328-344, 1971.

45. Serber M, Wolpe J: Behavior therapy techniques, in *Sexual Behaviors: Social, Clinical and Legal Aspects*, Resnik HLP, Wolfgang ME (eds). Boston, Little, Brown and Company, 1972, pp 239-254.

46. Sturup GK: The treatment of chronic criminals. *Bul Menninger Clinic* 28: 229-243, 1964.

47. Sturup GK: *Treating the "Untreatables."* Baltimore, The Johns Hopkins Press, 1968.

48. Sturup GK: Castration: the total treatment, in *Sexual Behaviors: Social, Clinical, and Legal Aspects*, Resnik HLP, Wolfgang ME, (eds). Boston, Little, Brown and Company, 1972, pp 361-382.

49. Teitelbaum SH: The psychopathic style of life and its defensive function. *Amer J Psychother* 19: 126-136, 1965.

50. Vaillant GE: Sociopathy as a human process. *Mass J Mental Health* 3: 4-18, 1973.

Some Scientific, Clinical, and Ethical Issues in the Treatment of Aggressive Behavior

JOHN R. LION
MANOEL W. PENNA

Considering the prominent role that aggression as a concept has played in the psychodynamic theories of depression and psychosomatic disease, it is rather curious that much of the literature on aggression has been produced by scholars in the social sciences. Within the last few years a number of popularized books on the subject of aggression have been authored by ethologists or psychologists (5, 18, 23). Fewer works by psychiatric clinicians have appeared on this subject. Indeed, the field of aggression has generally been transplanted to forensic areas, and one is much more apt to find articles on the clinical aspects of aggression in journals of criminology and law enforcement (3).

Psychoanalysis has made important early contributions to the theoretical understanding of the dynamics of aggression. The insight gained into the role played by aggression in the human experience of intimacy in such areas as human psychosexual development, maternal attachment and separation, or mourning processes are paralleled by observations of socialization processes among animals where the development of bonds seems to be always associated with the display of aggression in mating behavior, territoriality or dominance. The love-hate continuum of both human and animal interpersonal relationships emphasizes the fact that the vast majority of acts of human violence are committed against persons in one's circle of relatives and friends. This truism is often ignored as periodic cries are heard for programs designed to detect the potentially dangerous members of society when family- and victim-oriented intervention programs are epidemiologically sounder.

The paucity of clinically oriented articles on the handling of aggressive patients stems in part from difficulties in conceptually clarifying the term "aggression". We have been trained to divide human experience into internal, reportable, psychological processes and external, observable behavior.

The insights regarding aggression obtained through psychoanalysis have been made through inference and through the studies of the internal and reportable processes of patients who describe angry thoughts, hostile feelings, or violent ideation. In contrast, other disciplines such as criminology, anthropology, and sociology have focused on the overt behaviors of aggression. Thus, two modes of looking at aggression have arisen, and a dichotomy has sprung up which perpetuates two literatures. This is not the case with the affective or thought disorders, where both inner psychological phenomena and external behavior have been given recognition within one literature in the discipline of clinical psychiatry. The solution to this problem in the study of aggression rests in the obvious. We need to see aggressive patients if we want to understand aggression. To study the normal course of anger in a depressed patient or the development of hostility in a nonviolent schizophrenic is insufficient.

Unlike depression, aggressive behavior has long been seen as less of a psychologic entity and more of a moral entity, behavior which reflects criminality rather than mental illness. Thus aggressive human acts have traditionally come to the attention of legal authorities rather than psychiatrists, and aggressive individuals have been subjects of concern to police and judges. Nonaggressive patients, on the other hand, have psychopathology which does not confront the clinician with the moral problems and issues of confidentiality and psychotherapeutic obstacles in treatment (8, 9). Fear and mistrust are compounded by unrecognized superego sanctions or prohibitions in making the development of therapeutic alliance painful and difficult. Hence, the shunting of these patients away from areas of clinical concern.

There are other clinical problems interfering with our work with the aggressive patient. Most of us have a clear idea of what a depressed patient is and there is essential cross-cultural agreement on the pathology of depression. There is the familiar insomnia, the despondency, and the somatic and psychomotor changes. But an "aggressive" patient is a diverse entity, ranging from an explosive personality to a psychotic murderer. Questions arise in our minds when we hear the word "aggressive." What is the nature of the patient's aggression, and how aggressive is he? Is he aggressive because of underlying and treatable psychopathology? If so, how do we determine and treat it? Then we move to less solid ground and wonder whether he is a "character disorder" or a criminal who is simply a morally inferior person in need of incarceration, not treatment (11, 13).

These are difficult questions which strike at the root of societal attitudes toward violence and penal reform, but they also mirror our own clinical anguishes when seeing an aggressive patient, for most clinicians have conflicts in evaluating the aggressive patient. We value introspection and the introjection of emotions and put a negative premium on outwardly directed behavior, labeling it as "acting out," a term with a pejorative ring to it, because it bypasses the verbalization we desire in a patient. We value insight, reflection and affective meditation; that is the premise of the discipline of psychiatry and we tend to be more in tune with the depressed patient and the patient who suffers. We usually, in fact, demand of most psychiatric patients that they suffer in some way as part of their therapy. This value on suffering may be therapeutically valid, but the initial failure of some aggressive patients to agonize over their behavior, even though they may well agonize in jail, coupled with their impulsive hedonism, is seen as reprehensible and is apt to lead to the perception of the patient as callous, hardened and indifferent to both society and treatment. There are hardened criminals, to be sure. Yet part of our task as clinicians is to convert what is syntonic to what is dystonic, and this involves probably the utmost of clinical skill. The point is that subtle value judgments shape the process of determining treatability in the first place.

Further value judgments confuse the clinical issues of assessing and treating aggressive patients. Strong concerns have been expressed regarding the danger that our growing knowledge of aggressive behavior may be used by dominant groups in society to control and eliminate acts of aggression which spring from social oppression, racial prejudice or economic discrimination. To what extent can aggression be justified as a legitimate social process? A clinician confronted with the militant patient whose activism has led to involvement in acts of social agitation may perceive those acts as "destructive" because civil disobedience often brings the patient in conflict with the police; the subtleties of defiance of authority and the covert or overt use of force by a patient may raise within us much uneasiness, facilitating the diagnosis of "aggressiveness." Thus, evaluation and treatment of aggressive patients requires much self-examination, much more so than with depressed patients, where the norms and goals are more clearly spelled out (8, 9). The issue of the "normality" of aggression appears in the phenomenon of intraspecific aggression in animals. Animal observations demonstrate that aggression does not naturally aim at the destruction of members of the same species, but it is regulated and directed at other animals of other species. This aggression is given expression regularly. Keeping animals under circumstances which tend to interfere with the expression of aggression leads to animals harming members of the same species. Ethologists have called this appetitive behavior, and in the human realm observers have noted increased expressions of aggression in an Antarctic naval base where men live under unusual hardship and isolation (25). The point is that socially repressive constraints on the expression of aggression have detrimental effects. In the clinical realm, we emphasize that the aim in handling aggressive patients is not to suppress violence and to quench assertiveness but to teach the patient to effectively modulate his own aggressiveness to serve his own positive interests. Thus there is "normal" and "abnormal" aggression.

Aggressive patients present with varied chief complaints and behaviors. Some patients talk about "tempers," others relate violent outbursts in association with drinking, some are sent to us with a history of antisocial acts or an isolated antisocial act such as murder. It takes work to clarify the aggressiveness of each act, and each case is unique. Each aggressive patient requires that we sit down and analyze the act, the appropriateness of the act, and the probability of future aggressive acts. This last endeavor, the prediction of aggressiveness, is another highly charged social and clinical issue. There is now sufficient data to demonstrate that the diagnosis of dangerousness is difficult if not impossible, and that such labeling of patients as "dangerous" is apt to be in itself dangerous because it can lead to the identification of false positives and to unjustified incarceration (2). It should be further noted that dangerousness usually connotes externally directed violence more than suicide. That is, the trouble with the words "violent" and "aggressive" is that they connote behaviors which are frightening and threatening. There is evidence that violent patients—those patients initially seen because of homicidal urges—are as prone to kill themselves as they are prone to kill anyone else (19). Again this points out the interesting if poorly understood relationship between aggression and depression.

Behaviorally, individuals have been observed to switch from one role to the other over a period of time. Psychodynamically, both aggression and depression have an intimate relationship to the experience of helplessness but it remains to be understood how that experience shapes the ultimate violent behavior. These considerations notwithstanding, it remains that clinicians fear work with violent patients and are afraid that such patients may hurt them. This is an interesting phenomenon, often a countertransference one, perhaps stemming out of less-than-conscious anxieties about the introjection of our own hostile urges (16). It is obvious that fear may be appropriate in some instances. Yet a violent patient is not necessarily more apt to bear a grudge against the clinician than a psychotic patient who evolves a delusional system which contains the physician as his enemy. The caution to be exerted with violent patients as with all patients is the monitoring of the transference and the observation and bilateral discussion of the therapy. We acknowledge that special hazards may exist in certain forensic settings with high-risk groups. Many psychiatrists have been assaulted during their careers to some degree by some patient who was not necessarily perceived as aggressive (21). In many instances of assault on professional staff, some provocation is noted to have occurred (20, 24). This is very much like the situation in the real world—many violent crimes involve some role of a victim—and there is no reason why the situation should be any different in psychotherapy, where intimacy exists.

Given that diagnostic homogeneity is lacking in the management of aggressive patients, it becomes incumbent on the clinician, as stated above, to clearly dissect the patient's behavior. The patient may be aggressive because of overwhelming provocation on the part of a spouse, or he may direct aggression at authority figures, or at children, or at those he sees as threatening. His ability to curb aggressive impulses may be hampered by life-style of behavioral aggression which perpetuates violence as a normal mode of action, or there may be psychological or organic factors which contribute to the poor control of hostile urges. Some patients appear intractably aggressive, just as some psychotic patients appear intractably incurable and just as some patients appear chronically depressed. Whether such patients should be helped is a separate ethical issue. We only wish to point out here that intractability is a relative term, actually descriptive of the hopelessness of the therapist, but implying some therapeutic attempts or, at the very least, some diagnostic enlightenment. Some recidivist criminals are not amenable to treatment and some are; others require a "trial of treatment," and for some, treatment is very stormy and full of risk. Risk is important in the treatment of aggressive patients, and again we encounter a phenomenon that is handled differently in the realm of depression. Most clinicians take some risks with depressed patients. One cannot lock up a depressed patient forever, and it is a truism that a suicidal patient, if he really wants to, can carry out his intentions despite all the precautionary measures we can take. This situation does not mean that clinical nihilism should prevail, but rather that the clinician should accept some degree of uncertainty in the hope that progress can be made. In the area of aggression, things are somewhat different, and even though ambivalence may exist, the clinician is less likely to tolerate the uncertainty of the patient's potential behavior and errs on the conservative side, if that side can be erred on. Thus if the patient is in jail, there is a tendency to keep him there. Such attitudes on our part — if we play a role in the decision-making — is understandable, as we do not want to see anyone else get hurt. Or, to put the matter in another way, we feel that the suicidal patient will kill himself and that is all, but the homicidal patient may kill one person or a large number of other people in, say, a mass murder act. This thought is not entirely valid, however, for the suicidal patient is also capable of killing others before he kills himself. The issue here, given the confusion surrounding the clinical problem, is not so much that the aggressive patient will kill others and that we may be held liable, but that the aggressive patient is viewed as unpredictable, while the suicidal patient will "cry for help" and keep in closer contact with us. This view is also not accurate. Violent acts do not occur in a vacuum, and close supervision of an aggressive patient reveals many dynamic factors that will play a role in the genesis of the violent behavior (12). Most aggressive patients respond to definite and defined psychopathological events which surround their lives. Violent patients are not necessarily any more predictable or unpredictable than other types of patients unless we allow them to be so by lax follow-up policies, by a refusal to see other relevant members of the family who we know incite the patient, and by a belief that they are "bad" and will show their true colors in the course of time. Also, the need on our part to covertly foster aggressive behavior must be observed. We are all familiar with the clinician in practice or the aide in our ward who always gets involved in altercations with patients and who seems, on closer observation, to provoke them for his own inner needs.

The problems of treating aggressive criminals within a prison system are formidable and include allegiance problems and strategic problems. Since therapy involves some degree of modification of the patient's behavior, we are confronted with complex ethical and technical obstacles whenever we become agents of an institution rather than being directly hired by the patient. A therapeutic alliance is even more difficult to accomplish when the institution concerned is a prison, and the patient is always justifiably suspicious that the clinician is the person who shapes his future. There is no way out of this dilemma, even if the psychiatrist is an outside psychiatrist, for that psychiatrist, too, can potentially communicate with parole boards. If one is to engage in this kind of activity, the only solution to the problem is to face the issue squarely, much as one tries eventually to face the issue with the adolescent sent to therapy by his parents. The lack of trust is a severe obstacle but a surmountable one, provided the clinician and patient can discuss it and come to understand it. The entire subject lends itself to the evolution of one large resistance, and efforts must be made to proceed on other therapeutic issues in the face of bilateral mistrust. The aim of therapy is to create insight and lead the patient to reflect on his life and curb the hostility and impulsivity which has led him into difficulties in the first place (10). That is a large job, a painful one for both parties, but one which can be accomplished in both group and individual experiences, even in coercive surroundings. A prison, of course, is not the best place to do psychotherapy, and few psychiatrists spend an appreciable amount of time in prisons, for prisons are dreary places, full of hostility perpetuated by the structure. Therapy is viewed with suspicion and anxiety, as is the entire process of introspection. It is necessary to realize this: introspection is a painful experience and is something which no criminal is going to immerse himself in easily. There is a structurally facilitated system of projection which negates introspection, and the clinician's job is to align himself with the patient in this process in such a way that the patient comes to understand that introspection may be useful, though anxiety-producing. Or, more precisely, the need to reflect must be made palatable, or it will be crushed by the powerful forces surrounding the society of inmates. The development of insight and the whole procedure of introspection is, unfortunately, perceived by some civil libertarians as "brainwashing," as though meditation and inner reflection were alien to freedom. Brainwashing is a mental process which teaches a patient one thing and one mode of thinking and one type of thought; our job, as clinicians, is not to "brainwash" prisoners but to get them to anticipate the consequences of their antisocial and aggressive behavior effectively and in such a way that the thought of such behavior, and its attendant consequences, may have some deterrent value. This is not brainwashing; this is mature, psychologically adaptive thinking. Like the "acting-out" adolescent, the prisoner needs to learn that freedom implies a capacity to choose rather than a blind and uncontrollable drive to maladaptive action. But this type of process is difficult without the inner conviction of the clinician that he is doing something reasonable in the face of social opposition. We do believe that psychiatrists have some role to play in prisons; to say they do not is to say that prisoners have no definable psychopathology. This is not to say that attention paid to psychopathology obviates the need for social reform; psychiatry can be misused in prison settings, but psychiatry can also be insidiously misused in the office just as well, and probably is misused there more than any other place. The point is that the isolation of those prisoners with treatable psychopathology is still both a scientific and ethical problem for our society. This is demonstrated by the chronic publicity given to and legal actions taken against indeterminate sentence facilities such as Patuxent Institute in Jessup, Maryland, where "defective delinquents" are grouped together with the rationale that they constitute a risk to society and possess psychopathology requiring treatment by the mental health staff of that prison.

Recent and intense social and scientific criticism of psychosurgical techniques to control behavior has focused on epileptic and nonepileptic patients prone to violent outbursts who have been used as subjects for surgical procedures such as amygdalectomy (6). These procedures have cast some light on the neurophysiology of aggression. The very fact that certain neurophysiologic circuits have been discovered to be related to the integration and release of aggressive behavior in both animals and man makes the subject of aggression far different from that of depression, for there is no set of cerebral structures currently known to be implicated in depression to the same extent that it is present for aggression. Another important implication of the existence of such circuitry is that it provides all individuals with a preset neurophysiologic mechanism which can be translated into aggressive behavior given appropriate and adequate stimulation. The neurosurgical treatment of violent patients is a modality of therapy whose efficacy remains questionable at this point in time, and more research is needed to clarify indications and justifications. However, the fact that a neurosurgical procedure exists at all which may reduce the aggressiveness of certain patients raises a number of anxieties of a moral, ethical and psychological nature. Setting aside the more global issue of behavior control, the manipulation of aggression represents the potential infringement of a drive, innate or learned, which is so deeply rooted and prized in this culture so as to make its mitigation a distinct cultural threat. Part of this threat can be seen in society's contradictions in social attitudes toward crime and violence: the cry for controls and restraints on violence and the demands for an effective penology on the one hand, and a heightened sensitivity to the civil rights of prisoners and an abhorrence of vindictiveness on the other. These issues require the most urgent discussion; suffice it only to point out here that the "aggressive" patient evokes in the clinician and those around him a multiplicity of anxieties which hamper diagnosis and treatment.

The diagnosis and treatment of violent individuals are topics often viewed with clinical skepticism and nihilism, especially when one bolsters such negativism by citing prison statistics—it is all too easy to dismiss the "efficacy" of penal reform as one measure of "treatment" of aggressive patients by pointing to the persistent high recidivism levels in criminals in this country. But we submit that progress can be seen both in this country and other countries where more vigorous therapeutic approaches are used to treat aggressive individuals. Concepts such as the indeterminate sentence, behavior therapy, hormone treatment and others induce justifiable apprehension in society, but such concepts can be judiciously used in a humane way to assist aggressive patients in their struggles with society. They, of course, can also be utilized in a repressive way, as can all modalities of therapy and social manipulations which alter behavior or influence the mind.

As we return to the issue of psychosurgery, we are confronted with the fact that, like it or not, there are severely violent patients who are so disabled by their aggressiveness that they will require more drastic forms of treatment. These patients are exceedingly few in number. Yet there must be available to clinicians ways of treating such individuals besides locking them up forever; incarceration is no alternative to caution, and we must press forward in furthering our scientific knowledge on these problems. On a number of occasions we have been asked to see in consultation a small variety of aggressive patients who have been labeled by responsible clinicians as "intractable," and it has been clear on review of data in such cases that much has been tried and exhausted in an attempt to control such patients. Usually these patients have been refractory to a variety of medications and several psychotherapies. They are usually patients who are borderline or psychotic, and they are kept in chronic isolation and restraints because they are so assaultive and self-mutilative. An extreme burden to nursing staff and an obvious danger to themselves and others in society, they are hopelessly incarcerated and doomed to remain so unless a newer and more innovative form of therapy exists. No therapy is perfect for such patients, and sacrifices must be made. More specifically, a sacrifice of some cerebral integrity may have to be considered for the sake of social usefulness and personal freedom, though this is an ominous decision and one which needs to be made with as many safeguards as possible, after the fullest medical regimens have been tried for supervised intervals and under review by knowledgeable teams of clinicians. Incidentally, one difficulty in this area is the availablility of clinicians knowledgeable in the area of aggression and the limitations and indications for various therapeutic tactics. Most clinicians who come in contact with aggressive patients handle such individuals dispositionally and are unfamiliar with evaluative techniques.

Neurosurgical treatment of aggressive patients is not the only therapeutic modality to come under social and scientific criticism lately. Drug treatment has also received closer scrutiny, and drug suppression of aggression in man is a subject which has caused ferment. The issue is somewhat puzzling, and again appears to relate to a deeper underlying fear of behavior control. Most violent patients, even in prison settings, value some curbs on their impulsivity and generally welcome measures which put them in charge of their emotions. Few patients like being aggressive, and a greater number freely admit that the loss of control which accompanies violent outbursts or temper tantrums is frightening. This clinical axiom must be understood. Violence is unpleasant for most people, and the restoration of controls is welcomed by most patients, provided that the medication given to restore such controls does not in fact worsen the situation, as large doses of any neuroleptic can do (7). Any drug which renders a patient lethargic or helpless is apt to increase violence, not decrease it, as the patient comes to feel that he is losing even more control over his body and mind. Dynamically, the issue for most violent patients is helplessness and fear of passivity and weakness, and medications which enhance such anxieties do the patient no good. This is the issue in prison settings. Patients need to be alert to defend themselves from abuse, sexual and otherwise. They do not take kindly to any form of medication, unless that medication is rendered with some understanding of his anxieties and unless the medication helps restore controls, not weaken them.

An array of pharmacologic agents has been used in aggressive patients, including major and minor tranquilizers, antidepressants, lithium, the anticonvulsants, the central nervous system stimulants and hormonal agents. The multiplicity of such agents attests to the fact that there is no one drug for aggression. Aggression, unlike depression, has multiple etiologies and results from multiple underlying pathologies (7). The aggressive patient may be psychotic, paranoid, depressed, epileptic; he may have charcter pathology, brain dysfunction, a circumscribed neurosis or any combination of these things. Each drug will affect a different target symptom and hence affect the aggressiveness differently. The clinician's job is to recognize whether the aggressiveness springs from a thought disorder or a paranoid personality structure or an underlying "ictal" disturbance, and to administer, when appropriate, the right drug (15).

The problem of evaluating an aggressive patient is further made difficult by the fact that aggression is not a constant but, rather, a recurring behavior. Impulsivity plays a prominent role in the phenomenology of aggression. A depressed patient, as previously mentioned, usually shows little variation in the level of his depression during the course of his illness unless the illness is cyclical and recurring; in the latter case, we are apt to describe the illness as either the manifestation of a cyclothymic personality or a manic-depressive disease process. Depression is a disorder with a relatively constant mood; those small variations in the mood process which occur in the evening or night are considered to be inherent in the psychopathological process of depression. Aggressive patients, however, are rarely aggressive for sustained periods. The psychomotor excitation which normally accompanies aggressiveness would, if sustained, lead to physical exhaustion; few patients, except manic individuals or severely psychotic patients, such as those in a state of catatonic excitement, are agitated for sustained periods. In these instances, the clinical picture is more apt to be that of disorganization of thought processes and intense, disregulated psychomotor behavior. Goal-directed aggressive behavior is less present in such cases, though, of course, assault can always occur under appropriately provocative conditions.

The aggressive patient, then, is characteristically an individual who demonstrates labile hostile outbursts rather than sustained, chronic aggressiveness (17). That is, aggressiveness in such patients occurs suddenly, with or without premeditation, and is superimposed upon a less aggresive baseline of behavior. A depressed patient can be depressed for many months and show relatively stable behavioral patterns. An aggressive patient may be aggressive for minutes or hours, possibly days, but the time periods of such behavior are much shorter.

It is our belief that both lability of affect and behavior, referred to as impulsivity, is a distinct clinical feature of aggressive patients, irrespective of the causality of their aggressiveness. That is, the symptom of aggression is intimately bound up with impulsivity from the phenomenological point of view. This is important, since the diagnosis of the impulsive act requires elucidation. An isolated aggressive act, whether representing a characterological, neurotic or psychotic process, must be examined and accounted for, etiologically speaking. Two diagnostic processes, then, are usually necessary to understand the phenomenon of aggression. First, one must understand the long-term processes underlying the aggressive act, namely, the patient's personality pattern, his life-style and its psychopathological deviations. Second, one must understand the aggressive act, its precipitants, its dynamics and the surrounding conditions which contribute to its pathogenesis (role of the victim, weapons). Particular attention must be paid to the organic process, which, in our experience, can reflect some degree of brain dysfunction, often of an epileptoid nature. This topic, the role of epilepsy in aggression, is as highly charged as the psychosurgical techniques which have been advocated to control both, and there is literature to support and refute the existence of ictal aggression; there is probably more evidence to support the notion that aggressiveness as an epileptic phenomenon is rare, and when, as-sociated with epilepsy, usually occurs interictally or postictally, rather than representing a direct seizure state (6, 9).

Brain dysfunction, an ambiguous term itself, is difficult to document with the rigor approaching that for other organic conditions in medicine. It is easier to acquire evidence for altered hepatic or renal functioning or cardiac functioning, but the intricacies and overlapping functions of cerebral processes, together with the subjectivity inherent in the evaluation of all cortical processes makes documentation of such brain function difficult. The electrencephalograph still provides only indirect evidence of brain dysfunction, and even greater variability is inherent in the evaluation of such testing. While great caution is entailed in the evaluation of brain dysfunction, the skilled use of neurological assessment, psychological testing, and EEG evaluation can nonetheless provide some degree of clinical information which may be useful, in a pragmatic sense, to the clinician who treats patients.

An unfortunate dichotomy exists today, in our experience, regarding the neuropathology and psychopathology of violence. Given observational data which support the existence of organic factors in the treatment of these types of patients, it is incumbent on the clinician to maintain a bilateral orientation and to assess organic factors which may underlie the "ego" defects in those patients who do demonstrate difficulties with aggression, particularly labile, hostile outbursts (1, 12).

We have discussed the fact that aggressive individuals are sporadically so, and it may be argued that many aggressive individuals are chronically aggressive. Fromm, in his recent book, presents brief bibliographic data on historical figures such as Stalin and Hitler to illustrate, among other things, that these individuals harbored persistent levels of vindictiveness, hatred and lust for violence (5). That these men were indeed evil is indisputable, but the clinical fact remains that their own isolated aggressive acts appear to have been sporadic and impulsive; both men, for example, had tempers and both were given to labile hostile outbursts. To be sure, they were aggressive men, but the social machinery of aggressiveness which they set into motion made their violence chronic and widespread. We do need a good deal of humility and restraint, however, as we move from observations of aggression in individuals to generalized formulations about the origins and manifestations of violence in a given society.

Tolerance of aggressive behavior varies in cultures, and man's concerns about aggression are actually not concerns about anger or hostility as much as they are concerns about destructiveness and physical harm, areas that have come into increasing individual and social consciousness as the technology of destructiveness has advanced. Hence, it is interesting to remember that Freud himself did not deal significantly with the concept of aggression until confronted with its destructiveness in World War I. Paradoxically, man's increasing awareness of his destructiveness has made him defensively more aggressive, not less, and has led to the familiar arms-race phenomenon. Therefore, aggression is a phenomenon that paradoxically has no satiation as far as cultural or societal expression is concerned, and we appear to be at a point in this culture where the expression of aggression and violence is taken for granted by the media and within our cities and towns. The immersion of our society in violence may be the reasons we overlook the obvious, may make us forget Kozol's statement (4) that a dictator or king or even president may be far more violent than a single isolated mass murderer—that is, those in power in government or the military may use their aggressiveness in sanctioned ways or unsanctioned ways to produce widespread social harm. This fact needs to be remembered as we discuss the concept of aggression.

The phenomenology of aggression in man remains a poorly studied subject, which presented great conceptual problems even to Freud. The development of knowledge about such behavior has been retarded by confusion regarding its validity as a genuine psychopathological entity versus its existence as morally inferior behavior. Aggression awakens internal conflict in physicians, and confronts students with deep personal and social value judgments. Both the evaluation of the process and the treatment of persons afflicted with the illness of aggression deserve recognition in scientific clinical psychiatry (14).

REFERENCES

1. Bach-y-Rita G, Lion JR, Climent C, et al: Episodic dyscontrol: A study of 130 violent patients. *Am J Psychiatry* 127: 1473-1478, 1971.
2. *Clinical Aspects of the Violent Individual*, Task Force Report #8, American Psychiatric Association, Washington, DC, 1974.
3. Ibid, p 27.
4. Kozol HL, Boucher RJ, Garofalo RF: The diagnosis and treatment of dangerousness. *Crime and Delinquency* 18: 371-392, 1972.
5. Fromm E: *The Anatomy of Human Destructiveness.* New York, Holt, Rinehart and Winston, 1973.
6. Goldstein M: Brain research and violent behavior. *Arch Neurol* 30: 1-36, 1974.
7. Lion JR: Conceptual issues in the use of drugs for the treatment of aggression in man. *J Nerv Ment Dis* 160: 76-82, 1975.
8. Lion JR: *Evaluation and Management of the Violent Patient.* Springfield, Ill., Charles C Thomas, 1972.
9. Lion JR: The development of a violence clinic, in *Violence and Victims.* Pasternack SA (ed.). New York, Spectrum Publications, 1975.
10. Lion JR: The role of depression in the treatment of aggressive personality disorders. *Am J Psychiatry* 129: 347-349, 1972.
11. Lion JR (ed): *Personality Disorders: Diagnosis and Management.* Baltimore, Williams & Wilkins, 1974.
12. Lion JR, Azcarate C, Christopher R, et al: A violence clinic. *Maryland State Med J* 23: 45-48, 1974.
13. Lion JR, Leaff LA: On the hazards of assessing character pathology in an outpatient setting. *Psychiat Quart 47-52:* 104, 1973.
14. Lion JR, Monroe RR: Editorial: Clinical research of the violent individual. *J Nerv Ment Dis* 160: 75, 1975.
15. Lion JR, Monroe RR (eds): Special section on drugs in the treatment of human aggression. *J Nerv Ment Dis* 160: 75-145, 1975.
16. Lion JR, Pasternack SA: Countertransference reactions to violent patients. *Am J Psychiatry* 130: 207-210, 1973.
17. Lion JR, Penna M: The study of human aggression in *Neuropsychology of Aggression*, Whalen RE (ed). New York, Plenum Publishing Corp., 1975.
18. Lorenz K: *On Aggression.* New York, Bantam Books, Inc, 1967.
19. Macdonald JM: *Homicidal Threats.* Springfield, Ill., Charles C Thomas, 1968.
20. Macdonald JM: *The Murderer and His Victim.* Springfield, Ill., Charles C. Thomas, 1961.
21. Madden DJ, Lion JR, Penna M: Physical assaults on psychiatrists by patients. *Am J Psychiatry* (In Press).
22. Maryland's Defective Delinquent Statute: A progress report. Dept. of Correctional Services, Patuxent Institution, Jessup, Maryland, 1973.
23. May R: *Power and Innocence: A Search for the Sources of Violence.* New York, W.W. Norton & Company, 1973.
24. Pasternack SA: *Violence and Victims.* New York, Spectrum Publications, 1975.
25. Pierce CM: Psychophysiological studies in Anarctica. Paper presented at Grand Rounds, Institute of Psychiatry and Human Behavior, Department of Psychiatry, University of Maryland School of Medicine, Baltimore, October, 1967.

Subject Index

DATE DUE

JUN 2 3 198 ~~SEP - - 1999~~		
MAR 2 7 198 ~~"RESERVE"~~		
DEC 1 2 1986 ~~PJCS 313~~		
DEC 1 4 1988 8/17/00		
MAR 1 7 1989 "RESERVE"		
OCT 1 5 199 AUG - - 2000		
NOV 0 4 199 ~~~~		
MAR 3 0 199 "RESERVE"		
JAN 27 199 AUG - - 2001		
~~RESERVE~~ ~~PJCS 313~~		
~~SEP - - 1996~~		
PJCS 313		
AUG - - 1997		
"RESERVE"		
~~		
~~		
PJCS 313		
GAYLORD		PRINTED IN U.S.A.